Of Sondry Folk

What Examples, Similitudes, Times, Places, and
above all, Persons, with their speeches, and attributes, doe as in his *Canterbury*-tales (like
these threds of gold, the rich *Arras*) beautifie
his worke quite thorow.

HENRY PEACHAM, *The Compleat Gentleman*, 1622

Oure governour, And of our tales juge and reportour

Of Sondry Folk

The Dramatic Principle in the
Canterbury Tales

By R. M. LUMIANSKY
Illustrated by MALCOLM THURGOOD

AUSTIN
UNIVERSITY OF TEXAS PRESS

To my wife, Janet

International Standard Book Number 0-292-76017-5
Library of Congress Catalog Card Number 80-53433
Copyright © 1955, 1980 by R. M. Lumiansky
Printed in the United States of America

First Paperback Printing, 1980

Contents

CONTENTS

Illustrations

ILLUSTRATIONS

Preface

Many scholars have written about the dramatic interplay present in various segments of the *Canterbury Tales*, but a detailed investigation from this point of view of the book as a whole has not been made available. This study offers analyses of the dramatic contexts within which each of the twenty-three performances by Chaucer's Canterbury Pilgrims is delivered; and from these analyses I have deduced a statement—more detailed and, I think, more illuminating than has hitherto appeared—concerning the operation of the dramatic principle which contributes so effectively to the lasting appeal of the *Canterbury Tales*. This statement, which forms a framework for the book, is developed at length in Part I and the Conclusion. The dramatic function of the General Prologue and the Links is treated in Part II. These framing statements and large elements in many of the twenty-three analyses (Part III) represent new ideas; in other instances I have attempted to select in sensible fashion from among numerous and often conflicting interpretations advanced by earlier commentators.

I am greatly indebted to many scholarly writers whose publications have treated matters of textual, literary, and cultural history. I also acknowledge gratefully a grant from the Tulane University Council on Research that allowed me time for work on this book.

Some material in this book first appeared in the *Explicator* (V [1946], item 20); Tulane *Studies in English* (I [1949], 1–29,

[ix

and III [1952], 47–68); *PQ* (XXVI [1947], 313–20); *Journal of General Education* (III [1949], 309–12); *UTQ* (XX [1951], 344–56); and *PMLA* (LXVIII [1953], 896–906). This material is reprinted here in revised form with permission of the editors concerned.

R. M. LUMIANSKY

Tulane University
September 15, 1954

Preface to the Paperbound Edition

This book was first published in 1955 in hard covers, the fifth reprinting of that edition appeared in 1972, and the decision against further reprinting of the hard-cover edition was made in 1978.

For better or for worse, my view of the matters discussed in the book has not changed substantially over the years of studying and teaching the *Canterbury Tales* since 1955. During that period, however, Chaucerians have not been idle, and numerous publications have appeared in which "diverse folk diversely they demed" about these matters. To provide a beginning guide to those varying views, I have provided an addendum to the Selected Bibliography; but it should be noted that because space was limited I have not been able to include all pertinent items. I hope that the excluded authors will forgive.

It remains for me to express my appreciation to the University of Texas Press for the decision to bring out a paperbound edition of this book.

August 1980   R.M.L.

Of Sondry Folk

LIST OF ABBREVIATIONS

The following abbreviations are used in the notes and in the Selected Bibliography:

CT   *Canterbury Tales*
ELH   *English Literary History*
JEGP   *Journal of English and Germanic Philology*
MLN   *Modern Language Notes*
MP   *Modern Philology*
MLQ   *Modern Language Quarterly*
MLR   *Modern Language Review*
NED   *New English Dictionary*
PMLA   *Publications of the Modern Language Association*
PQ   *Philological Quarterly*
RES   *Review of English Studies*
SP   *Studies in Philology*
TLS   London *Times Literary Supplement*
UTQ   *University of Toronto Quarterly*

The following shortened titles are used in the notes:

Robinson, *Works:* for F. N. Robinson (ed.), *The Complete Works of Geoffrey Chaucer* (1933). Line numbers, regularly inserted in the body of the present volume to facilitate reference to pertinent passages of the *Tales*, refer to Chaucer's text as it appears in Robinson, *Works.*

Sources and Analogues: for W. F. Bryan and Germaine Dempster (eds.), *Sources and Analogues of Chaucer's Canterbury Tales* (1941).

Bowden, *Commentary:* for Muriel A. Bowden, *A Commentary on the General Prologue to the Canterbury Tales* (1948).

Manly, *New Light:* for J. M. Manly, *Some New Light on Chaucer* (1926).

Curry, *Sciences:* for W. C. Curry, *Chaucer and the Mediaeval Sciences* (1926).

I : INTRODUCTION

The Point of View and the Assumptions

or centuries readers of Chaucer's *Canterbury Tales* have in various ways understood and commented upon its dramatic aspect. From twentieth-century critics who attempt to indicate this essential feature of Chaucer's literary genius, we have such remarks as the following: "The conception of the *Canterbury Tales* as drama is Chaucer's masterpiece"; ". . . the most astonishing characteristic of Chaucer's art is . . . what is commonly called the dramatic method"; ". . . the abundance of [Chaucer's] genius finds expression in terms of character, and, however much humour and pathos come into play, it is human character that starts him at his best."[1] And additional statements stressing the dramatic nature of the *Canterbury Tales* could be gathered by the score from the writings of other commentators.

The indisputable point here seems to be that Chaucer not only came in contact with human beings of all sorts in the course of his long public career as diplomat and civil servant, but that he took full advantage of the opportunity to observe closely the features, dress, habits, manners, quirks, affectations, and eccentricities of the people he met; and then, because of his interest in, and his keen observation of, mankind, he regularly conceived and developed his narratives as vehicles for character portrayal. Thus many of the individuals we meet in Chaucer's writings strike us as actors in a play, whom we come to know almost intimately from their performances. Upon this foundation—stated

[1] These passages, in the order quoted, are from J. L. Lowes, *Geoffrey Chaucer and the Development of His Genius*, 206; Manly, *New Light*, 294; and H. R. Patch, *On Rereading Chaucer*, 137.

here in its barest simplicity—Chaucer builds the intricate structure of his dramatic method.

Nowhere in Chaucer's work is this dramatic method so extensively employed as in the *Canterbury Tales*, for it was through the use of a pilgrimage as the framing device for a series of stories, and particularly through the creation of the Pilgrims as tellers of these stories, that Chaucer's dramatic genius found its fullest outlet late in his career. In fact, the *Canterbury Tales* seems to have originated and taken shape with the Pilgrims— the actors in the drama—as the steady center of focus. It will be my purpose in this book to analyze the performances given in the *Canterbury Tales* by Chaucer's actor-Pilgrims. Such analyses will serve a worth-while end in themselves if they in any way illuminate their various subjects; but these analyses taken together will also enable us to state, with a precision beyond that usually encountered, those specific techniques which make up Chaucer's dramatic method in the *Canterbury Tales*, and which constitute the dramatic principle for the book.

One conclusion which immediately emerges from this dramatic approach to Chaucer's book is that the stories, rather than being ends in themselves, are meant to be taken as complementary to the portraits and actions of their individual tellers. This does not imply that the tales are of little importance or that Chaucer was not greatly interested in good storytelling; it is to say, however, that the stories should be read in context. And the proper context for a given story consists primarily of the individual traits and the dramatic purposes of the Pilgrim telling that story. Accordingly, in attempting to interpret a particular Pilgrim's performance in the *Canterbury Tales*, a critic must first establish, to his own satisfaction at least, the traits that Chaucer intended us to associate with that Pilgrim, and the dramatic forces that govern not Chaucer as author but the Pilgrim as teller of the tale.

Although commentators are almost unanimously agreed upon the general view which I have been developing as a point of departure for this study of the *Canterbury Tales*, the possibility for considerable difference of opinion exists when we attempt a comprehensive statement treating the detailed workings of Chaucer's dramatic principle in the book. This difference of opinion seems to stem from three conflicting conceptions, which can perhaps be set forth most clearly by three representative quotations.[2] First, there is an almost complete negation of the dramatic approach:

Very few of the tales in the collection have much value for the characterization of their tellers. Chaucer shows, it is true, a due sense of propriety in assigning tales to pilgrims; thus, the gentry tell stories befitting their social respectability, and the smutty stories are put in the mouth of the common herd. But it would be a great mistake to interpret a given story as serving primarily to characterize its teller as an individual. Indeed, some of the tales seem quite unsuitable to their tellers as we find them described in the general prolog.

The second view is represented by the following comment on the Knight's Tale:

Chaucer always has two familiar rules or purposes in the *Canterbury Tales:* the more important is to tell a good story in accord with the literary climate of the day, and the other is to blend it with the temper and prejudices of the given pilgrim-narrator. The successful formula appears again and again; the "verray parfit gentil knyght, of his port as meeke as is a mayde," provides an illustration as authentic as those of the Wife of Bath or the Pardoner. It is therefore in keeping that, in its narrative essentials, the Knight's story shall cleave to the courtly line, the more so perhaps as this tradition is beginning to acquire a substantially antiquarian tinge by the time of Richard II.

According to this view, for Chaucer the quality and type of the tale were of first importance, and its suitability to its narrator secondary.

The third conception was set forth by Professor Kittredge, without doubt the leading exponent of a dramatic approach to the *Tales.* The often-quoted core of his argument follows:

The Canterbury Pilgrimage is . . . a Human Comedy, and the Knight and the Miller and the Pardoner and the Wife of Bath and the rest are the *dramatis personae.* The Prologue itself is not merely a prologue:

[2] The three quotations, in the order listed, are from Kemp Malone, *Chapters on Chaucer,* 211; E. B. Ham, *ELH,* XVII (1950), 256–57; and G. L. Kittredge, *Chaucer and His Poetry,* 154–56. Émile Legouis has an illuminating statement similar to Kittredge's; see his *Geoffrey Chaucer* (English trans.), 180–86.

it is the first act, which sets the personages in motion. Thereafter, they move by virtue of their inherent vitality, not as tale-telling puppets, but as men and women. From this point of view, which surely accords with Chaucer's intention, the Pilgrims do not exist for the sake of the stories, but *vice versa.* Structurally regarded, the stories are merely long speeches expressing, directly or indirectly, the characters of the several persons. . . . Thus the story of any pilgrim may be affected or determined,—in its contents, or in the manner of telling, or in both,— not only by his character in general, but also by the circumstances, by the situation, by his momentary relation to the others in the company, or even by something in a tale that has come before.

According to Kittredge, for Chaucer a tale exists primarily to characterize its narrator, and the quality of that tale—a question of secondary importance—cannot be considered apart from the presentation of its narrator.

The examination to be presented in this book is certainly more indebted to Kittredge's point of view than to either of the other conceptions. But throughout I shall use an approach which differs somewhat from his. In connection with the twofold problem of a tale by itself and the same tale in its dramatic context, I assume that both the stories and the storytellers in the *Canterbury Tales* have at least two purposes and that these two purposes regularly and intentionally mesh, so that the stories and the tellers, considered from the point of view of either purpose, gain vastly from their coexistence. On the simpler level, the story and the teller exist as separate entities—indeed, as types of medieval storytelling and of medieval society—but this existence then provides the firm foundation for the more complex level, on which the story and the teller serve a dramatic purpose and thereby add to, and gain from, each other. Which of these two purposes is more important is manifestly a question wide of the mark, since in terms of the book as a whole a given story or teller cannot be finally considered as existing solely for either purpose. Obviously, a tale's or a teller's separate existence contributes much to the dramatic existence of each; but there can be no final isolation of either tale or teller.

To be sure, there can be and there are, as we shall see, varying degrees of complexity among the various segments of the *Can-*

terbury Tales in the manner whereby one purpose meshes with the other; and there is also considerable variation in the success with which Chaucer employed this principle of double purposes for both his stories and his tellers—after all, his book was never completed, nor were the completed portions ever finally revised. But, in the light of his vivid introduction of the individual Pilgrims by means of the General Prologue, in the light of his setting up, by means of the Links and the Host, a movable stage from Southwark to Canterbury upon which the Pilgrims are to perform, and in the light of his assigning specific tales to individual tellers—however hazy this assignment may be in two instances—we are committed to the necessity of assessing a given tale or teller on the level of dramatic existence as well as on the level of existence as a separate entity. The "Pilgrims do not exist for the sake of the stories," nor do the tales exist for the sake of their tellers; rather, the crowning genius of Chaucer's enveloping plan for the *Canterbury Tales* derives from the fact that the Pilgrims and their stories exist for the sake of themselves and, at the same time, for the sake of each other.

Probably the most widely used generalization concerning this dramatic principle in the *Canterbury Tales* is that Chaucer gains dramatic effectiveness *by suiting the tale to the teller.* A generalization of this sort will be useful in the analyses which make up the body of this book so long as we understand, in accord with the preceding two paragraphs, that the statement must include its corollary that *the teller is suited to his tale.* In fact, the most pat generalization would be that Chaucer *suits the tale and the teller.* But, most importantly, we should observe that Chaucer suits the tales to the tellers—and the tellers to the tales—in a variety of ways.[3] The interpretations in Part III of this book of the performances by the Canterbury Pilgrims lead me to maintain that Chaucer employs three stages of dramatic development, or three techniques of dramatic presentation, in dealing with the Pilgrims and their performances in the *Canterbury Tales.* Let me define and illustrate each of them.

First of all, there is the simple suiting of tale and teller. We

---

[3] J. R. Hulbert has commented upon this variety from a point of view different from that used here; see *SP*, XLV (1948), 565–77.

are introduced to the teller by means of his portrait in the General Prologue; when his turn comes to perform, this teller recounts a story that fits what we earlier learned of his character. Such is the case with the Squire, a gay, lighthearted young man who tells, or begins to tell, the romantic tale of far-off Tartary, in which are evident certain attitudes that the Squire has acquired from his father, the Knight. There are no dramatic complications—no antagonisms pursued or axes ground—as contexts for the performances in this category.

Second, we find a large number of recitals for which there is motivation beyond the nature of the particular teller as revealed by means of his sketch in the General Prologue. For example, there is the Friar-Summoner controversy; these two worthies are professional enemies, whose enmity breaks into the open at the end of the Wife of Bath's Prologue. The tale each tells, as well as the prologue by which each introduces his tale—in other words, his whole performance—is aimed at discomfiting his adversary. It is important to note that this second technique of dramatic presentation includes the first. That is, the tales which the Friar and the Summoner tell are well suited to their characters as established in the General Prologue; but, in addition, their performances represent motivated drama, rather than the simple suiting of tale and teller. And the motivation for the performances in this category is essentially external, in that the drama here springs from outside circumstances, such as the professional enmity of the Friar and the Summoner.

Third and last, there is in several instances a complete dramatic revelation of a Pilgrim: first, by means of his portrait in the General Prologue; second, through his actions and words in his own prologue; and third, by means of his tale. Thus all the lines which Chaucer devotes to these particular Pilgrims combine to give us extended, well-rounded character studies. The Wife of Bath's performance illustrates this situation: we learn certain things about her from the General Prologue; her own prologue gives further details about her and sets up her antagonism to the antifeminists; then her tale, which certainly fits her character, serves as an *exemplum* illustrating her argument for female sovereignty. Thus this third technique of dramatic presentation includes not only the first (suiting of tale and teller) but also the second (external motivation of the drama); and then it goes beyond the second in the completeness and detail of character revelation. Present also is internal motivation for the performances in this third category. Not only do external circumstances come into play, but also the tensions within the individual Pilgrims dictate the performance. Important, too, in this technique is the fact that the teller is not fully aware of his detailed self-revelation.

These three techniques of dramatic presentation, the ranking of which obviously depends upon the complexity of dramatic interrelations surrounding the performances by the Canterbury Pilgrims, will be fully illustrated by the analyses which make up Part III and will be used for purposes of summary in the Conclusion. Since among Chaucerians "diverse men deem diversely" about these matters, it will perhaps be well to state here the five principal assumptions concerning the *Canterbury Tales* that will be used throughout this study.

First, in the interpretations I shall not be concerned with analyzing the action of the characters within the various stories except where such analysis contributes to establishing Chaucer's probable conception of a particular storyteller. Thus, in the Pardoner's performance, the presence of the *exemplum* involving the three rioters who seek and find Death is of importance to the analysis of the Pardoner's motives; but a detailed discussion of the old man who appears in that *exemplum* would be beside the point. Similarly, the Franklin's choice of a story stressing gentilesse and marital happiness is of importance here; but the literary function of the black rocks of Brittany within that story is not. On the other hand, the story told by the Wife of Bath bears detailed relation to the drama underlying her whole performance; consequently, specific analysis of many aspects of that story is quite in order. In short, this book is limited to the drama of the Canterbury Pilgrims, and does not pretend to consider the full drama within each of the narratives. The dramatic interplay within the stories is of great interest and importance to any student of the *Canterbury Tales*, but it is not always relevant to the aims of this study.

A second assumption is called for because of the unfinished nature of the *Canterbury Tales*. In a number of places we think that we have evidence of Chaucer's earlier intentions in the assignment of tales. The Sergeant of the Law promises a tale in prose, but relates in verse the story of Constance; and the Shipman uses feminine pronouns in referring to himself. Probably we are to infer that at one stage in the composition of his book, Chaucer meant to assign the prose Tale of Melibeus to the Lawyer and the Shipman's Tale to the Wife of Bath. Now a question arises: To what extent do these traces of earlier assignment interfere with the working out of the dramatic patterns of which these tales are a part? It seems to me that whereas the traces of earlier assignment are immensely interesting, in that they furnish glimpses of Chaucer's working habits, they present no real barrier to interpretation of the drama; rather, they are an aid to such analysis. Presumably Chaucer had good reason for each of his changes in assignment of tales, and it is highly likely that these good reasons were chiefly a matter of dramatic suitability. Although the fabliau which the Shipman tells is adequately suited to the Wife of Bath, certainly the tale Chaucer finally gave her serves to a greater degree in making her performance an immortal creation; and, at the same time, the fabliau concerning the merchant of St. Denis is a fitting story for the Shipman to tell. Thus I am not bothered greatly by the faulty reference of pronouns, or by other minor evidences of earlier assignment of tales and lack of revision. Our main interest lies in the dramatic principle present in as final a version of the *Canterbury Tales* as is available. But it must be granted that because of the unfinished nature of the book, all the performances are not equally well worked out dramatically, and in several instances, as we shall see, the effect is not particularly successful.

The third assumption concerns the question of Chaucer's conscious artistry in the dramatic development of the Pilgrims. Although the view advanced by a number of critics in previous centuries of a naïve Chaucer, possessed of a fumbling native genius, has been thoroughly refuted by the writings of more recent Chaucerians, there are still many who hesitate to go very far in granting the subtleties of literary composition present in the *Canterbury Tales* except in specific matters concerning Chaucer's alteration of his sources for particular tales. Thus it is that we hear talk of this or that critic "reading meanings into" Chaucer's work, rather than illuminating the methods used in that work. In preparing this book I have assumed that in view of our limited knowledge of the fourteenth century, and in view of Chaucer's amazing understanding of human psychology and his equally amazing artistry in the techniques of utilizing that understanding in presenting his Pilgrims, it is unlikely in the extreme that a critic can illuminate to the full his portrayals; nor is the critic likely to "read into" these portrayals complexities of a degree not intended, so long as he bases his theories solidly on Chaucer's text itself and on the established findings of over one hundred years of steadily industrious and often brilliant scholarship. Look, for example, at the almost unbelievable "tightness of the weave" in the Merchant's story of January and May, where every sentence carries suggestions aimed at heightening the unlovely picture of an old man blinded by lust, a picture that reveals much of dramatic interest concerning the storyteller himself, the Merchant. In 1936, Professor Tatlock commented brilliantly upon Chaucer's skillful use of detail in this story, but there remained a number of aspects of Chaucer's possible dramatic purposes in this performance to which Professors Schlauch, Baugh, and Sedgewick, and Mrs. Dempster could call attention.[4] And doubtless future critics will have additional things to say about the Merchant's Tale. Of course, these interpretations differ at many points, and where they do, the intelligent reader will try to decide who presents the best case; he will not simply dismiss all the interpretations as "meanings read into" the Merchant's Tale.

My fourth assumption concerns what Professor Lawrence has called the combination of "artifice and realism" in the *Canterbury Tales*.[5] By "artifice" is meant those arbitrary characteristics of the book which are inherent in the conventions of late medieval storytelling and in Chaucer's framing plan; and liter-

[4] For these studies, in the order mentioned, see *MP*, XXXIII (1935–36), 367–81; *ELH*, IV (1937), 201–12; *MP*, XXXV (1937–38), 15–26; *UTQ*, XVII (1947–48), 337–45; *MP*, XXXVI (1938–39), 1–8.

[5] W. W. Lawrence, *Chaucer and The Canterbury Tales*, 24–63.

ary realism, we should remember, is not the same thing as full reality, but "a collective term for the devices that give the effect of reality." Thus, as artifice, we are asked to accept such facts as that most of the Pilgrims can speak in skillful verse, that thirty-odd people can all hear the storyteller despite the narrow, muddy road, that many of the Pilgrims know expert short stories and have considerable familiarity with learned material, that this whole company agrees to complete supervision by an innkeeper, that the omniscient Narrator remembers everything word-for-word, that no more than one person in the group from each class is the general rule, and that the telling of the tales would take neither more nor less time than seems available for them. These matters are far more bothersome to the critic who makes a list of them than to the reader who goes his way through the *Canterbury Tales* for the fun of it. For Chaucer, by his minute observations of dress and manners, by his frequent recording of personal likes and dislikes, and by numerous other devices which will be discussed in later sections, treats his company as a group of real people on a real pilgrimage, and it is as such that we shall examine them. Actually, the *Canterbury Tales* presents the effect of dramatic realism within a framework leading to the easy acceptance of certain artificialities.

The fifth and final assumption involves the frequently discussed question of the order that Chaucer intended for the stories in his unfinished book. All of the numerous manuscripts are dated later than Chaucer's death, and thus no one of them possesses any absolute authority. Further, these manuscripts show wide variation in the sequence of the stories, in the connections among stories, and in the presence and position of the Links. It was early seen, however, that the work falls into ten clearly defined groups or fragments, within each of which the order of the tales is relatively stable. Very careful examination of the manuscript evidence and of such internal evidence as references to time or place and cross references among groups has led to various theories as to the sequence of groups which Chaucer would have used had he completed the *Tales*; and, in addition, some scholars have argued that we cannot hope to determine Chaucer's intention in this matter.

The two theories that editors of the *Canterbury Tales* have followed are called the "Chaucer Society Order" and the "Ellesmere Order"; the former term results from the sequence employed for the editing of various manuscripts published by the Chaucer Society, the latter term from the sequence found in the Ellesmere manuscript. The following tables show the differences:

CHAUCER SOCIETY ORDER

Group A: General Prologue, Knight, Miller, Reeve, and Cook
Group B^1: Man of Law
Group B^2: Shipman, Prioress, "Sir Thopas," "Melibeus," Monk, and Nun's Priest
Group C: Physician, Pardoner
Group D: Wife of Bath, Friar, and Summoner
Group E: Clerk, Merchant
Group F: Squire, Franklin
Group G: Second Nun, Canon's Yeoman
Group H: Manciple
Group I: Parson, Retractions

ELLESMERE ORDER

Fragment I: General Prologue, Knight, Miller, Reeve, and Cook
Fragment II: Man of Law
Fragment III: Wife of Bath, Friar, and Summoner
Fragment IV: Clerk, Merchant
Fragment V: Squire, Franklin
Fragment VI: Physician, Pardoner
Fragment VII: Shipman, Prioress, "Sir Thopas," "Melibeus," Monk, and Nun's Priest
Fragment VIII: Second Nun, Canon's Yeoman
Fragment IX: Manciple
Fragment X: Parson, Retractions

It is immediately apparent that these two orders differ in the positions of VI (C) and VII (B^2); but neither order is without difficulties. According to the Ellesmere sequence, certain geo-

[13

graphical references do not make sense: Sittingbourne, forty miles from London, is mentioned much earlier than Rochester, thirty miles from London (III, 847, and VII, 3116); according to the Chaucer Society sequence, various artistic considerations are violated: for example, the Pardoner's interruption of the Wife of Bath (III, 163–92) meaninglessly follows his prologue and tale.

Recently, Professor Pratt[6] has convincingly defended a third order:

Fragment   I: General Prologue, Knight, Miller, Reeve, and Cook
Fragment   II: Man of Law
Fragment   VII: Shipman, Prioress, "Sir Thopas," "Melibeus," Monk, and Nun's Priest
Fragment   III: Wife of Bath, Friar, and Summoner
Fragment   IV: Clerk, Merchant
Fragment   V: Squire, Franklin
Fragment   VI: Physician, Pardoner
Fragment   VIII: Second Nun, Canon's Yeoman
Fragment   IX: Manciple
Fragment   X: Parson, Retractions

This sequence, which will be followed in Part III of this book, resolves the difficulties occasioned by the two orders set forth earlier. Further, it seems very likely from manuscript evidence that the whole problem of Chaucer's intended order for the *Tales* arose simply because at the time of his death the series which we call Fragment VII had been removed—perhaps to his work-table—from its proper place between Fragments II and III in his master set of manuscripts.

Here, then, are the point of view and the five fundamental assumptions which will be used for this study of the twenty-three performances by Chaucer's Canterbury Pilgrims. But before we begin to examine these performances discretely, it will be well to consider the function of the General Prologue and of the Links.

6 R. A. Pratt, *PMLA*, LXVI (1951), 1141–67. This article includes a full discussion of earlier views.

II : THE MOVABLE STAGE

The General Prologue and the Links

Chaucer's originality in selecting a pilgrimage as the framing device for the *Canterbury Tales* is often noted.[1] This framework he built by means of the General Prologue and the Links, i.e., the individual prologues and epilogues that occur between tales. It will not, however, be my purpose to remark further on his originality; nor is this the place to examine in detail many of the sketches of the various Pilgrims included in the General Prologue, or many of the individual Links; rather, I shall treat those aspects of the General Prologue which serve as preparation for the later dramatic performances by the Pilgrims, and shall emphasize the opportunity furnished by the Links for sustaining dramatic development. In other words, we are here concerned with Chaucer's use of the General Prologue and the Links to set up and to keep before us an adequate stage upon which to present his Pilgrims.

Look first at the opening sentence of the *Canterbury Tales:*

> Whan that Aprille with his shoures soote
> The droghte of March hath perced to the roote,
> And bathed every veyne in swich licour
> Of which vertu engendred is the flour;
> Whan Zephirus eek with his sweete breeth
> Inspired hath in every holt and heeth
> The tendre croppes, and the yonge sonne
> Hath in the Ram his halve cours yronne,

[1] See the chapter by R. A. Pratt and Karl Young in *Sources and Analogues*, 1–81. For a different view, see J. V. Cunningham, *MP*, XLIX (1951–52), 172–81.

[15

> And smale foweles maken melodye,
> That slepen al the nyght with open ye
> (So priketh hem nature in hir corages);
> Thanne longen folk to goon on pilgrimages,
> And palmeres for to seken straunge strondes,
> To ferne halwes, kowthe in sondry londes;
> And specially from every shires ende
> Of Engelond to Caunterbury they wende,
> The hooly blisful martir for to seke,
> That hem hath holpen when that they were seeke.
>
> I, 1–18

For our purposes, this passage deserves close attention because of its appropriateness as an introductory statement to a narrative in which we are to meet realistic human beings rather than stock figures. Many critics have commented favorably upon this eighteen-line sentence, most frequently because of its "poetic" nature. It appears that they have generally used "poetic" to refer not to the rhyme and meter but to the treatment of various aspects of the arrival of spring: April showers, plants, Zephyrus, the new shoots, the sun, the small birds. The truth is, however, that such descriptions of the coming of spring are not at all unusual in the literature of the Middle Ages; in fact, they are present even in scientific writing. In other occurrences the critics have not judged these descriptions of spring "poetic," and we are not often told why Chaucer's lines deserve the term while similar passages do not. Perhaps "poetic" needs further qualification before it fits Chaucer's opening sentence. James Russell Lowell, in a well-known comment, said that after repeating it to himself a thousand times, "still at the thousandth time a breath of uncontaminate springtide seems to lift the hair upon my forehead." But Lowell did not state convincingly just why this is true of Chaucer's sentence and not true of other medieval descriptions of spring.

The sentence is made up of two main parts: the description of spring and the statement of the longing which people feel to go on pilgrimages. The former idea is expressed in the two *when*-clauses, the latter in the *then*-clause; thus the relationship of these two parts of the sentence—and therefore of the two ideas they express—is causal rather than parallel. The truth of the second part results from the truth of the first part: because of certain characteristics of spring, people long in that season to go on pilgrimages. The sentence opens with the natural world and shifts, in its second part (the *then*-clause) to the world of human beings. Or, rather, the second part correctly places human beings in their relation to the natural world during a particular season of the year. And, within the world of human beings, the application is rapidly narrowed from pilgrimages in general to the specific English pilgrimage to Canterbury. "A breath of uncontaminate springtide" seemed to lift Lowell's hair when he read this passage chiefly because Chaucer specifically applied his description of the arrival of spring to the world of human beings.

Another important result of the combination of ideas which Chaucer included in this sentence is that therein the purposes and implications of a pilgrimage are examined in terms broader than the usual religious ones. In its simplest form the sentence says: "When spring comes, then folks long to go on pilgrimages." The fundamental spiritual nature of a pilgrimage is not thereby overshadowed or obscured, but the significance of a pilgrimage as a social event is also given emphasis. The long, hard English winter is just over; people are tired of living indoors, feeding fires, and bundling up in heavy clothes to go outside. Therefore, when April comes, they long to go on pilgrimages. And this statement of the social appeal of a pilgrimage—a vacation in the spring—strikes a familiar note in the experience of most human beings. Then, behind this broadened point of view from which Chaucer examines a pilgrimage, there lies the whole question of man's relationship to religion (the afterlife) and to nature (this life). The implication is that most people perhaps cannot successfully deal with religion, represented here by a pilgrimage, unless the spiritual aspects of religion are modified by natural, earthly considerations, represented here by the coming of spring. Chaucer's sentence surpasses similar medieval passages mainly because in it the often-used description of the arrival of spring serves to broaden and to make more humanly realistic the purposes of a pilgrimage.

It is immediately apparent that, when so understood, the opening sentence of the *Canterbury Tales* has an important introductory bearing on the rest of the General Prologue and on the *Tales* as a whole. As has been frequently said, the General Prologue is especially remarkable because the Pilgrims who are portrayed therein are realistic human beings. There are among these Pilgrims those who, like the Parson and the Plowman, are making the pilgrimage because of sincere devotion. There are others, like the Miller and the Shipman, who seem more concerned with the vacation in the spring. But the presence of most of the Pilgrims is the result of a combination of motives. For Chaucer, unlike most other medieval writers, knew enough about people to realize that unmixed black and white are colors which should seldom be used when painting living portraits. As we have seen, the first sentence of the General Prologue skillfully introduces the human element into the idea of a pilgrimage.

To say that Chaucer's choice of a pilgrimage as the framework for his collection of stories was a stroke of genius is to risk triteness. But it should be observed that the opening sentence, by placing the social appeal of a pilgrimage alongside its religious significance, serves an important function in adequately preparing for the use of this framework throughout the *Tales*. It not only prepares for our meeting realistic rather than one-sided people in the General Prologue, but it also makes us ready for Chaucer's keeping these people alive—that is, many-sided—during the pilgrimage itself by means of the three techniques of dramatic presentation defined in Part I.

Following this opening sentence, Chaucer begins his narrative:

> Bifil that in that seson on a day,
> In Southwerk at the Tabard as I lay
> Redy to wenden on my pilgrymage
> To Caunterbury with ful devout corage,
> At nyght was come into that hostelrye
> Wel nyne and twenty in a compaignye,
> Of sondry folk, by aventure yfalle
> In felaweshipe, and pilgrimes were they alle,
> That toward Caunterbury wolden ryde.   I, 19–27

At once these lines introduce the story of the pilgrimage. With his usual expert economy in handling narrative openings, Chaucer rapidly gives here the answers to all the necessary questions: when?—one day in April; where?—in Southwark, at the Tabard Inn; why?—to go on the previously mentioned pilgrimage to Canterbury; and who?—"I" and a group of some twenty-nine other pilgrims. The second and perhaps less obvious purpose of the passage is to continue the combination, established by the opening sentence, of the two motivating aspects of a pilgrimage: religious devotion and a vacation in the spring. On the one hand, Chaucer here points out that he looks forward with "ful devout corage" to his pilgrimage; he will not slight the religious aspects of his trip. But on the other hand, he is well aware of the social possibilities and is quick to interest himself in the "sondry folk" who have already formed a "compaignye" that will make possible "felaweshipe" during the journey. And—most importantly, from his point of view as author—there can from such fellowship arise opportunities for the varied dramatic performances which the individual Pilgrims will give.

Fortunately, the atmosphere of the Tabard is conducive to fellowship, for no one could find fault with its accommodations (I, 28–29). Such an atmosphere is just what the sociable Chaucer, or our Narrator, as he might better be called, likes.[2] Everybody is in good spirits and busily goes about getting acquainted. The Narrator also moves easily about as he makes himself one of the group (I, 30–34). In these lines we quickly observe another introductory device for the drama that is to come later. For the Tabard possesses an air of pleasant, everyday informality in which the Pilgrims can relax and be themselves; furthermore, the reader can now guess that the Narrator is to be depended upon to get about and learn what is going on. He is a man who will miss none of the details in the gossip, the antagonisms, and the animosities that will inevitably spring up among the Pil-

---

[2] The idea of a sociable and gregarious Narrator in the *CT* is rejected—for no good reason, as I see it—in an article by Ben Kimpel in *ELH*, XX (1953), 77–86. See also the chapter on the *CT* in Henry Ludeke, *Die Funktionen der Erzählers in Chaucers epischer Dichtung.*

grims during the course of the pilgrimage. Also the narrative has progressed one step further, in that we have learned of the "forward" to get up early the next morning to start the journey, about which the Narrator promises to tell us.

Next comes the perfectly natural sentence to prepare us for meeting the Narrator's new companions (I, 35–42). By this time we realize sufficiently the probable keenness of the Narrator's powers of observation to feel that his descriptions of the other Pilgrims will be entertaining, and we begin to share his interest in these people as individuals to an extent that makes us willing for him to postpone his account of the trip in order to present the travelers. Moreover, his argument is a thoroughly sound one: if we are to understand and enjoy his account, we should first get to know the people who are taking the trip. The next 672 lines of the General Prologue present the portraits of the Pilgrims. In Part III, where we consider the individual performances, we shall examine carefully the particular traits set forth in many of these sketches. Here we are concerned with two technical devices which Chaucer uses in presenting the portraits, and which lead the reader to accept the Pilgrims as realistic persons. For in their form, as well as in their content, the portraits are a vital part of Chaucer's preparation for the dramatic events that will occur during the pilgrimage and the storytelling game.

First is the conversational ring of the style in which the individuals are described. This style continues the informal friendliness established by the Narrator's telling of his making himself a part of the group that entered this excellent inn, and it thus aids our acceptance of the Pilgrims' reality. One obvious means by which the conversational tone is conveyed to the reader is the Narrator's several references to the mechanics of what he is doing. He has taken this opportunity, while he has "tyme and space," to *tell*—not to write—about his companions; and he does not hesitate to remind us that this is an oral account, aimed at preparing us for understanding the coming narrative of the trip. Regularly a Pilgrim is introduced by the phrase "there was with us," or "there was," for we are dealing with the members of a particular group. After describing the Knight's character and travels, the Narrator will *tell* us of his array, but of the Lawyer's array he will *tell* no longer tale. Then, as he nears the end of the list, we are told "Ther was also a Reve, and a Millere,/A Somnour, and a Pardoner also,/A Maunciple, and myself—ther were namo." We are not allowed to forget that these sketches represent a rapid, oral interpolation which the Narrator kindly furnishes to help us understand the behavior of the Pilgrims after the journey begins.

Another means by which we are led to think of these sketches as parts of a natural, oral account is the Narrator's use of conversational exaggeration. The Friar is the best beggar in his order; no "vavasour" is so worthy as the Franklin, and no navigator so expert as the Shipman; the Physician is the world's best for talk of medicine and surgery; there could not be a better priest than the Parson; and so on. This sort of exaggeration is not unusual in everyday talk, and Chaucer had doubtless listened to enough stories around the Customs House to realize its value for producing conversational effects.

Chiefly, however, the conversational informality with which the sketches are delivered results from the Narrator's trick of halting momentarily his factual description of the clothes, appearance, or experience of a particular Pilgrim in order to insert a brief comment embodying his personal opinion. For example, in the sketch of the Sergeant of the Law, we are first told in a factual fashion:

> A Sergeant of the Lawe, war and wys,
> That often hadde been at the Parvys,
> Ther was also, ful riche of excellence.
> Discreet he was and of greet reverence—   I, 309–12

But in the next line the Narrator inserts his personal judgment: "He semed swich, his wordes weren so wise." Then the factual account is resumed for eight lines:

> Justice he was ful often in assise,
> By patente and by pleyn commissioun.
> For his science and for his heigh renoun,
> Of fees and robes hadde he many oon.
> So greet a purchasour was nowher noon:
> Al was fee symple to hym in effect;

His purchasyng myghte nat been infect.
Nowher so bisy a man as he ther nas.   I, 314–21

Then suddenly the Narrator puts in his evaluative remark: "And yet he semed bisier than he was." After that, the objective description is continued for the remaining eight lines of the sketch. Aside from the value of the Narrator's two brief personal comments in bringing alive his otherwise completely factual portrait of the Lawyer, these rapid expressions of opinion give this sketch the sound of everyday talk, in which a tinge of prejudice or gossip regularly turns up. Similar methods and results are present in the Narrator's pun on the philosophers' stone in the portrait of the Clerk; in the little joke he makes concerning "goldwasser" while describing the Physician; in the censure he passes on the Cook's "mormal"; in the mock innocence with which he suggests that the Shipman hails from "Dertemouthe"; in his sympathy with the Wife of Bath's deafness; in the bluntness with which he states a priest's responsibilities; and in his speculation concerning the Pardoner's physical defect. These instances, taken together, give to the sketches a ring of familiarity which inevitably leads the reader to think about the people described as living individuals who can play a part in the coming drama.

There is a second very effective device that Chaucer uses in the General Prologue to aid the reader in accepting the Pilgrims, from their portraits, as realistic people. Many critics have described this device as the combination of typical and individual traits; that is, a Pilgrim possesses certain characteristics which make him representative of a type, but, in addition, there is something about him which makes him stand out as an individual distinct from his type. Since the argument for the Pilgrims as representatives of types will not hold in some instances, a more exact way of describing this technique is to call it a combination of the expected and the unexpected. In any event, this latter terminology has the advantage of placing the emphasis upon the reader's reaction to the technique. Look, for example, at the Knight, with whose portrait the Narrator "first begins":

A Knyght ther was, and that a worthy man,
That fro the tyme that he first bigan

> To riden out, he loved chivalrie,
> Trouthe and honour, fredom and curteisie.   I, 43–46

So far, there is nothing surprising to a reader in these lines about the Knight. We expected to meet a brave and honorable representative of the age of chivalry. Neither are we surprised by the next twenty-one lines of the sketch, from which we learn of the Knight's wide travels and consistent success in campaigning. But then comes the unexpected shift:

> And though that he were worthy, he was wys,
> And of his port as meeke as is a mayde.
> He nevere yet no vileynye ne sayde
> In al his lyf unto no maner wight.
> He was a verray, parfit gentil knyght.
> But, for to tellen yow of his array,
> His hors were goode, but he was nat gay.
> Of fustian he wered a gypon
> Al bismotered with his habergeon,
> For he was late ycome from his viage,
> And wente for to doon his pilgrymage.   I, 68–78

From this latter part of the sketch we learn that the Knight is prudent, humble, circumspect in speech, modest in dress, and serious in religious devotion. And these are not traits we would expect to encounter in a professional military man. Thus, Chaucer's Knight is both courageous in battle and humble in manner, widely traveled and gently spoken, highly successful in war and truly devout. As a result of this combination of expected and unexpected traits, the Knight assumes memorable individuality in the mind of the reader.

It would seem, then, that in large part because of the conversational informality used in the portraits, and by the combining of expected and unexpected traits within a given portrait, we are led to accept the Pilgrims as convincing characters who can participate fully in the dramatic recital which we have been promised. But first the Narrator must pick up matters where he left them. The sketches completed, we therefore have a passage (I, 715–24) which serves as conclusion for the series of portraits and as reintroduction for the narrative of the pilgrimage. This passage refreshes our memory—possibly a bit hazy after the lengthy

[23

series of portraits—of the where, when, and why of this account, information that we had gained from the second sentence in the General Prologue. Now that we have met the people concerned, we can be sure that an account of their trip will be of interest. More specifically, this passage prepares for a report of the happenings in the Tabard Inn "that ilke nyght." But before giving this report, the Narrator wishes to make clear just where he stands with regard to certain dubious aspects of his responsibility. He accordingly launches at this point his mock apology (I, 725–46) : we should not consider him vulgar if he speaks plainly in reporting the words of his companions, for everyone knows that any reporter must either repeat matters as exactly as he can, no matter how crude they are, or else be guilty of lying. He also wishes forgiveness if he does not treat the Pilgrims according to rank. The effect of this mock apology is, of course, a whetting of the reader's appetite for what is to follow. The account will not be refined; if people act or speak improperly (as people sometimes do) we shall hear about it. And there will be no formalities about "degree"; these Pilgrims will be handled informally, not stiffly according to protocol. As preparation for convincing dramatic performances, this apology is a superb touch, suitably capped by the Narrator's "My wit is short, ye may wel understonde" ("After all, I'm just an ordinary sort of fellow, the same as you"). Now we are to get the report of the night's happenings, in which the Host, Harry Bailly, plays an important part.

The Host performs marvelously, making everyone "greet chiere," and we see why at the Tabard a guest was "esed atte beste." Soon a fine supper is served; "Strong was the wyn, and wel to drynke us leste." For the time being, the social aspects of the pilgrimage are uppermost. The Host is an impressive person, fit to be a major-domo of a palace:

> A large man he was with eyen stepe—
> A fairer burgeys is ther noon in Chepe—
> Boold of his speche, and wys, and wel ytaught,
> And of manhod hym lakkede right naught.   I, 753–56

He is also a merry man, but his love of mirth does not interfere with his business acumen:

> Eek therto he was right a myrie man,
> And after soper pleyen he bigan,
> And spak of myrthe amonges othere thynges,
> Whan that we hadde maad our rekenynges.   I, 757–60

And the Host's merry speeches include his proposals for the storytelling game.

Actually, the drama of the Canterbury pilgrimage can be said to commence right here in the Host's proposals (I, 761–821), if it did not start in the thirty-first line of the poem, with the Narrator's making himself one of the group. Certainly it is worthy of note that the Host's speech represents the first words spoken by anyone other than the Narrator. So far we have had expert preparation for dramatic effectiveness, but the drama has been static. Now the curtain rises, and the action begins. And this first action, in which the Host makes his proposals to the Pilgrims, is characterized by interesting dramatic overtones that include a rather subtle play of human relationships between the Host and the company of Pilgrims. In his first and very flattering speech, Harry tells the Pilgrims that he has just thought of a game which will entertain them while traveling and which will cost them nothing. He states, however, that before he will tell them his idea, they must all agree "For to stonden at my juggement,/And for to werken as I shall yow seye." At that, he orders the group to make evident by a show of hands whether or not they accept his stipulation, and he pauses for their decision.

The next four lines, in which the Narrator reports the group's acceptance of the Host's stipulations, show a bored and indifferent reaction on the part of the Pilgrims to Harry's first speech. At first glance, this reaction is a bit puzzling. The Narrator says, in effect: "We did not worry much about how we voted, for the matter seemed unimportant. The easiest thing to do was to let him tell his idea as he pleased." The indifferent attitude shown here by the Pilgrims is understandable when we realize that the easy assumption of authority and the concern for money apparent in the Host's speech might well have caused the Pilgrims to form an unfavorable first impression of him and to be somewhat suspicious of any idea to which he asked their blind agreement

That Harry felt this coolness and undercurrent of dislike is evidenced by the second line of his next speech: "But taak it nought, I prey yow, in desdeyn."

In his second speech the Host advances his suggestion of the storytelling game as a means of entertainment on the trip and offers his services—without charge—as guide. At the conclusion of this speech, he again asks for a vote from the Pilgrims. This time the agreement to his suggestion is enthusiastically unanimous. Oaths are sworn with "ful glad herte," and the Pilgrims voluntarily increase the Host's authority over them, making him their "governour," "juge," and "reportour," as well as "gyde." This warm reaction on the part of the Pilgrims to Harry's second speech, in striking contrast to the coolness they evidenced after his first, is an indication that they now feel somewhat relieved to find that his idea involves neither annoyance nor expense for them. Therefore, in an effort to offset their former indifference, they now bend over backwards in agreeing to Harry's proposal and to his leadership of the pilgrimage. On the basis of the friendly confidence thus established, the wine is fetched and drunk, and "to reste wente echon,/Withouten any lenger taryynge."

By means of this brief scene after supper in the Tabard, the Host is adequately introduced as the central unifying device for the *Tales*. He will control the company as best he can, and we shall often see the various Pilgrims through his eyes, as he appoints a new storyteller, comments upon a tale just finished, or attempts to bring forth private information from one or another of his company. But Harry is no mechanical master of ceremonies, to be used only as background against which the other Pilgrims are projected. By having the Host furnish many insights into his own character, Chaucer effects a complex dramatic development whereby we learn of such matters as Harry's married life, his taste in literature, and his political views. There can be no doubt that the drama of the Canterbury Pilgrims is made possible in large part by Chaucer's use of the Host as the unifying device.

From some points of view, the General Prologue should end at line 821, when the company goes "to reste"; the remaining lines

(I, 822–58) might better be considered the first link, a prologue to the Knight's Tale. As we have seen, the General Prologue, exclusive of this introduction to the Knight's Tale, is aimed primarily at preparing for the dramatic activities of the Pilgrims as they travel. It is now necessary to notice briefly the device Chaucer employs for retaining a movable stage throughout his book.

This device is the use of Links between the tales—short dramatic scenes in which various Pilgrims take part. The presence of these links allows for the appearance in action of the people whom we met at rest in the portraits that make up the bulk of the General Prologue. As an example, look at the introduction to the Knight's Tale which we just noticed. On the first morning of the pilgrimage, Harry gathers his "flok" together and leads them a short distance from Southwark. Then, with lordly authority, he reminds them of their agreement, the night before, to the storytelling game and to obeying his decisions. With that, he has them draw straws to see who shall tell the first tale. Whether by chance or through Harry's respect for "degree," the "cut fil to the Knyght," at which everyone is pleased. The Knight, behaving exactly in accord with what we learned about him from his portrait, says:

> Syn I shal bigynne the game,
> What, welcome be the cut, a Goddes name!
> Now lat us ryde, and herkneth what I seye.   I, 853–55

From this introduction we are in a position to look upon the story of Arcite and Palamon as a recital by the Knight, not just as one tale in a collection by Chaucer.

Immediately after the Knight's Tale we find another Link, the Prologue to the Miller's Tale, which offers even greater dramatic complication than the scene introducing the Knight's story. Not only is the Miller's Tale skillfully introduced by this link, but the Miller-Reeve antagonism is made evident and the way is thus also prepared for the Reeve's performance after the Miller's. By no means are all the Links in the *Canterbury Tales* so fully developed, and in some instances Chaucer provided no link to introduce a Pilgrim's tale. We can be almost certain, however, that had Chaucer finished his book, he would have given full attention to furnishing additional ones. And it is worth noting, I think, that the Links which come at the end of the *Tales*—Fragments VIII, IX, and X: Second Nun, Canon's Yeoman, Manciple, and Parson—represent as full and careful development as do those in Fragment I. Although Chaucer certainly did not start with the General Prologue and write straight through the Parson's Tale, there is every indication that throughout the composition of that portion of the *Tales* which he did complete, he realized fully the importance of the Links as a dramatic device.

At times we find within the *Tales* short scenes that are actually links even though they are not labeled as prologue to this tale, or epilogue to that. We have seen one example of this at the end of the General Prologue, in the lines introducing the Knight's Tale. Another occurs in the Friar-Summoner controversy near the end of the Wife of Bath's Prologue (III, 829–56). The Friar takes exception to the length of this prologue, and the Summoner attacks the Friar for meddling. Here, even before the current performance—that of the Wife—is completed, Chaucer has set up a motivated situation for the next two performances, those of the Friar and the Summoner. The opportunity for such flexibility in the use of links is one of the most prominent evidences of their value as a dramatic technique by means of which the Pilgrims are kept as the center of focus throughout the *Tales*. We turn now to the first of the performances by Chaucer's actor-Pilgrims.

III :

The Twenty-three Performances

1. THE KNIGHT

*I*n the past, the Knight and his recital in the *Canterbury Tales* have been favorite topics for critical comment, and, judging from the half-dozen or more studies which have recently appeared, this interest is in no danger of slackening.[1] Two aspects of the Knight's sketch in the General Prologue have received careful attention: his travels, and his possible connections with the Lollard movement. But his tale is a subject for investigators far more frequently than his sketch. Comparison of the tale with its chief source, the relation of the tale to the perhaps lost "Palamon and Arcite" mentioned in the Prologue to the *Legend of Good Women*, the significance of the astrological material in the tale, and analysis of the characters of Palamon and Arcite— these are topics which have interested most of those who have written about the Knight's Tale. Yet one fact emerges from a reading of all these studies: very seldom has this story been seriously considered in its dramatic context as a performance by the Knight, who is presented to us in the General Prologue and who also appears briefly elsewhere in the *Canterbury Tales*.[2]

[1] E. B. Ham surveyed many of these studies recently; see *ELH*, XVII (1950), 252–61.
[2] William Frost analyzed the tale from this point of view; see *RES*, XXV (1949), 289–304.

[29

He loved chivalrie, Trouthe and honour, fredom and curteisie

Any discussion of the Knight and his tale from this point of view requires as preliminary the answering of three pertinent questions: (1) Are we justified in reading the story as a speech by the Knight? (2) In what ways have earlier commentators considered this story and its teller suited to each other? (3) How did Chaucer handle his source materials in forming this story?

The first of these questions can certainly be answered in the affirmative. The opening ten lines of the tale establish the narrative of Theseus' victory over the Amazons, his marriage to Hippolyta, and his journey homeward with his wife and her sister Emily. Then we have a series of direct comments from the Knight to his audience; for example:

> Lete I this noble duc to Atthenes ryde.   I, 873
>
> I wolde have toold yow fully. . . .   I, 876
>
> But al that thyng I moot as now forbere.
> I have, God woot, a large feeld to ere,
> And wayke been the oxen in my plough.
> The remenant of the tale is long ynough.
> I wol nat letten eek noon of this route;
> Lat every felawe telle his tale aboute,
> And lat se now who shal the soper wynne;
> And ther I lefte, I wol ayeyn bigynne.   I, 885–92

Such comments leave no doubt about the dramatic situation: the Knight is talking directly to the Pilgrims. The end of the tale also makes this clear; the Knight says: "Thus endeth Palamon and Emelye;/And God save al this faire compaignye!" (I, 3107–3108). And the Miller's Prologue begins: "Whan that the Knyght had thus his tale ytoold" (I, 3109). The Knight is speaking to the company throughout his tale, and even though Chaucer should probably have revised line 1201,[3] critics err when they read passages in the tale as direct statements from "the author of the Wife of Bath," or state that in one instance "Chaucer himself steps outside the story [the Knight's Tale] long enough to remark that everything which may transpire in this world is precisely as God planned it."[4]

[3] "But of that storie list me nat to write."
[4] H. B. Hinckley, *Notes on Chaucer*, 113; Curry, *Sciences*, 161.

Consideration of the second question listed above indicates that though commentators generally find the Knight and his story well suited, there is a noticeable lack of detailed treatment of this subject. We encounter only such short remarks as that the tale "seems as if made for the Knight,"[5] that "a specimen of chivalric romance" is a proper story for a knight to tell,[6] that realistic military details in the story come naturally from the mouth of a fourteenth-century knight,[7] or that the tale is "perfectly suited" to its teller.[8] I find only one writer who feels that the tale is not well-suited to the Knight; he says: ". . . to this elderly, crusading Knight is assigned a tale of young love in a Grecian setting. Certainly this story would have suited the Esquire much better."[9] But the integrated Boethian elements of the Knight's Tale would indeed sound strange in the mouth of the youthful and inexperienced Squire.

As to the third question, concerning Chaucer's handling of his source materials, numerous scholars have compared this story with its primary source, Boccaccio's *Teseida*.[10] Chaucer increased the pace of the story by considerable cutting of his original and adapted the tale to the life of his own time. Most importantly, from our point of view, he made significant additions to his original.[11] Outstanding among these additions are passages from Boethius' *Consolation of Philosophy*. B. L. Jefferson indicated the extent of Chaucer's borrowing from Boethius[12] and stated, in connection with the *Troilus* and the Knight's Tale: "Chaucer did not use the Boethian material haphazardly for the interest that might be attached to the particular lines in themselves, but . . . he brings its consideration of the fundamental questions of human existence to bear in a large way on the lives of his characters."[13] However, Jefferson did not show in any detail just how

[5] Bernhard ten Brink, *History of English Literature*, II, 156.

[6] Robinson, *Works*, 4.   [7] Stuart Robertson, *JEGP*, XIV (1915), 226–55.

[8] Marchette Chute, *Geoffrey Chaucer of England*, 259.

[9] J. R. Hulbert, *SP*, XLV (1948), 575.

[10] See the chapter by R. A. Pratt in *Sources and Analogues*, 82–105.

[11] See Robinson, *Works*, 4–5.

[12] *Chaucer and the Consolation of Philosophy of Boethius*, cited hereafter as *Chaucer and the Consolation;* see also Curry, *Sciences*, 154–63.

[13] Jefferson, *Chaucer and the Consolation*, 120.

Chaucer brought the Boethian material to bear on the lives of the characters in the Knight's Tale.

Too often the Knight's Tale is considered only as an adaptation of the *Teseide*, as a romance of spectacle and movement, suited to the Knight merely by reason of his profession. Yet there is a clearly defined philosophical theme which dominates the Knight's Tale and which is not apparent to any large degree in the *Teseide*.[14] This theme derives from the inclusion of terms and passages from the *Consolation* at crucial places in the chivalric narrative. And the resulting philosophical romance is thus skillfully suited to its teller, who is interested both in warfare and in man's relation to God. In order to see this suitability in full detail, let us first examine the Knight's character as it appears from the sketch in the General Prologue, enlarging upon an idea already presented in Part II, and then analyze the working out of the philosophical theme in his tale.

When, near the beginning of the General Prologue, Chaucer says that he will now describe the Pilgrims whom he met at the Tabard, we have just before the Knight's sketch the line, "And at a knyght than wol I first bigynne" (I, 42). From this line the reader naturally expects to meet a man who is courageous and who is both widely experienced and outstanding in warfare. Such expectations are fulfilled; the Knight is outstanding in his profession. But there is an unexpected element in his thirty-five-line portrait: this man is also notable for courteous conduct and piety, and these are not qualities regularly found in professional military men of any age. In the fourteenth century, "everyone knew how the true knight should conduct himself and everyone knew how seldom he was encountered in the world of actuality."[15] This statement gains support from consideration of Chaucer's comment about the Knight: "And though that he were worthy, he was wys,/And of his port as meeke as is a mayde" (I, 68–69). We can hardly fail to miss the force of the introductory "and though": even though the Knight was brave, he was pru-

---

[14] See H. S. Wilson, *UTQ*, XVIII (1948–49), 131–46, for a statement of the philosophical theme in the *Teseide* and in the Knight's Tale.
[15] Bowden, *Commentary*, 45.

dent and as modest as a maiden, contrary to the usual characteristics of "worthy" knights.

We now come to a consideration of the passages in the Knight's Tale which Chaucer took from Boethius' *Consolation of Philosophy*. This influential book Chaucer himself had earlier translated, and it seems to have been his favorite philosophical treatise. Three speeches in the tale contain the bulk of the borrowings: the speech of Arcite in *Prima Pars* (I, 1251–74), wherein he blames himself for seeking false felicity; the speech of Palamon in *Prima Pars* (I, 1303–33), wherein he finds the gods at fault; and the speech of Theseus in *Pars Quarta* (I, 2987–3040), wherein he discusses an established beneficent order in the universe. These three passages account for only about 100 lines among the more than 2,200 which make up the Knight's Tale.[16] Most of the 100 lines deal with one point, "the relation of Providence to man's happiness," and this point is, of course, at the very center of the *Consolation*.[17] Moreover, these three passages from the *Consolation* which Chaucer chose to add to his primary source represent the core of Boethius' argument and conclusion. It is also particularly noteworthy that Chaucer placed these passages at crucial positions in the Knight's Tale. The speeches of Arcite and Palamon come shortly after the two young knights are introduced, and furnish a key to the point of view held by each; Theseus' "bond-of-love" speech is placed near the end of the tale and sets forth the conclusion to which Lady Philosophy leads Boethius. Thus, as we shall later see in detail, the 100 philosophical lines in the Knight's Tale, coming from the *Consolation*, both motivate the characters and reflect upon the action occurring in the remaining 2,100 lines, which present the chivalric narrative of the *Teseida*.

But, in addition to the three speeches mentioned above, there are a number of shorter passages in the Knight's Tale either derived from, or reminiscent of, the *Consolation*. The very striking

[16] Jefferson, *Chaucer and the Consolation*, 130–31, 142–43.
[17] *Ibid.*, 118, 131.

34]

fact about these passages—so far unnoticed, I think—is that they regularly occur as explanation for the important events in the narrative. When Theseus decides to go hunting—a decision vital to the narrative, since it causes him to find Arcite and Palamon fighting in the wood, to learn of their love for Emily, and to arrange for the tournament—we have the following passage, based on Book IV, prosa 6, of the *Consolation:*

> The destinee, ministre general,
> That executeth in the world over al
> The purveiaunce that God hath seyn biforn,
> So strong it is that, though the world had sworn
> The contrarie of a thyng by ye or nay,
> Yet somtyme it shal fallen on a day
> That falleth nat eft withinne a thousand yeer.
> For certeinly, oure appetites heer,
> Be it of werre, or pees, or hate, or love,
> Al is this reuled by the sighte above.
> This mene I now by myghty Theseus,
> That for to hunten is so desirus.   I, 1663–74

It is the Boethian Destiny that causes Theseus to go hunting.

Examination of the chain of important events, step by step through the Knight's Tale, shows that almost without exception the Knight accounts for each event by suggesting that it resulted from an influence outside the individual. This influence comes, in the majority of cases, from agents who hold established places in the hierarchy, set forth by Boethius in the *Consolation*, through which God deals with human beings. Providence, Destiny, Fortune, Nature, "cas," "aventure"—these are the Boethian terms that appear in the passages under discussion. A listing of the chain of important events in the Knight's Tale, together with the passages accounting for these events, shows this relationship:

1. The noble ladies persuade Theseus to fight against Creon; thus Arcite and Palamon come to be prisoners in Athens.

> Now be we caytyves, as it is wel seene,
> Thanked be Fortune and hire false wheel,
> That noon estaat assureth to be weel.   I, 924–26

2. Emily walks in the garden; thus Palamon and Arcite can see her.

> The sesoun priketh every gentil herte,
> And maketh hym out of his slep to sterte,
> And seith, "Arys, and do thyn observaunce."
> This maked Emelye have remembraunce
> To doon honour to May, and for to ryse.   I, 1043–47

3. Palamon looks out of the window; thus he falls in love with Emily.

> And so bifel, by aventure or cas,
> That thurgh a wyndow, thikke of many a barre
> Of iren greet and square as any sparre,
> He cast his eye upon Emelya.   I, 1074–77

4. Arcite, released through Perotheus' request, must return to Thebes to suffer the malady of love and leave Palamon near Emily in Athens.

> Wel hath Fortune yturned thee the dys,
> That hast the sighte of hire, and I th'absence.
>   I, 1238–39
>
> For possible is . . .
>
> .   .   .   .
>
> That by som cas, syn Fortune is chaungeable,
> Thow maist to thy desir somtyme atteyne.   I, 1240–43

5. A vision of Mercury causes Arcite to return to Athens.

> . . . To Atthenes shaltou wende,
> Ther is thee shapen of thy wo an ende.   I, 1391–92

6. Palamon escapes from prison.

> Were it by aventure or destynee—
> As, whan a thyng is shapen, it shal be—
> That soone after the mydnyght Palamoun,
> By helpyng of a freend, brak his prisoun.   I, 1465–68

7. Arcite goes to the wood where Palamon is hiding.

> Now wol I turne to Arcite ageyn,
> That litel wiste how ny that was his care,
> Til that Fortune had broght him in the snare.
>   I, 1488–90

8. Arcite selects a path near Palamon's bush; thus Palamon can overhear him.

> And in a path he rometh up and doun,
> Ther as by aventure this Palamoun
> Was in a bussh. . . .   I, 1515–17

9. Theseus decides to go hunting, thereby finding Palamon and Arcite. Lines 1663–75, quoted and analyzed on page 35.

10. Theseus is moved to have mercy on the two knights.

> For pitee renneth soone in gentil herte.   I, 1761

11. Theseus proposes the tournament to settle the love-debate.

> Thanne shal I yeve Emelya to wyve
> To whom that Fortune yeveth so fair a grace.
>   I, 1860–61

12. The gods arrange the defeat of Palamon in the tournament and the subsequent injury to Arcite.

> Now weep namoore, I shal doon diligence
> That Palamon, that is thyn owene knyght,
> Shal have his lady, as thou hast him hight.
> Though Mars shal helpe his knyght. . . .   I, 2470–73

13. Arcite dies.

> Nature hath now no dominacioun.
> And certeinly, ther Nature wol nat wirche,
> Fare wel phisik! go ber the man to chirche!   I, 2758–60

14. Palamon and Emily marry.

> Thanne is it wysdom, as it thynketh me,
> To maken vertu of necessitee.   I, 3041–42

Of these fourteen events forming the narrative skeleton of the Knight's Tale, nine (Nos. 1, 3, 4, 6, 7, 8, 9, 11, and 13) are clearly explained as resulting from influences exerted by agents who appear in the Boethian hierarchy. For each of the remaining five events, a definite cause is assigned, and in three instances possible connection with the Boethian hierarchy is fairly obvious. The season (May) causes Emily to walk in the garden. "May" can here be understood as a representative of Nature.

"Pitee" causes Theseus to have mercy on Palamon and Arcite when he finds them fighting in the wood. Although this "pitee" is not an outside agent, it is often the equivalent, in Chaucer's usage, for the gentilesse, or noble conduct, which Lady Philosophy explained to Boethius.[18] The "necessitee" of which Theseus speaks in urging the marriage of Palamon and Emily is, of course, a result of the whole system set forth in the *Consolation*. The two remaining events involve the gods. A vision of Mercury sends Arcite back to Athens; and Saturn, Venus, Mars, and Pluto are involved in Arcite's mortal injury. Although these influences lie outside the Boethian system and are best regarded as a necessary part of the machinery of the story, they perform exactly the same function as do the agents from the *Consolation* in the motivation of the other events.

We are justified in concluding, then, that rather than being limited to the three speeches by Arcite, Palamon, and Theseus, the Boethian influence is so pervasive as virtually to control the action in the chivalric narrative which Chaucer took from the *Teseide*. This conclusion can be strengthened by careful examination, within the framework of the narrative, of the function and effect of the three speeches, and of the philosophical shifts which Palamon and Arcite experience.

Of the three Boethian speeches, the two by Arcite and Palamon (I, 1251–74, 1303–33) present an inescapable contrast. After his release from prison, Arcite says:

> Allas, why pleynen folk so in commune
> On purveiaunce of God, or of Fortune,
> That yeveth hem ful ofte in many a gyse
> Wel bettre than they kan hemself devyse?   I, 1251–54

And, he continues, "We seken faste after felicitee,/But we goon wrong ful often, trewely." Finally, he applies these views to his own situation and concludes that, since he cannot see Emily, he is as good as dead. Thus Arcite takes full blame for his miserable state and acknowledges the "purveiaunce of God." Meanwhile,

[18] Jefferson, *Chaucer and the Consolation*, 101–102.

Palamon entertains no such sweet reasoning. When he learns that Arcite is now at liberty "Swich sorwe he maketh that the grete tour/Resouneth of his youlyng and clamour." He thinks Arcite will be able to raise an army in Thebes and thereby win Emily, while he rots in prison. Then he cries out against the "crueel goddes," who, caring no more for mankind than for sheep, often permit the innocent to suffer. Consequently, he asks: "What governance is in this prescience,/That giltelees tormenteth innocence?" Palamon leaves the answer "to dyvynys," but he is convinced "that in this world greet pyne ys." His particular "pyne" is twofold: as a Theban he is kept in prison because of Saturn and Juno; and Venus torments him with jealousy and fear of Arcite. Thus Palamon finds no benevolent order or justice in the universe.

Although the two knights were indistinguishable when they were found in the pile of bodies after the battle, it is immediately apparent that at this point in the story, in their contrasting reactions to adversity, Arcite and Palamon represent to some degree the two states of mind that Boethius experiences in the *Consolation*. Arcite's view here is similar to that which Boethius has attained at the end of the book, after assimilating the teachings of Lady Philosophy; but Palamon here holds views similar to those of Boethius at the opening of it. The question at once arises as to just what shifts occur in the course of the Knight's Tale in the attitude held by each of the young men, as a result of the impact upon them of the series of incidents which they experience. Consideration of this question involves examining the characters of Palamon and Arcite in Boethian terms, and such an approach may well supplement the numerous studies, based almost exclusively on Chaucer's alterations of the *Teseida*, which treat the two heroes of the Knight's Tale.[19] The answer is relatively simple in the case of Palamon. With Arcite, however, we have an extremely complex problem.

Palamon's behavior preceding his Boethian speech is quite

---

[19] See, for example: H. N. Fairchild, *JEGP*, XXVI (1927), 285–93; J. R. Hulbert, *SP*, XXVI (1929), 375–85; P. F. Baum, *MLN*, XLVI (1931), 302–304; A. H. Marckwardt, University of Michigan *Contributions in Modern Philology*, No. 5 (1947); H. S. Wilson, *UTQ*, XVIII (1948–49), 131–46; W. H. French, *JEGP*, XLVIII (1949), 320–28.

consistent with the view expressed in that speech. In prison he impatiently roams back and forth (I, 1065, 1071) and steadily complains about his situation: " 'That he was born,' ful ofte he seyde, 'allas!' " (I, 1073). Then, at the sight of Emily, whom he mistakes for Venus, he prays for his and Arcite's release from prison (I, 1107). Finally, in the dispute as to who has pre-emption in loving Emily, Palamon addresses Arcite with the same injured air (I, 1129–51) that he later adopts in crying out against the cruel gods because Arcite is at liberty while he remains in prison. The point is that, throughout *Prima Pars*, Palamon has no conception of his place in a benevolently ordained universe and is intent only on attaining earthly happiness, or what Lady Philosophy calls "false felicity."

We see no change in his attitude until Arcite dies. Rather than accept his adverse situation with Boethian passivity, he manages, after seven years in prison, to drug his jailer and to escape with the help of a friend (I, 1467–75), and hides in the wood in great fear of death (I, 1518). His terrible anger (I, 1576–78) when he overhears Arcite's complaint causes him to force the duel in the wood (I, 1587). Similarly, in his prayer to Venus he says:

> Fynd thow the manere hou, and in what wyse:
> I recche nat but it may bettre be
> To have victorie of hem, or they of me,
> So that I have my lady in myne armes.   I, 2244–47

But with Arcite's death after the tournament, Palamon gives up his impatient complaining and his restless striving to fulfill his desires. He marches in the funeral procession "in clothes blake, ydropped al with teeres" (I, 2884), and after "certeyn yeres" (I, 2967) he is still in "blake clothes" and in haste comes sorrowfully in answer to Theseus' summons (I, 2975–80). Indeed, he is now called "gentil Palamon" (I, 2976), and is apparently most receptive to the Boethian philosophy that Theseus advances in his "bond-of-love" speech (I, 2987–3074). As "gentil Palamon" (I, 3077), who has now realized the folly of his blind pursuit of false felicity and has thus reached some understanding of an established benevolent order in the universe, he deserves Emily's hand and is a fit partner in a marriage which accomplishes wide political benefits (I, 2970–74): "And thus with alle blisse and melodye/Hath Palamon ywedded Emelye." The Knight takes his leave of this couple in words which suggest that Palamon's happy state results, in part at least, from his realization of his former misconceptions and his present acceptance of the Boethian view:

> And God, that al this wyde world hath wroght,
> Sende hym his love that hath it deere aboght;
> For now is Palamon in alle wele,
> Lyvynge in blisse, in richesse, and in heele,
> And Emelye hym loveth so tendrely,
> And he hire serveth al so gentilly,
> That nevere was ther no word hem bitwene
> Of jalousie or any oother teene.
> Thus endeth Palamon and Emelye.   I, 3099–3107

Palamon has bought God's love "deere," but he *has* "aboght" it.

As suggested earlier, Arcite wrestles far more often than Palamon with the questions of man's relation to God and the individual's place in the universe. Arcite's first speech comes as advice to Palamon when the latter cries out at the sight of Emily:

> ... Cosyn myn, what eyleth thee,
> That art so pale and deedly on to see?
> Why cridestow? who hath thee doon offence?
> For Goddes love, taak al in pacience
> Oure prisoun, for it may noon oother be.
> Fortune hath yeven us this adversitee.
> Som wikke aspect or disposicioun
> Of Saturne, by som constellacioun,
> Hath yeven us this, although we hadde it sworn;
> So stood the hevene whan that we were born.
> We moste endure it; this is the short and playn.
>   I, 1081–91

Here Arcite shows full awareness of, and compliance with, an established order, an order which "for Goddes love" should be accepted patiently. This Boethian view is, as we have seen, directly opposite to that held by the impatient Palamon in *Prima Pars* of the Knight's Tale. But almost immediately, when Palamon explains the cause of his outcry, Arcite looks at Emily and also falls in love with her. Falling in love brings an entirely new problem into his life, a problem of greater importance to him than imprisonment (I, 1118–22), and we soon see him giving up his former patient acceptance of his lot. He now argues bitterly with Palamon about pre-emption in loving Emily. When Palamon reminds him of their sworn brotherhood, Arcite quotes an "olde clerkes sawe": "Who shal yeve a lovere any lawe?" (I, 1164). Here is certainly a change from Arcite's former belief in immutable laws that produce situations which "may no other be." He continues:

> Love is a gretter lawe, by my pan,
> Than may be yeve to any erthely man;
> And therfore positif lawe and swich decree
> Is broken al day for love in ech degree.   I, 1165–68

Arcite now accepts love as a greater force than "positif" or man-made law,[20] and is eager to win Emily's "mercy and hir grace" (I, 1120).

It is of some importance to notice that the proverb which Arcite quotes here is from the *Consolation* and occurs in the course of the brief recital of Orpheus' loss of Eurydice, a story used as an *exemplum* pointing up the folly of seeking worldly happiness. In fact, the following moral is drawn from the story:

This fable apertenith to yow alle, whosoevere desireth or seketh to lede his thought into the sovereyn day *(that is to seyn, into cleernesse of sovereyn good)*. For whoso that evere be so overcomen that he ficche his eien into the put of helle *(that is to seyn, whoso sette his thoughtes in erthly thinges)*, al that evere he hath drawen of the noble good celestial he lesith it, whanne he looketh the helles *(that is to seyn, into lowe thinges of the erthe)*.[21]

This context for Arcite's "sawe" indicates his possible knowledge of the risk he runs in shifting from his former patient acceptance of his lot, for "Orpheus lokede abakward on Erudyce his wif, *and lost hire, and was deed.*"[22] The point is, I think, that Ar-

---

[20] See G. C. Macauley, *MLR*, IV (1910), 17.
[21] *Boece*, Bk. III, m. 12, ll. 67–78, as presented in Robinson, *Works*, 418.
[22] *Ibid.*, ll. 65–67. (Italics mine.)

cite has now encountered an earthly end which he strongly desires to fulfill; in the face of this desire, his patient acceptance of prison, stated in his earlier speech, goes by the board.

Although as a result of falling in love he becomes, like Palamon, extremely impatient with his imprisonment, Arcite still maintains his former opinion that he and Palamon must spend their lives in the tower because of Fortune and the stars; he draws an analogy to the hounds, the bone, and the kite (I, 1177–80) and concludes his argument as follows:

> And, therfore, at the kynges court, my brother,
> Ech man for hymself, ther is noon oother.
> Love, if thee list, for I love and ay shal;
> And soothly, leeve brother, this is al.
> Heere in this prisoun moote we endure,
> And everich of us take his aventure.   I, 1181–86

It would seem that Arcite feels that he is controlled by two forces —Love and Fortune. He is determined to serve Love, but he realizes that his imprisonment is a part of an established plan.

Before long, however, it happens that Perotheus comes to visit Theseus and brings about Arcite's release. But Arcite is forbidden to remain in Athens and consequently can never see Emily again. His reaction to this event is stated in his Boethian speech, which shows him once more in the position of passive acceptance of his lot, for his experience has now taught him that it does no good to wish for changes.

Upon his return to Thebes he suffers the malady of love for "a yeer or two" (I, 1381). This alters his appearance beyond recognition; he becomes so feeble that there is every indication of approaching death. The two controlling forces, Fortune and Love, are leading him to destruction. At this point "hym thoughte how" the winged god Mercury appeared to him as he slept. Mercury says: "To Atthenes shaltou wende,/Ther is thee shapen of thy wo an ende" (I, 1391–92). Arcite awakens and decides to go to Athens to see Emily, no matter how much he suffers for it; he says, in fact: "In hire presence I recche nat to sterve" (I, 1398). This passage has been explained as an example of the deceitful oracle employed for dramatic irony.[23] Thus Mercury, possessing a supernatural foreknowledge, knows that the end "shapen" for Arcite's woe is death, while Arcite, a mere mortal, understands Mercury's ambiguous prophecy as a prediction of a happy reunion with Emily. In other words, we are told, the irony results from Mercury's foreknowledge and Arcite's misinterpretation through ignorance. To read the passage in this fashion is, I think, to disregard the preceding events and the consequent shifts in attitude experienced by Arcite earlier in the Knight's Tale. Actually, he seems well aware of the possibility of death as a result of his return to Athens; but he nevertheless chooses to follow Mercury's suggestion because of the misery of his present situation, which only the sight of Emily can alleviate.

Arcite has found in Thebes that Fortune and Love have placed him in a thoroughly unsatisfactory situation. The way in which the Knight states the appearance of Mercury suggests that the messenger of the gods is not a visitant sent to Arcite by a supernatural controlling agency to play the role of a deceitful oracle. Rather, Arcite, in his unsatisfactory situation and his preoccupation with the idea of returning to Athens and to Emily, seems to have conjured up Mercury to instruct him as he wants to be instructed—"Hym thoughte how that the wynged god Mercurie/ Biforn hym stood and bad hym to be murie" (I, 1385–86). Here is a situation strikingly similar to Africanus' appearance to the dreamer Chaucer in the *Parlement of Foules* (95–105), after Chaucer had read all day in Macrobius. And there are certain ominous circumstances about Mercury's visit of which Arcite seems well aware.

Arcite "took keep" that Mercury is dressed just as he was when "Argus took his sleep," that is, Mercury is dressed as a shepherd, and carries his "slepy yerde" (I, 1387–90). It is not absolutely clear that Arcite understood the danger foreshadowed for him when he quoted a part of the Orpheus legend as it appears in the *Consolation;* but here, in the reference to Argus, there can be no doubt as to Arcite's realizing that Mercury appears before him dressed exactly as he was when he visited Argus. The conclusion is inevitable that he must recall at this moment the story of Ar-

[23] David Worcester, *The Art of Satire*, 116.

gus' death: Jupiter, desiring Io, sent Mercury to kill Argus, whom Juno had set to watch Io.[24]

Further, Arcite's words after Mercury's statement indicate his awareness of the danger for him in returning to Athens (I, 1394–98); and his earlier experience has shown him the folly of striving against Fortune. Nevertheless, his alternatives at the moment are either to die of the malady of love in Thebes or to follow the dictates of Love and risk death by returning to Athens. Since Arcite is here a human being struggling for happiness under the control of Fortune and Love, he chooses the second alternative. But he is by no means the blind plaything of a deceitful oracle.

Having returned to Athens as Philostrate, Arcite serves "a yeer or two" (I, 1426) as page to Emily. Ennobled by love, he is "so gentil of condicioun" (I, 1431) that his reputation spreads through the court and Theseus makes him a squire. In this capacity Arcite prospers for three years (I, 1446). One day in May he gaily goes to a nearby wood to do honor to the season. But after his jollity he falls into sadness, for neither his being in Athens, where he can see Emily, nor his material prosperity has brought him happiness. In fact, as a servant of Love he is "Now up, now doun, as boket in a welle" (I, 1533). His melancholy calls forth an audible complaint (I, 1542–71) in which he states his great dissatisfaction with his present situation: the gods (i.e., Fortune) still oppress him bitterly by forcing him to maintain his disguise as a squire, and also Love leads him to his death, "That shapen was . . . erst than my sherte" (I, 1566). Arcite's decision, made four or five years earlier, to return to Athens has not brought him happiness. He still considers himself controlled by two governing plans, that of Fortune and that of Love. Within the two, the hardships brought on by Love seem to him far more grievous (I, 1569–71). He feels so little hope of solving his problems that he falls down in a trance (I, 1572–73).

Palamon has overheard this complaint and angrily challenges Arcite to a duel, again upbraiding him for breaking the oath of sworn brotherhood. Arcite once more states his defiance of positive law where love is concerned (I, 1604–1607), fetches the armor, and engages in the duel. When Theseus appears, halts the

[24] Ovid, *Metamorphoses*, i, 671–77.

duel, and asks who they are, it is Palamon rather than Arcite who answers. Arcite could, of course, have argued that he, as Theseus' faithful squire, was fighting in an effort to recapture Theseus' escaped prisoner. Such dishonesty would not have been surprising in a man who had lived as an impostor for many years. But when Palamon reveals the true situation to Theseus, Arcite remains silent. Death will not come to him unexpectedly: from the time of his imprisonment he has believed that Fortune was his foe, and he realized fully when he returned to Athens that Love might lead him to death. Moreover, once before, in desiring release from prison, he had seen the folly of striving against "purveiaunce of God." He is ready to consider himself as deserving death for not having passively accepted his destiny. But the ladies' pleading brings forth Theseus' sense of humor and his "pitee," and plans for the tournament are arranged. Arcite readily agrees to terms whereby Emily will be given "To whom that Fortune yeveth so fair a grace" (I, 1861). He perhaps sees in these arrangements the possibility of his attaining happiness within the spheres of both Fortune and Love, his controlling agents. If he should gain victory in the proposed tournament, he not only would win Emily and thus avoid death from Love (I, 1563–68) but also would escape the imprisonment and the exile brought upon him by Fortune (I, 1542–62).

This possibility seems uppermost in his mind when, shortly before the tournament, he prays to Mars for victory. Whereas Palamon in his prayer to Venus states that he does not care for military glory or victory in the tournament so long as he can have full possession of Emily (I, 2242–43), Arcite directs his prayer to the god of war, who, he thinks, can help him to win the tournament and thus to gain happiness within the two ordained plans which, in his opinion, govern his life. He consequently asks Mars to "have routhe upon my sorwes soore" (I, 2419)—all his "sorwes," not just those occasioned by Love—and to "Yif me the victorie, I aske thee namoore" (I, 2420). When, in answer to his prayer, the statue of Mars rings and murmurs "Victorie!" Arcite is "fayn as fowel is of the brighte sonne" (I, 2437).

In the tournament Arcite wins victory and expects an end to

the torments of both Fortune and Love; but the machinations of Saturn cause his horse to throw him, and he is mortally injured. When he knows that he must die, he sends for Emily and Palamon (I, 2762–63), in order to urge that, if Emily should ever "ben a wyf," she remember Palamon. In taking leave of Emily, Arcite speaks the well-known lines in which he not only attempts to summarize all his "sorwes smerte" (I, 2766), but also states his final bewilderment at the workings of a universe which, though ordained by "purveiaunce of God," has defeated him at every turn. He says:

> What is this world? what asketh men to have?
> Now with his love, now in his colde grave
> Allone, withouten any compaignye.
> Fare wel, my sweete foo, myn Emelye!
> And softe taak me in youre armes tweye,
> For love of God. . . .   I, 2777–82

Within the course of the Knight's Tale, Arcite begins with a patient acceptance of an established order whereby Fortune made his imprisonment inevitable; then, upon falling in love, he desires release from prison, but Perotheus' intervention and his own exile from Athens show him the folly of desiring things other than those which fall to his lot; next, at the point of death as a result of the workings of Love and Fortune, he chooses to return to Athens as Philostrate, but several years of prosperity within sight of Emily do not bring him happiness; finally, when he thinks the tournament furnishes him an opportunity of winning freedom from the adversities of both Love and Fortune, he prays to Mars for victory; but even victory leads only to death, and Arcite dies with no satisfactory solution to the problem of his relation to the governing forces of the universe. After all his wrestling with this problem, he can only make a final effort at a sensible reconciliation by urging Emily to remember Palamon if she ever decides to marry.

In conclusion, it is worthy of notice that Chaucer elected to alter his source in order to leave Arcite's philosophical questions unanswered. In the *Teseida*, Arcite goes up into the heavens and,

A janglere and a goliardeys

realizing there the meaning of true felicity, laughs at those, in-
cluding himself, who seek earthly happiness; but the Knight
simply says:

> His spirit chaunged hous and wente ther,
> As I cam nevere, I kan nat tellen wher.
> Therfore I stynte, I nam no divinistre;
> Of soules fynde I nat in this registre,
> Ne me ne list thilke opinions to telle
> Of hem, though that they writen wher they dwelle.
> Arcite is coold, ther Mars his soule gye!   I, 2809–15

It remains only for Theseus in his "bond-of-love" speech to state
the benevolence of God's ordained plan and to point out that
there is no reason for lamenting Arcite's death at the height of
his powers and reputation. Thus the way is prepared for the marriage of Palamon and Emily, which brings matters to a happy
ending. The story is by no means a complete tragedy; as we learn
later, the teller of this story does not like tragedy. In fact, the
Knight says, when interrupting the Monk's recital, that it is
much better to tell stories of a poor man who "clymbeth up and
wexeth fortunat,/And there abideth in prosperitee" than to tell
of prosperous ones who fall to low estate (VII, 2767–79).

2. THE MILLER

The Knight's recital, representing simple suiting of tale and
teller, is followed by those of the Miller and the Reeve. These
performances form a complementary pair within the structure
of the *Canterbury Tales* and represent the second stage of dramatic development discussed in Part I. Not only do the fabliaux
which these two Pilgrims relate fit with the coarse natures of
their tellers, but, as we shall see, there is the added complication
of an externally motivated antagonism, probably based on their
personal experience as well as on traditional trade hostility.

From the Miller's sketch in the General Prologue (I, 545–66) our chief impression is of his strength and roughness. He is a "stout carl," muscular and of large stature, with broad shoulders and a thick chest. Expert in wrestling, he can heave a door from its hinges or butt it down with his head. Chaucer also gives a clear picture of his face: a broad red beard, a bristly wart on his nose, wide black nostrils, and an exceedingly large mouth. The Miller's behavior is in keeping with his appearance. He likes to gossip and tell dirty jokes, and he is not above stealing grain and overcharging for his work. He plays the bagpipe well and with this music leads the company from Southwark. We later learn that his name is Robin (I, 3129).

The pilgrimage is hardly under way before we get evidence of the Miller's disregard for good manners and of his liking for gossip and off-color stories. When the Knight completes his tale, the Host compliments him and then calls for a story from the Monk, next in rank to the Knight. But the Miller, who is drunk, has no respect for rank and loudly and profanely interrupts:

> . . . By armes, and by blood and bones,
> I kan a noble tale for the nones,
> With which I wol now quite the Knyghtes tale.
>
> I, 3125–27

Harry Bailly, who has noted the Miller's drunken state and has strong suspicions about the "nobility" of any tale he might tell, tries tactfully to silence him, but is unsuccessful and prudently withdraws from the argument. Now the Miller launches into his preamble. He knows from the noise he is making that he is drunk and asks that the company blame the ale of Southwark for any faults in his narration. For, he continues:

> . . . I wol telle a legende and a lyf
> Bothe of a carpenter and of his wyf,
> How that a clerk hath set the wrightes cappe.
>
> I, 3141–43

At once the Reeve breaks in:

> . . . Stynt thy clappe!
> Lat be thy lewed dronken harlotrye.

It is a synne and eek a greet folye
To apeyren any man, or hym defame,
And eek to bryngen wyves in swich fame.
Thou mayst ynogh of othere thynges seyn. I, 3144-49

It is here that the Miller-Reeve quarrel begins. The natural antagonism between a miller, who grinds grain, and a reeve, who, as overseer of a farm, has grain to be ground, has in the past been pointed to as the motivation for this quarrel, along with the fact that we are told in the General Prologue of the Reeve's being a carpenter in his youth (I, 613-14); and the Miller announces as his topic the cuckolding of a carpenter.[1] Recently, however, there appeared a better explanation of the basis for the quarrel.[2] It seems likely that the Miller-Reeve acquaintanceship must be of long standing, that the Miller worked years ago as servant boy in the Reeve's household at the time when the Reeve, then a carpenter, was made a cuckold by a cleric. This background makes the Reeve's violent interruption much easier to understand. If objection were being made to the Miller's topic simply on the ground that a carpenter is cuckolded, we would expect the Carpenter, one of the five Guildsmen present, to voice the complaint rather than the Reeve. But the Reeve probably knows the content of the coming story and is therefore able to tell the Miller that he will be both sinful and foolish to ridicule or insult any man and to circulate such a rumor about a wife. Naturally the Reeve wants the Miller to tell a story about "othere thynges."

We find further support for this explanation when we look at the story that the Miller relates. In the remaining lines of his prologue (I, 3151-66), he seems greatly to enjoy taunting the Reeve. Also, Robin the Miller knows the Reeve's name, Oswald, and knows that he is married. Further, he seems aware that Oswald is certainly not going to answer his question: "Why are you so angry about my tale now?" The force of the "now" apparently means: "You were cuckolded a long time ago; why worry about it now?" The Miller makes clear to Oswald in this speech

[1] Frederick Tupper, *JEGP*, XIV (1915), 265-70.
[2] R. A. Pratt, *MLN*, LIX (1944), 47-49. For different views, see W. C. Stokoe, Jr., *UTQ*, XXI (1951-52), 120-27; and C. A. Owen, Jr., *MLN*, LXVII (1952), 336-38.

that he is not suggesting that all wives are unfaithful; he is simply showing how one—namely, Oswald's wife—made her husband a cuckold. His point is, of course, that the Reeve just used bad judgment in selecting a wife. It may be that the Miller is considerably more sober than he pretends; under the guise of drunkenness he has enjoyed overriding the Host, and now he is having the fun of discomfiting the Reeve.

After this exchange, the Narrator enters his apology for having to repeat the Miller's low tale and advises anyone not interested to choose another story. In the narrative we meet an elderly and gullible carpenter named John, who has a young and skittish wife named Alice. Nicholas, a young cleric on the lookout for amorous adventure, has a room in their home. By convincing John of the imminence of a second flood, Nicholas manages to spend a night in John's bed with Alice, while John sleeps in a tub tied under the roof, which he is to cut loose when the floodwaters rise. But there is another young man, Absolon, also desirous of Alice's favors. When he asks for a kiss at her bedroom window, he suffers indignities which drive thoughts of love from his mind. Then he gets his revenge upon Nicholas by means of a red-hot iron. Nicholas screams for water to cool his scorched flesh; old John, hearing the one word "water," thinks the second flood has now come, cuts the ropes holding up his tub, crashes to the floor, breaks his arm, and becomes a laughingstock for all the neighbors, who believe Alice and Nicholas when they say the old man is mad.

Obviously the element in this tale which the Miller means to apply to the Reeve is the character of the carpenter. Old John, jealous of his young wife, is made a cuckold and an object of ridicule. Perhaps there is also another personal application to be made in the story: Robin the Miller may be Robin the servant boy in the carpenter's household. Two parallels in their descriptions support this identification: first, "The Millere was a stout carl for the nones" (I, 545), and "His knave was a strong carl for the nones" (I, 3469); second, in the Miller's sketch we learn "Ther was no dore that he nolde heve of harre" (I, 550), and, in the tale, Robin the servant boy "by the haspe he haaf it [the door] of atones" (I, 3470). Although it is true that Nicholas caused John to send Robin to London before the merry night described in the tale, we suspect strongly that upon his return Robin lost no time in finding out how John came to break his arm.

If our speculations adequately describe the basis for the Miller-Reeve quarrel, we see good reason for the distance separating these two Pilgrims as they travel: the Miller is at the head of the company leaving Southwark, while the Reeve rides always last.

3. THE REEVE

Most of the Pilgrims enjoyed the Miller's tale, and the Narrator tells us that only the Reeve seemed disturbed by it (I, 3859–63). We now know the probable reason for Oswald's anger; but the Narrator, as well as the other Pilgrims, does not know that the Miller's narrative probably resembled an actual incident, for Robin did not come right out with that fact. Thus the Narrator, a separate person from Chaucer the author of the *Tales*, can only conclude that the Reeve's displeasure stems from the fact that old John was a carpenter. We note, however, that Oswald's ire is now much less than when he interrupted the Miller *before* he had told his tale; the reason for this may well be that Oswald is considerably relieved to find that the Miller's account of John's cuckolding did not include a direct connection with him. At any rate, when he begins to talk now, he finds fault with the tale only a "lite."

The Reeve first says that he could easily tell a story about the cuckolding of a miller if he cared to stoop to ribaldry, but he is old and does not want to enter into such a game. The mention of his advanced years leads him to a lengthy personal statement concerning the loss of virility in old age.[1] No inconsistency exists

[1] For an analysis of this speech, see G. R. Coffman, *Speculum*, IX (1934), 272–77.

Noon auditour koude on him wynne

here with the picture of the Reeve gained from the General Prologue (I, 587–622). There he was an unattractive lean man of unpleasant disposition, skilled in farm management and very capable in detecting thievery in others, as well as in feathering his own nest dishonestly. Furthermore, his long calfless legs give evidence, according to medieval science, of his lustful, sensual desires, an interest fully apparent in his lecture on old age.[2] The General Prologue also suggests that the Reeve is no longer young: he has had charge of the accounting "Syn that his lord was twenty yeer of age"—presumably for considerable time, since his managing to become wealthy by secret dealings must have been done bit by bit over many years to escape detection.

The Host does not care much for the Reeve's remarks on old age and interrupts, speaking "as lordly as a kyng":

> ... What amounteth al this wit?
> What shul we speke alday of hooly writ?
> The devel made a reve for to preche,
> Or of a soutere a shipman or a leche.
> Sey forth thy tale, and tarie nat the tyme.
>
> I, 3901–3905

The Reeve, forgetting his earlier determination not to tell a bawdy tale, now asks the company's indulgence for a tale in which a miller is cuckolded. We find also that the Reeve tries here to cover up the real reason for his former anger by offering the lame excuse that he is a carpenter:

> This dronke Millere hath ytoold us heer
> How that bigyled was a carpenteer,
> Peraventure in scorn, for I am oon.
> And, by youre leve, I shal hym quite anoon;
> Right in his cherles termes wol I speke.
> I pray to God his nekke mote to-breke;
> He kan wel in myn eye seen a stalke,
> But in his owene he kan nat seen a balke.   I, 3913–20

The tale which follows, like that told by the Miller, is among the most brilliant in the whole collection. Two college boys from

---

[2] Curry, *Sciences*, 71–90. On the Reeve's position and duties, see H. Y. Moffett, *PQ*, IV (1925), 208–23.

Wel koude he knowe a draughte of Londoun ale

Cambridge University, John and Allan, set out to catch the arrogant Miller Simkin in the act of stealing their college's grain while he grinds it. Simkin, realizing their purpose, unties their horse, which runs away. Then he grinds the grain honestly, as the boys look on. But when they prepare to return to the college, they find their horse gone and must chase it; Simkin now steals half a bushel of their meal, which he has his wife bake into a loaf. Not until after nightfall do John and Allan get back with their horse. Because of the lateness of the hour, they ask Simkin to give them lodging for the night, and he agrees, celebrating his success at outsmarting these educated young men by drinking a great deal of ale. During the night the boys manage to take their revenge: Allan sleeps with Simkin's daughter, John with his wife. When Simkin discovers what is going on, the students beat him roundly, take their horse and meal, and go back to the college, picking up the stolen loaf, about which the daughter had told Allan, on the way out. "Lo, swich it is a millere to be fals!"

The application of this tale to its dramatic context is obvious. Simkin, in his rough, bullying ways, in his dishonesty, and in his drunkenness, bears close similarity to the loudmouthed Robin, whom Oswald seeks to spite. Thus the Reeve has settled his score with the Miller.

4. THE COOK

The Cook's performance presents difficulty to anyone analyzing the dramatic situation in which the tale is to be read; this difficulty stems primarily from the tale's being so brief a fragment that the reader has little indication of what its exact purpose would have been had the tale been completed. Nevertheless, from the fragment and the prologue which introduces it, we can see, first, positive evidence of its suitability to its teller as he is described in the General Prologue; and, second, some faint indication of its being used in a Cook-Host antagonism, though this dramatic antagonism is more hinted at than functional.

The fifty-eight-line fragment (I, 4365–4422) which the Cook relates does little more than introduce the chief character, Perkin Reveller. This gay young man well deserves his name, for he much prefers dancing, love-making, attending weddings, and drinking in taverns to remaining at work in the victualer's shop where he is an apprentice. He is always in attendance at parades and often plays dice in the street with companions of a similar stamp. With these companions Perkin is so generous that often his master finds the cashbox empty. Finally, Perkin is discharged and goes to live with an accomplice, whose wife keeps a shop for appearance' sake but practices prostitution for a living. At this point the tale breaks off, an unfortunate fact which those of us who find Chaucer's fabliaux to our taste will ever regret.

Considerable discussion has ensued as to why Chaucer left this tale unfinished. Although there may be some merit to the view that he abandoned the tale because he felt that three fabliaux in succession would be too much of a good thing,[1] or to the opinion that since he was in this instance not working from a direct source, as was often his custom, he therefore could not finish the story easily,[2] it seems to me a more likely explanation is simply that other duties or interests caused him to put aside the tale, which he never found opportunity to return to. Be that as it may, there is no denying the suitability of this fragmentary fabliau to the earthy Cook.

Three points stand out in the sketch of the Cook (I, 379–87): he is in the employ of the Guildsmen for the duration of the pilgrimage; he is very expert in his trade; and he unfortunately has a sore. Certain aspects of the first and third points are worthy of brief mention here. The main emphasis in the sketch of the Guildsmen (I, 361–78) is upon their *nouveau riche* characteristics.[3] Their equipment and clothing are ostentatiously new, and

---

[1] R. K. Root, *The Poetry of Chaucer* (rev. ed., 1922), 179–80.

[2] See the chapter by E. D. Lyon in *Sources and Analogues*, 148–54.

[3] E. P. Kuhl, *Transactions* of the Wisconsin Academy of Sciences, Arts, and Letters, XVIII (1916), 652–75.

their wives, who have no reason to complain about lack of money, are extremely appreciative of their place in society. We are not surprised, therefore, to find that these wealthy middle-class Londoners have brought along a cook for this pilgrimage, and the contention is not convincing that if the sketch of the Guildsmen were added to the General Prologue late—as is unlikely—we are to understand that the Cook was brought along by the Lawyer and the Franklin.[4]

More pertinent to our present interest are several comments that bear upon the Cook's "mormal." We cannot be absolutely sure whether this is a running or a dry sore,[5] or whether it is on the Cook's shin or chin.[6] It does seem clear, however, that this mormal indicates that the Cook is given to a disregard for sensible dietary habits and to lechery and love of licentious living.[7] The mormal, therefore, is not only a memorable individualizing trait in the picture of the Cook; it also helps explain the gusto with which he describes the gay doings of Perkin Reveller.

There is in the Prologue of the Cook's Tale (I, 4325–64) evidence of a Cook-Host antagonism. The "gentils" may not have liked the fabliau which the Reeve has just completed, but the Cook, Hodge [i.e., Roger] Ware, certainly enjoyed it. He expresses his approval by beating the Reeve on the back and exclaims at length on the fitting punishment the two college boys meted out to scornful Miller Simkin. Then he urges that the fun not be halted and volunteers to tell the company as best he can about a little "jape" that occurred in "oure citee." The Host agrees to this suggestion but feels called upon to warn the Cook that the tale must be good. Harry explains the need for this warning by pointing out that Hodge has sold many twice-cooked pies in his cookshop and has been bitterly cursed by many pilgrims who were sickened by the food he sold them, for there are numerous flies in his shop. After these thrusts, the Host attempts to placate the Cook by implying that he is only jesting:

[4] Carroll Camden, Jr., *PQ*, VII (1928), 314–17; Kemp Malone, *ELH*, XIII (1946), 41–42.

[5] Curry, *Sciences*, 48; Haldeen Braddy, *MLQ*, VII (1946), 265–67.

[6] See Manly and Rickert, *The Text of the Canterbury Tales*, V, 33. The better manuscripts have *shin*.

[7] Curry, *Sciences*, 50–52.

> Now telle on, gentil Roger by thy name.
> But yet I prey thee, be nat wroth for game;
> A man may seye ful sooth in game and pley.
>
> I, 4353–55

The statement that a man may speak the truth openly so long as he is jesting does not, of course, do much toward taking the sting from Harry's earlier remarks. But Roger Ware, like the Miller, is not the man to be intimidated by Harry Bailly. He comes back immediately with a Flemish proverb to the effect that a joke which is true is a poor joke, and then states his determination to even the score with the Host by telling a tale, presumably true, in which an innkeeper will play a part (I, 4358–64).

This lively scene not only gives us the names of both the Cook and the Host but also admits us as spectators to a brisk clash of tradesmen in late fourteenth-century London. There was at that time an actual innkeeper named Harry Bailly[8] and an actual proprietor of a cookshop named Roger Ware.[9] Further, for a contemporary reader the antagonism that we have just examined would have seemed perfectly natural in the light of legal restrictions at that time.[10] The laws governing victualers strictly prohibited cookshops from selling food not freshly prepared and for which reasonable rules of cleanliness were not observed; but the records show that many London cooks did not pay close attention to these laws. Thus the Host's thrusts at the Cook strike home. But, on the other hand, there were also laws to the effect that London innkeepers must not sell food or drink in competition with victualers, such as the Cook; consequently, many innkeepers moved outside the city limits to Southwark, where these laws could not be enforced. Accordingly, there is little reason for Roger Ware, a London cook, to love Harry Bailly, a Southwark innkeeper. And their antagonism in the Cook's Prologue is a natural development of their relationship as tradesmen.

Despite this expert dramatic framework which Chaucer has provided for a fully developed controversy, we cannot be sure just what Roger has in mind when he says that his tale of an inn-

[8] Manly, *New Light*, 77–83.
[9] Edith Rickert, *TLS* (1932), 761; E. D. Lyon, *MLN*, LII (1937), 491–94.
[10] Frederick Tupper, *JEGP*, XIV (1915), 256–70.

keeper will not come now but will come before "we parte." It may be that at this stage in the writing of the *Canterbury Tales* Chaucer was still working according to the plan set forth in the General Prologue, whereby each Pilgrim would tell two tales going to, and two tales returning from, Canterbury, a plan he seems to have abandoned later. Or it may well be that the Cook's fragment treating Perkin, the idle apprentice, would have, if completed, constituted an indirect ridiculing of the Host, and that his saying that he will postpone his thrust at Harry is simply a device aimed at putting Harry off his guard. But such speculation is useless, for we have no shred of information about the matter. The Cook will reappear when in the Manciple's Prologue he is again involved in a controversy; but before then he must have opportunity to become "ful pale and no thyng reed" (IX, 20) as a result of too much strong drink.

5. THE SERGEANT OF THE LAW

Five sections in the *Canterbury Tales* concern the Lawyer: (1) the sketch in the General Prologue; (2) the Introduction to the Man of Law's Tale; (3) the Prologue of the Man of Law's Tale; (4) The Man of Law's Tale; (5) a part of the Epilogue to the Man of Law's Tale. The tale itself, in which we meet the steadfast Constance, has many similarities to a saint's life; however, the framework for the tale involves not only the Lawyer and the Host, but also Chaucer himself and possibly John Gower. As a result, this performance presents an even more difficult problem to a critic analyzing the dramatic relationships surrounding the tale than did that of the Cook. It will be well to grant at the outset that there are certain aspects of the problem which apparently cannot be explained completely.

First of all, there is the station of the teller of this tale: he is a

He semed bisier than he was

Sergeant of the Law in the General Prologue but simply a Man of Law in the remaining sections. As Professor Manly showed, a sergeant of the law in the fourteenth century was not just another attorney; rather, he was an extremely important and wealthy member of the legal profession.[1] One therefore wonders why in the performance by this Pilgrim the much less specific term "Man of Law" is used. The only workable hypothesis is that generally adopted: the Man of Law who tells the tale is the Sergeant of the Law in the General Prologue. It is the Host who, in calling for a tale from the Lawyer, originates this confusion of terms. Harry says: "Sire Man of Lawe, . . ./Telle us a tale anon, as forward is" (II, 33–34). One explanation, of course, for this shift in names is that the Host, though realizing that he is addressing a member of the legal profession, does not know that this Pilgrim has the high rank of Sergeant of the Law. Such a mistake might have arisen from the modesty of the Sergeant's clothing: "He rood but hoomly in a medlee cote" (I, 328). Sergeants seem generally to have dressed more richly. As an innkeeper the Host would have the habit of arriving at an estimate of a person's status by reference to his clothing—witness his comments about the Canon's shabby clothing (VIII, 629–39).

There can be little disagreement, I think, with Professor Manly's suggestion that Chaucer took a contemporary sergeant of the law, Thomas Pynchbek, as model for his Sergeant of the Law. This is not to say that the literary creation equals Pynchbek; it is to say, however, that there are humorous overtones in the literary sketch that would have been meaningful to anyone who knew much about Pynchbek—for example, the line "Ther koude no wight *pynche* at his writyng." A brief review of Manly's findings will perhaps be helpful here in making clear the outlines, at least, of the Pilgrim who is later to poke fun at Chaucer's literary efforts and then to tell the tale of Constance. Pynchbek was made a sergeant of the law not later than 1376, and he dealt extensively in land, his family thereby becoming extremely well to do. He belonged to the political faction opposite to that with which Chaucer seems to have been sympathetic, and the Pynchbek estates were near the estate of Chaucer's sister-in-

[1] Manly, *New Light*, 131–57.

law, Katherine Swynford, whom Chaucer's wife often visited. Furthermore, there is a story that Pynchbek had a quarrel with one of Chaucer's friends, William Beauchamp. Then, too, Chaucer most likely studied law at one of the Inns of Court, where he almost certainly would have known Pynchbek.

These facts seem to offer an acceptable explanation for the satiric tone which Chaucer uses when introducing his Sergeant of the Law (I, 309–30). These lines show that Chaucer does not wish us to take the Sergeant of the Law at the same high value which that worthy attaches to himself. Rather, we derive the picture of a high-ranking legal personage, who not only is markedly pompous in his words and actions but who also busies himself steadily in amassing money and land.

When we consider the Introduction to the Man of Law's Tale, we first find thirty-two lines of rather heavy admonition to the company by the Host. Although Harry is "nat depe ystert in loore" (II, 4), he computes from the sun that the time is ten o'clock, and he delivers to the Pilgrims a little lecture against wasting time in idleness. Then he calls on the Lawyer to tell a tale:

> Sire Man of Lawe, . . . so have ye blis,
> Telle us a tale anon, as forward is.
> Ye been submytted, thurgh youre free assent,
> To stonden in this cas at my juggement.
> Acquiteth yow now of youre biheeste;
> Thanne have ye do youre devoir atte leeste.   II, 33–38

Note the legal terminology in this speech: "forward," "submytted," "free assent," "cas," "juggement," "acquiteth," "biheeste," and "devoir." Harry intends to leave no doubt that he can address a professional man in the proper professional terms.

The Lawyer at once states his desire to keep his promise; there is, however, one trouble: he does not know any worth-while story which that writer Chaucer has not already told in such English as he could muster—though he was not very skillful with meters and rhymes. Indeed, the Lawyer continues, if Chaucer has not recounted these tales in one book, he has in another, "For he hath toold of loveris up and doun/Mo than Ovide made of mencioun" (II, 53–54). To prove this point the Lawyer refers to

Chaucer's early work *The Book of the Duchess*, and then to the later *Saint's Legend of Cupid* (*Legend of Good Women*), citing the individual stories in the *Legend* (II, 57–76).

It would seem from the bantering tone of the Lawyer's comments about Chaucer as a writer that the way is being prepared for some entertaining dramatic complexity. When we recall Chaucer's satiric treatment of the Sergeant of the Law in the General Prologue, we are not particularly surprised to find that this Pilgrim now pokes fun at Chaucer. A factor deserving consideration in this situation is that possibly we should understand that the Lawyer recognizes Chaucer, whereas the other members of the company do not. Certainly the contemporary London court-and-business circle was not so large but what a comptroller of the customs and a sergeant of the law would have met, and the close connection which Manly showed between Pynchbek and Chaucer certainly does not hinder such an assumption. Yet these two are the only Pilgrims drawn from that circle. That the Franklin accompanies the Lawyer (I, 331) does not indicate necessarily that the former knew the exact identity of his companion, though if the Franklin understands the banter here, the joke is the better. Clearly, the Host does not know the Sergeant of the Law, since he calls him Man of Law; and we see from the prologue to "Sir Thopas" that Harry certainly does not know Chaucer (VII, 695). The Lawyer's jests about Chaucer's clumsiness in poetic composition, about his writing in English rather than in Latin or French, and about his prolificness in telling love stories may result from his recognizing the poet as a member of the company. If so, we can see here the germ, at least, for a dramatic antagonism which might have been intended as a framework for the story the Lawyer is to tell. But this possibility is not developed.

Indeed, the Lawyer next shifts to a kind of defense of the moral content of Chaucer's stories. He says that Chaucer has never written about "Canacee,/That loved hir owene brother synfully" (II, 79), about Apollonius of Tyre, or about any other such abominable topics: "Of swiche cursed stories I sey fy!" (II, 80). This defense of Chaucer by the Lawyer has been interpreted as a thrust at John Gower, who in his *Confessio Amantis* did tell the two stories mentioned.[2] It is further argued that this jibe caused the two friends, Chaucer and Gower, to fall out. However that may be, the mention of these stories treating of incest seems to cause the Lawyer to abandon his jocular attitude toward Chaucer as poet; on the contrary, he goes on to pay Chaucer compliments:

> But of my tale how shal I doon this day?
> Me were looth be likned, doutelees,
> To Muses that men clepe Pierides—
> *Methamorphosios* woot what I mene;
> But nathelees, I recche noght a bene
> Though I come after hym with hawebake.
> I speke in prose, and lat him rymes make.   II, 90–96

The Pierides are, of course, the daughters of Pierus of Emathia, who, according to Ovid's *Metamorphoses*, vied with the Muses and were changed into magpies. Thus the Lawyer is saying that he is loath to vie with Chaucer as a storyteller. Yet he must tell a tale, and he does not really care if he comes after Chaucer "with hawebake," that is, with plain fare, a narrative which is not a brilliant literary production. Therefore, the Lawyer will tell a tale in prose and leave rhyming to Chaucer. This statement represents a complete reversal from the Lawyer's earlier jokes about Chaucer's lack of skill with meter and rhyme. It also seems to indicate that Chaucer at one time intended to have the Lawyer tell a prose tale rather than the rhymed story of Constance, and it is argued that the Tale of Melibeus was at that time assigned to him.[3] At any rate, despite these several seemingly impossible problems, we have seen that the possibility of an entertaining dramatic antagonism between the Lawyer and Chaucer, hinted at earlier, has been abandoned. From the last two lines of this introduction we learn that the Lawyer's earlier jocularity has now shifted to "a sobre cheere."

That the material we are now examining does not represent Chaucer's final revision for the Lawyer's performance is suggested by the fact that the last line of the Introduction would

[2] Margaret Schlauch, *Constance and the Accused Queens*, 132–34; this book includes references to earlier treatments of the question.

[3] J. S. P. Tatlock, *The Development and Chronology of Chaucer's Works*, 197.

lead us to expect the tale to begin immediately. Instead, we first have the Prologue of the Man of Law's Tale; and this prologue, which treats the evils of poverty and is practically a translation of a section in Pope Innocent's *De Contemptu Mundi*, jars oddly with the Introduction and with the story which follows. Of the thirty-four lines that make up this prologue, the first twenty-two set forth the dire results of lack of money. Of course, recollection of certain lines from the Lawyer's sketch in the General Prologue makes clear that this Pilgrim, to whom large fees and unentailed land were so important, is completely in character when he holds forth against the "condicion of poverte." However, such comments do not seem to fit with the preceding thrusts at Chaucer and possibly at Gower, nor are they especially apposite as an introduction to the tale of Constance, whose hardships do not result primarily from poverty.

The last twelve lines of this prologue do represent a more easily understandable transition from the stanzas on poverty to the tale itself. Here the Lawyer praises "riche marchauntz" as the ideal of happiness and prudence. Furthermore, since such merchants travel to distant lands, they are bearers of news of all sorts. Indeed, says the Lawyer:

> I were right now of tales desolaat,
> Nere that a marchant, goon is many a yeere,
> Me taughte a tale, which that ye shal heere.
>
> II, 131–33

For the second time, the way is cleared for the tale, and a further connection with the prologue is established when we find that the Sultan of Syria learns of Constance from the tidings brought by "chapmen riche" (II, 135).

The story which the Lawyer tells permits far simpler and clearer analysis from the dramatic point of view than do its introduction and prologue. Although this tale has been considered inappropriate to its teller,[4] more recent critics have discovered an increasing body of evidence for its dramatic suitability. Three aspects of the tale, to be examined, are particularly pertinent in this connection: the narrative method employed in the tale, the

---

[4] *Ibid.*, 172; T. R. Lounsbury, *Studies in Chaucer*, III, 436.

literary type to which the tale belongs, and the occurrence in the tale of terms from canon law. We should bear in mind that for Chaucer's tale of Constance the direct source is Nicholas Trivet's *Anglo-Norman Chronicle*, and that here, as elsewhere in the *Canterbury Tales*, Chaucer's alterations of his source constitute some of the surest evidence as to his efforts at suiting tale and teller.[5]

First, concerning the suitability to a lawyer of the narrative method used here, two quotations will perhaps suffice:

1. He [the Lawyer] tells his tale as if he were pleading before a jury, using every oratorical device, anticipating objections and answering them; quoting Scripture; at emotional points working on their feelings with bursts of horror or pity, praying, execrating, or breaking into passionate outcries.[6]

2. The narrative order is sound, the transitions are clear. The presentation is very sympathetic. The digressions from the narrative proper are comments pertinent to the course of action; the apostrophes arouse the emotion of the listener still further in behalf of the sufferer, or temporary client.[7]

Second, what seems to me a strong case has been made recently to the effect that the story told by the Lawyer should be classified as a sentimental tale rather than as a romance, and that as such it would have satisfied middle-class taste.[8] In the tale "blatant emotionalization, a show of verisimilitude, common piety, and broad, trite characterization are clothed incongruously in a semblance of the romantic manner." Such a sentimental tale is well suited to the Lawyer, a member of the middle class, who would not be disposed to tell the kind of romance most popular with the nobility.

Third, a more specific kind of evidence to show that Chaucer aimed at suiting this tale and its teller is to be found in the discussion by the Syrian privy council of the Sultan's marriage to Constance (II, 204–24); this section represents an addition by

[5] See the chapter by Margaret Schlauch in *Sources and Analogues*, 155–206. Recently an important study has appeared by E. A. Block in *PMLA*, LXVIII (1953), 572–616.

[6] W. H. Browne, *MLN*, XXIII (1908), 53.

[7] E. C. Knowlton, *JEGP*, XXIII (1924), 83–93.

[8] B. I. Duffey, *ELH*, XIV (1947), 181–93.

Chaucer to Trivet's version. "The Man of Law first thinks of the proposed marriage as a problem in canon law to be solved by the Sultan's advisers, presumably men of some legal background, and this reveals the interest of his own legal mind." The problem is *disparitas cultus*—the difference between the Sultan's Mohammedanism and Constance's Christianity—and canon law required that this difference be resolved by the Sultan's baptism.[9]

Another specific passage has point here. When Constance stands before King Alla to be tried for the murder of Hermengild, of which she is falsely accused, the Lawyer interrupts his narrative and uses one of the few realistic analogies to be found in the tale:

> Have ye nat seyn somtyme a pale face,
> Among a prees, of hym that hath be lad
> Toward his deeth, wher as hym gat no grace,
> And swich a colour in his face hath had,
> Men myghte knowe his face that was bistad,
> Amonges alle the faces in that route?
> So stant Custance, and looketh hire aboute.   II, 645–51

This offhand reference to a courtroom scene comes quite naturally from the lips of the Lawyer, who must have seen the pale faces of condemned criminals many times.

A further aspect of the tale deserves notice: throughout, despite her extreme hardships, Constance never seems to dispute the necessity for obedience to authority. When she is to leave for Syria, she unquestioningly obeys her parents, though to depart grieves her sorely:

> Allas! unto the Barbre nacioun
> I moste anoon, syn that it is youre wille.   II, 281–82

And she never for a moment attempts to act against the supposed command from her husband, King Alla, that she leave Northumbria within three days. Closely connected to this respect which Constance shows for authority is the possibility that the Lawyer's Tale should be regarded as, among other things, preparation for the discussion of "maistrye" in marriage, a topic which will assume great importance in a number of later performances by the

9 P. E. Beichner, *Speculum*, XXIII (1948), 70–75.

Pilgrims. The question at issue then will be whether or not women should have sovereignty over their husbands. In the Lawyer's Tale, at least four specific passages set up clearly the accepted antifeminist view, widely advocated by the contemporary clergy, who held that Eve first brought about man's fall, that women have duplicated her action ever since, and that a wife is a lesser being whose natural role is subordinate to that of her husband.[10] The Lawyer, as a conservative proponent of established authority and of law and order, might be expected to espouse these antifeminist arguments. In his tale we find the following pertinent comments:

> Housbondes been alle goode, and han ben yoore;
> That knowen wyves; I dar sey yow na moore.
>
> II, 272–73

> I, wrecche womman, no fors though I spille!
> Wommen are born to thraldom and penance,
> And to been under mannes governance.   II, 285–87

> For thogh that wyves be ful hooly thynges,
> They moste take in pacience at nyght
> Swiche manere necessaries as been plesynges
> To folk that han ywedded hem with rynges,
> And leye a lite hir hoolynesse aside,
> As for the tyme,—it may no bet bitide.   II, 709–14

> Sooth is that thurgh wommanes eggement
> Mankynde was lorn, and damned ay to dye.
>
> II, 842–43

The first and third of these comments are interpolated into the narrative by the Lawyer, while the second and fourth are spoken by Constance herself. Not only is the point of view which these passages set forth that to be expected from the Lawyer, but also this theme might well pave the way for the lively altercations to occur in future performances.

Perhaps the clearest indication of the suitability of the tale and the Lawyer comes in the opening lines of the Epilogue to the tale:

---

[10] See F. L. Utley, *The Crooked Rib*, for a survey of the argument about women in the Middle Ages.

> Owre Hoost upon his stiropes stood anon,
> And seyde, "Goode men, herkeneth everych on!
> This was a thrifty tale for the nones!"   II, 1163–65

The Host's "thrifty tale" takes us back to the Lawyer's opening protest: "I kan right now no thrifty tale seyn" (II, 46). Harry Bailly, at least, found the tale to his liking and, in calling upon the Parson for the next performance, shows that in his opinion the Lawyer has acquitted himself well, despite his learning:

> Sir Parisshe Prest, . . . for Goddes bones,
> Telle us a tale, as was thi forward yore.
> I se wel that ye lerned men in lore
> Can moche good, by Goddes dignitee!   II, 1166–69

6. THE SHIPMAN

As in the case of the Lawyer, the Shipman's performance shows vestiges of an earlier plan on Chaucer's part and a lack of final revision. The problems here, however, occasion a critic somewhat less discomfort than do those just considered in connection with the Introduction and Prologue to the Man of Law's Tale, for we can be fairly certain that the story known as the Shipman's Tale was previously assigned to the Wife of Bath. But before examining this situation in detail, we should look closely at the character of the Shipman, since, despite Chaucer's shift in assignment of the tale in question, one can maintain—successfully, I think—that the story and its teller are not completely unsuited and that there are also several hints of a dramatic antagonism to be observed.

In some ways the Shipman's presence is the hardest to account for among the Pilgrims who make up the Canterbury company. He is surely not going to the shrine of St. Thomas to ask forgive-

Of nyce conscience took he no keep

ness for his lack of scruples, his murdering of prisoners, or his thefts of wine—matters of which we learn from his sketch in the General Prologue (I, 388–410). His behavior on the pilgrimage, particularly his refusal to listen to a tale from the Parson (II, 1178–90),[1] is anything but devout. On the other hand, neither does a pilgrimage seem the kind of vacation the ship's captain would likely choose. Whatever the reason for his presence, the fact remains that the Shipman is a very likable person, who makes no bones about what he is. As with most sailors, his horsemanship leaves much to be desired, but he is ready for any emergency and seems to get a great deal of pleasure from life. Since this Shipman comes from Dartmouth and has a vessel named the *Madelaine*, it seems likely that he is modeled after Peter Risshenden, a shipmaster for the well-known contemporary freebooter John Hawley.[2] But despite the Shipman's lack of scruples, he is a valuable and experienced man: "Hardy he was and wys to undertake;/With many a tempest hadde his berd been shake." And in his profession he is thoroughly competent.

Further, as we have noted, the Shipman has little sympathy with preaching and religious hairsplitting; rather, his is a comfortable acceptance of the fundamentals. He tells the Host, who after the Lawyer's Tale has called upon the Parson, that the clergyman shall not be allowed to preach:

> He schal no gospel glosen here ne teche.
> We leven alle in the grete God ...
> He wolde sowen som difficulte,
> Or springen cokkel in our clene corn.   II, 1180–83

We gather also that the Shipman did not find much pleasure in the sober tale of Constance that the Lawyer has just finished; the master of the *Madelaine* greatly prefers stories of a gayer sort:

> And therfore, Hoost, I warne thee biforn,
> My joly body schal a tale telle,

[1] There is some difficulty with the manuscript situation of the Epilogue to the Man of Law's Tale. The lines in question, however, seem perfectly in keeping with the character of the Shipman as presented in the General Prologue. See R. A. Pratt, *PMLA*, LXVI (1951), 1148–57.

[2] Manly, *New Light*, 169–81; F. E. White, *MP*, XXVI (1928–29), 249–55, 379–84, and XXVII (1929–30), 123–28; Margaret Galway, *MLR*, XXXIV (1939), 497–514.

And I schal clynken you so mery a belle,
That I schal waken al this compaignie.
But it schal not ben of philosophie,
Ne phislyas, ne termes queinte of lawe.
Ther is but litel Latyn in my mawe!   II, 1184–90

Such remarks are suitable to the sort of person we judged the Shipman to be from the sketch of him in the General Prologue.

The Shipman's story of the merchant of St. Denis satisfactorily fits the literary specifications that he set forth in the lines just quoted. It is an entertaining fabliau and belongs to a group of narratives that has been given the name "The Lover's Gift Regained." As in his other fabliaux, such as those told by the Miller and the Reeve, Chaucer seems here to have had no specific source;[3] but because of its narrative economy, its large proportion of natural dialogue, and its inevitable motivation of events by means of character, the Shipman's Tale is representative of Chaucer's mature work.[4]

That Chaucer at one time apparently intended to assign this tale to the Wife of Bath we surmise from the feminine pronouns in the opening lines of the story (VII, 1–19). Although it has been suggested that the Shipman is here reporting a view which he considers typical of wives, and that therefore lines 11–19 should be placed in quotation marks,[5] the text gives absolutely no support for this assumption. Consequently, our only alternative is to consider the speaker a woman. Three women are present in the company of Pilgrims—the Prioress, the Second Nun, and the Wife of Bath. Since this fabliau could by no stretch of the imagination be assigned to either of the first two, we conclude that the Wife of Bath was meant to be its original teller.[6] Even so, lines 5–10 still occasion some difficulty, for it is unlikely that the Wife would say that a woman's attracting attention at feasts and dances is not worth the money it costs. This statement, however, can best be considered as preparation for the emphasis which the

---

[3] See the chapter by J. W. Spargo in *Sources and Analogues*, 439–46; R. A. Pratt, *MLN*, LV (1940), 142–45.

[4] See Gardiner Stillwell, *RES*, XX (1944), 1–18.

[5] Frederick Tupper, *JEGP*, XXXIII (1934), 352–71.

[6] J. S. P. Tatlock, *The Development and Chronology of Chaucer's Works*, 205–19; R. F. Jones, *JEGP*, XXIV (1925), 512–47.

wife in the story places on the necessity for her having sufficient money to dress in such a manner as to do honor to her husband (VII, 179, 420–24). It is this argument, along with her readiness to afford her husband pleasure in bed, which the wife of the merchant of St. Denis uses to manage him as she wishes. And the Wife of Bath, as we know her from the General Prologue, seems also quite capable of using these devices for managing husbands. But her point here is that the merchant of St. Denis is to be the loser as a result of his accepting his wife's contention that she must have money for clothes in order to do him honor.

There is a more important aspect of the tale which clearly indicates its suitability to the Wife of Bath. The point of the story, I think, is that while the prosperous but boring merchant, completely wrapped up in his business, has little understanding of his wife and scant ability in managing her, the wife is expert in manipulating him and in conducting a secret affair. Although she tells the monk Don John that her husband is impotent and will not give her enough money (VII, 170–72), we have the merchant's own statement that she has enough for any thrifty housewife (VII, 245–48), and the reunion scene between the merchant and his wife at the end of the story shows that he is far from impotent. One suspects that the wife's statement to Don John of her pressing need for a hundred francs is simply a part of her attempt at rationalizing the night in bed which she hopes to spend with the attractive monk. From her point of view, her husband's most annoying trait is his absorption in making money (VII, 214–23), an absorption that occasions her considerable boredom, which she is eager to relieve by the closest means at hand—Don John, who she knows is not unmindful of her charms.

From the General Prologue we learn that Alice of Bath, who has had five husbands and who in her youth took lovers, is thoroughly familiar with all the intricacies of the art of love and therefore, like the merchant's wife in this story, is quite capable of having her cake and eating it too. In fact, in this tale the teller does not slight the merchant; almost as many lines are devoted to his wise comments upon, and successful conduct of, business affairs as are used for the account of his wife's success in the affair with Don John. And these two elements of the story are brilliantly, albeit somewhat frankly, brought together in the last two lines of the narrative:

> Thus endeth now my tale, and God us sende
> Taillynge ynough unto oure lyves ende.   VII, 433–34

The important word here is "taillynge," of course, upon which the teller puns. This word can refer to business dealings and to sexual intercourse: the merchant will be more than content with enough of the former, his wife with enough of the latter.[7]

There seems to me little support for the view that Chaucer, when he originally assigned this tale to the Wife of Bath, planned to work out "an exchange of hostilities, a polite quarrel between the Wife of Bath and the Merchant" on the pilgrimage.[8] For one thing, there is no motivation for such a quarrel in the sketches of either the Wife or the Merchant. Although it is true that in this tale a merchant is cuckolded and deprived of a hundred francs, his wife can hardly be regarded as the kind of protagonist the Wife would use if her chief purpose were to discomfit the Merchant. Neither in this tale nor in the sketch of the Wife of Bath do we find any emphasis on female sovereignty; in fact, the wife of the merchant of St. Denis, sincerely or not, ends by asking her husband's forgiveness (VII, 425). Moreover, the mention in the Merchant's Tale of the Wife of Bath (IV, 1685–87) seems clearly to stem from the Wife of Bath's Prologue, in which she describes her treatment of her husbands; since her prologue presumably was written after the Shipman's Tale, we are not justified in using passages from that prologue in an argument which assumes that she is the teller of the Shipman's Tale.

Our best conclusion, then, is that when Chaucer originally assigned the Shipman's Tale to the Wife of Bath, he considered the tale properly suited to her by virtue of its being a fabliau illustrating the kind of love-intrigue that the Wife herself had practiced in her youth. When, however, he worked out the far more dramatically complex performance which we know as the Wife

---

[7] Robinson, *Works*, 839, note to l. 434; Claude Jones, *MLN*, LII (1937), 570; R. A. Caldwell, *MLN*, LV (1940), 262–65; Albert H. Silverman, *PQ*, XXXII (1953), 329–36.

[8] Tatlock, *The Development and Chronology of Chaucer's Works*, 207.

of Bath's Prologue and Tale, he shifted the story of the merchant of St. Denis to the Shipman, presumably feeling that this fabliau would not sound strange in the mouth of the master of the *Madelaine*. To a considerable extent this view was justified.

The tale, as a story of cuckoldry, certainly falls in with the Shipman's dislike of highly moral and learned material, and fulfills his promise to "clynken" so merry a bell that he shall awaken all the company. There is also evidence in the narrative of the teller's rather specific knowledge of wine (VII, 70–73), which the Shipman could have gained in carrying cargo from Bordeaux (I, 396–97). Futhermore, the Shipman's telling a story of a merchant cuckolded is to a small degree motivated by the mention in the General Prologue of his regular success in outsmarting the "chapmen" for whom he works.[9] All in all, though it cannot be claimed that this performance is among the most effective examples of dramatic suitability in the *Canterbury Tales*, we are justified in finding it suitable to the character of its teller and in observing a trace, at least, of its suggesting a Shipman-Merchant antagonism.

So far as the Host is concerned, the Shipman has performed suitably and excellently:

> Wel seyd, by *corpus dominus*, . . .
> Now longe moote thou saille by the cost,
> Sire gentil maister, gentil maryneer!
> God yeve the monk a thousand last quade yeer!
> A ha! felawes! beth ware of swich a jape!
> The monk putte in the mannes hood an ape,
> And in his wyves eek, by Seint Austyn!
> Draweth no monkes moore unto youre in.
>
> VII, 435–42

Quite naturally, Harry interprets the tale in the light of his own circumstances. As an innkeeper he is concerned as to what sort of guests he harbors,[10] and he seems to miss the fact that the wife's boredom with her husband's constant concern for business brings about the cuckolding more than does the monk's perfidy.

[9] See M. R. Stobie, *PMLA*, LXIV (1949), 565–69.
[10] The meaning of Middle English "in" (VII, 442) is not equivalent to that of Modern English "inn"; it can also indicate a private home.

Al was conscience and tendre herte

7. THE PRIORESS

The character of Chaucer's Prioress has been most convincingly explained by Professor Lowes.[1] It appears that in the sketch of this lady (I, 118–62) Chaucer included many skillful touches which suggest the "delightfully imperfect submergence of the woman in the nun."[2] The result is a kind of gentle raillery, hardly sharp enough to be called satire but nevertheless indicative of certain limitations in the Prioress which result primarily from her concern with worldly matters.

In Chaucer's day the majority of nuns adopted their way of life for economic rather than for purely religious reasons, and they were most frequently from the upper classes.[3] Madame Eglentyne has risen to the office of prioress in her convent, and accordingly enjoys considerable prestige.[4] Professor Manly argued that she may be modeled to some extent after Madame Argentyn of St. Leonard's convent near Stratford-Bow.[5] However that may be, the Prioress is eager "to been estatlich of manere,/And to ben holden digne of reverence." She also makes great efforts to imitate "cheere of court": her table manners are above reproach, for her interest in etiquette is great. In this matter, as in the mention of her way of speaking French, her fine clothes, her ornaments, and her pets, Chaucer is laughing at this nun who interests herself in the behavior of fashionable people.

But an even more humorous touch is to be found in the description of the Prioress' physical appearance. Her smiling "ful

---

[1] J. L. Lowes, *Anglia*, XXXIII (1910), 440–51. See also E. P. Kuhl, *PQ*, II (1923), 302–309.

[2] See p. 442 of Lowes's article cited in n. 1 of this section, and his *Convention and Revolt in Poetry*, 60.

[3] Bowden, *Commentary*, 92.

[4] Eileen Power, *Medieval English Nunneries c. 1275 to 1535*, p. 69.

[5] Manly, *New Light*, 202–20. For different views, see Arthur Sherbo, *PMLA*, LXIV (1949), 236–46; and M. P. Hamilton's essay in *Philologica: The Malone Anniversary Studies*, 179–90.

[79

symple and coy," her name itself, her nose "tretys," her eyes "greye," her mouth "ful smal" and soft and red, her broad forehead—each of these characteristics represents the ideal for the heroine of the contemporary romances.[6] Then there comes the line, "For, hardily, she was nat undergrowe," in which we can find further fun at the Prioress' expense. The size of this lady, who has numerous features similar to those of a romantic heroine and who tries so hard to copy the dainty manners of a fashionable lady, is sharply out of keeping with the rest of her appearance and with her would-be fascinating manners. For she is a large woman—"nat undergrowe," that is, not small—and this line, coming as it does after the humorous emphasis on her delicacy and daintiness, represents a brilliant use of understatement.[7]

In addition to the Prioress' various feminine affectations so far noticed, there is the similar matter of her exaggerated tender sensitivity. She weeps if she sees a dead or bleeding mouse caught in a trap, and especially if one of her "smale houndes" dies or is beaten. At least in insignificant matters, "al was conscience and tendre herte" with this prioress. The sketch of the Prioress ends with mention of her shining gold brooch, "On which ther was first write a crowned A,/And after *Amor vincit omnia*." It is now generally agreed that the Love which here conquers all refers to divine love, rather than sensuous love. Chaucer makes considerable sport of Madame Eglentyne's fashionable affectations, but he does not accuse her of licentiousness.

After the Shipman has finished his tale, the Host speaks to the Prioress "As curteisly as it had been a mayde" (VII, 447–51). Harry Bailly's politeness here is doubtless understandable in view of her position and sex; but his excessive courtesy—"by your leave," "if I knew it would not annoy you," "if you so de-

[6] See the article by Lowes cited in n. 1 of this section and, for an opposing view, M. J. Brennan, *MLQ*, X (1949), 451–57.

[7] Miss Bowden (*Commentary*, 95), following Lowes, takes line 156 in the Prioress' sketch as a "quiet statement that she is well-proportioned ('nat undergrowe')." But the *NED* labels "undergrowe" an "obsolete variant of *undergrown*," which it defines as "imperfectly grown or developed," citing the line here in question; and Skeat (*Complete Works of Geoffrey Chaucer*, V, 18) explains "undergrowe" as "of short, stinted growth." Chaucer's "nat undergrowe" would therefore seem to mean, with reference to the Prioress, "markedly large." See also W. C. Curry, *The Middle English Ideal of Beauty*, 103; and G. H. Harper, *PQ*, XII (1933), 308–10.

sire," "if you would comply"—all within the space of five lines, suggests the possibility that Harry may be slyly poking fun at her extreme emphasis on "good manners," which was ironically stressed in her sketch in the General Prologue. In any event, the Prioress gladly complies with his request, and, after a prologue which is an invocation to Mary, she relates the story of the little schoolboy who, killed and hidden by the Jews, is later discovered through a miracle of the Virgin. Certain aspects of this story seem particularly suited to the combination of piety and affectation which we have observed in the Prioress.

First of all, the Prioress' Prologue and Tale show clearly, by means of their atmosphere of sincere religious devotion, that the bantering tone which Chaucer used in describing Madame Eglentyne in the General Prologue was not intended to indicate that she is open to adverse criticism on matters of fundamental faith. Although the material he assigned to her is taken from a large body of well-known miracles of the Virgin, which existed in the late Middle Ages, he has shaped this material in such a way as to have it convey to us a sense of her personal belief.[8] In the Prologue, made up in large part of borrowings from the services of the Church, Chaucer gave her what many critics consider some of the finest passages of lyric poetry in Middle English. Then, too, the Prioress takes occasion, when near the end of her story she speaks of the abbot who supervises the burial, to show her understanding of the proper behavior for a religious:

> This abbot, which that was an hooly man,
> As monkes been, or elles oghte be,
> This yonge child to conjure he bigan.   VII, 642–44

This comment, of course, seems to reflect particularly on the worldly monk, Don John, who makes a cuckold of the merchant in the immediately preceding Shipman's Tale. Perhaps it also reflects upon the luxury-loving Monk who is a member of the company of Pilgrims. Both her prologue and tale bear witness to the Prioress' earnest Christian humility. But what of the other aspect of her character, her feminine affectations?

We note at once that in her recital Madame Eglentyne keeps

---

[8] See the chapter by Carleton Brown in *Sources and Analogues*, 447–85.

hidden most of her leanings toward "cheere of courte." Three points, however, seem to fit with her exaggerated tenderness and sensitivity. First, Chaucer changed the age of the little schoolboy from ten to seven, thereby making him a more suitable recipient for the pathos of the Prioress' tale. Second, there seems to be a heightening of the mother's expression of grief when the little boy does not return home, and in this heightened grief we see some similarity with the Prioress' reaction to the loss of one of her pets. Third, there is the matter of the ending for the story. Chaucer apparently had the choice of a happy ending or the tragic ending that he selected, one that would seem to allow fuller revelation of the Prioress' character.

Miss Bowden finds a further matter which suits this tale and its teller.[9] For her, Chaucer implies in his sketch of the Prioress that Madame Eglentyne's charity and pity are aroused by such a matter as the suffering of a mouse, but that "she is not greatly concerned over the suffering of her fellow-man." In commenting on the passage in the Prioress' sketch which begins "But, for to speken of hire conscience" (I, 142–45), Miss Bowden continues:

This implication is later strengthened by her own *Tale* in which she tells with perfect blandness of the tortures visited upon the Jews [VII, 628–34]; and by the fact that when Chaucer writes of the charity of his Parson, he is explicit and clear in pointing out that here is a man who follows truly all the teachings of Christianity in loving his neighbour as himself. For Madame Eglentyne, then, the poet's *but* indicates a reservation. Despite her charm and dignity, she possesses a real imperfection not unmarked by the poet who has created her.

There are certainly those who will not be willing to agree with Miss Bowden on this last point. Personally, I think her interpretation defensible.[10] But, in any event, we have seen other details that indicate that Chaucer gave to the Prioress a story that mirrors the two facets of her personality. And, in conclusion, we should notice that the "quod she," inserted in line 581 of her tale, suggests strongly that this story was prepared with its teller well in mind.

[9] Bowden, *Commentary*, 99–100.
[10] A similar view is advanced by Sister Mary Hostia in *College English*, XIV (1953), 351–52.

8. THE PILGRIM CHAUCER

Following the Prioress' Tale, we have "Sir Thopas" and "Melibeus." These two recitals are set in a carefully developed dramatic framework provided by three exchanges between the Narrator and the Host. These exchanges are strategically placed before "Sir Thopas," between "Sir Thopas" and "Melibeus," and after "Melibeus," and are closely meshed with both the manner and the content of the two tales. To read these tales without careful regard for their dramatic framework would be almost certainly to neglect Chaucer's intentions. As we shall see, this whole performance by the Pilgrim Chaucer is aimed at exposing Harry Bailly to genial ridicule.

Until he is called on for a tale, our view of the Pilgrim Chaucer develops indirectly from his manner of telling us about the other people present and about the events on the pilgrimage. And, as we saw in Part II, our interest in, and enjoyment of, his book come to a considerable degree as a result of assumptions we are led to make about the character of the Narrator. From the General Prologue we conclude that here is a genial, sociable fellow who moves easily among any group of people and knows his way about in the world. Also, we recognize his acute powers of observation and effective reportorial ability. Then, when the storytelling game gets under way, we have reason to attribute to him a lively and delightful sense of humor. And we soon saw that the Narrator's sense of humor includes laughing at himself as well as at the other Pilgrims, for when the Lawyer poked fun at his clumsiness as a poet, the Pilgrim Chaucer let the joke stand unchallenged (II, 45–96). All in all, here is a man who well deserves attention and who can be counted on to entertain us. Consequently, we expect some fun when in the Prologue to "Sir Thopas" we see that the Host has called on the Pilgrim Chaucer to perform (VII, 691–711).

Now shul we heere Som deyntee thyng

Some critics have felt that in this passage the description of the Narrator as sober and retiring is inconsistent with the genial qualities attributed to him elsewhere.[1] Others maintain that his gravity here is to be explained by the moving effect of the immediately preceding Prioress' Tale.[2] It seems to me, however, not only that the Narrator is here consistent with his other appearances, but also that the scene is to be understood as his careful preparation—the present-day term"build-up" is apt here—for playing a joke on the Host. The core of the joke is to be that the Narrator, the literary sophisticate, will in his performance first make plentifully and entertainingly evident the fact that Harry Bailly lacks any real literary critical ability, despite the rapidity and certainty with which he criticizes the various tales; and, second, he will jockey the Host, a henpecked husband, into approving a tale in which a husband profits by accepting his wife's advice.

Since the glimpses of the Host are by design scattered through the *Canterbury Tales*, a reader may overlook the great care which Chaucer expended in portraying Harry's character. It must not be forgotten that the Host is Chaucer's chief unifying device for the group of stories and also for the group of Pilgrims. No other one of the Pilgrims is shown in so many situations which serve to delineate character, and Chaucer indicates a number of affectations and pretensions which Harry possesses. Most of these traits are those typical of an innkeeper, but we are here concerned with another sort of affectation which Chaucer has definitely stressed in his portrayal of the Host: Harry prides himself, without good reason for doing so, on his ability as a literary critic. In addition to his responsibility as guide and "governour" of the company, he is the self-appointed "juge and reportour" of the stories. Such a job demands literary critical ability, which Harry feels that he has; witness his statement "Fulfilled is my sentence and my decree" (X, 17).

As early in the *Canterbury Tales* as his second speech, the Host takes pains to exhibit with considerable pride his knowledge of the literary critical terms that qualify "best":

[1] T. A. Knott, *MP*, VIII (1910–11), 135–39.
[2] W. W. Lawrence, *PMLA*, L (1935), 90.

> And which of yow that bereth hym best of alle,
> That is to seyn, that telleth in this caas
> Tales of best sentence and moost solaas,
> Shal have a soper at oure aller cost
> Heere in this place, sittynge by this post.   I, 796–800

There is notable similarity between Harry's pride here (and in the Clerk's Prologue) in his knowledge of literary critical terms and in the manner in which he recites medical terms after the Physician's Tale (VI, 304–17). The hearty approval which he accords the tale by the Knight (I, 3115, 3119) is delivered with the air of one fully able to recognize a good story when he hears one, as is his admonition to the Cook to make sure his story is "good" (I, 4345). This "ex-cathedra" attitude which Chaucer has given the Host is perhaps most clearly seen in his response to the Reeve's philosophical comments on old age:

> Whan that oure Hoost hadde herd this sermonyng,
> He gan to speke as lordly as a kyng.
> He seide, "What amounteth al this wit?"
>   I, 3899–3901

There is little difference between the criterion for good literature which Harry implies here, as well as in his teasing rebuff of the Parson (II, 1174–77), and that which the Shipman later advances (II, 1185–90). But, unlike the Shipman, the Host does not openly admit his shortcomings; rather, he exaggerates his familiarity with literary material. Thus, in his remarks on the passing of time, just before he calls on the Lawyer for a story, Harry says:

> Wel kan Senec and many a philosophre
> Biwaillen tyme moore than gold in cofre,
> For "los of catel may recovered be,
> But los of time shendeth us," quod he.   II, 25–28

It does not seem to me pure chance that Harry is probably wrong when he attributes this axiom to Seneca,[3] or that of the five instances in which Chaucer uses the familiar proverb "Everything has its appointed time," Harry alone cites Solomon as his source

---

[3] W. W. Skeat, *The Complete Works of Geoffrey Chaucer*, V, 134–35.

(IV, 6). Such errors as *"corpus dominus"* (VII, 435) and *"corpus Madrian"* (VII, 1892) also suggest his pretentiousness.

Closely related to Harry's ex-cathedra critical attitude is the fact that Chaucer seems to give us more than a hint that the Host feels a certain condescension of the sort typical of the practical man of affairs toward the supposedly impractical man of books. Professor Lowes described this one of Harry's characteristics as "courtesy . . . touched with that benignant affability with which the man of the world indulges the scholar. . . ."[4] This attitude is noticeable in the Host's comment to the Parson, after the Lawyer has finished the story of Constance: "I se wel that ye lerned men in lore/Can moche good, by Goddes dignitee!" (II, 1168–69). Again, in Harry's words to the Clerk, this same feeling is evident:

> Youre termes, youre colours, and youre figures,
> Keepe hem in stoor til so be that ye endite
> Heigh style, as whan that men to kynges write.   IV, 16–18

When one recalls the Clerk's poverty and his not being worldly enough to get a job, it seems likely that Harry's implication that the Clerk will someday write to kings is more indulgent than courteous.

One of the surest indications that Chaucer intended the reader to see the wide gap between the Host's fancied ability at literary criticism and his actual lack of perception is to be found in Harry's missing the fact that the merchant of St. Denis' absorption in business contributes importantly to his cuckolding (VII, 435–42). Similarly, in his critique of the Merchant's Tale, the Host, no doubt thinking of his own wife, blames May, failing to see that January's lust has blinded him (IV, 2419–25). Such performances do not justify the claim to sure critical ability which the Host states in reprimanding the Monk for telling tragedies: "And wel I woot the substance is in me/If any thyng shal wel reported be." (VII, 2803–2804).

If Chaucer the poet intended throughout the *Canterbury Tales* for the reader to be aware of Harry's unwarranted pride in his ability as a literary critic,[5] one may infer that this affectation

[4] J. L. Lowes, *Geoffrey Chaucer and the Development of His Genius*, 205.
[5] For a different opinion, see Émile Legouis, *Geoffrey Chaucer* (English trans., 1913), 179–80.

would have furnished particular enjoyment to the Pilgrim Chaucer, whose surer critical ability had been developed by many hours spent with his books. Thus it may be that an interpretation of the scene between Chaucer and the Host in the Prologue to "Sir Thopas," and of the immediate purpose for "Sir Thopas" itself, should take into consideration the possibility of a desire on the part of the Pilgrim Chaucer to make humorously apparent Harry's affectation of great critical ability. The lines of that scene bear out this supposition.

In the first two lines the Narrator reports the sobering effect of the Prioress' story upon the group. The solemn and moving effect of such stories for the mass of people in Chaucer's day cannot be denied; but that is not to say that the Pilgrim Chaucer, certainly no stranger to miracles of Our Lady or to saints' legends in general, meant to picture himself as deeply touched by her performance. This is the same Narrator who smiled understandingly at those traits universally feminine which the Prioress' withdrawal from worldly life had not obliterated in her personality; it is also the same Chaucer who saw fit to give humorous emphasis in the Introduction to the Man of Law's Tale to having sufficient acquaintance with saints' legends to produce a parody of them (II, 60–61). In short, the Narrator is here simply reporting the effect of the Prioress' story on the group at large, without necessarily indicating his own reaction to that story.

Furthermore, to connect the opening statement concerning the sobering effect of the Prioress' Tale with the Host's reference to the Pilgrim Chaucer's staring at the ground does injustice to the text, for Chaucer plainly states in the third line of this passage that the Host dispels the solemn atmosphere by joking. This joking is not reported in any detail and, presumably, was of a general nature. The effect of the Prioress' Tale has gone before the Host directs his attention and jests toward Chaucer. It seems to me that the fourth line of the passage is often similarly misread, and that it also indicates that the usual gaiety has been restored before the Host speaks to Chaucer. The line goes "And thanne at erst he looked upon me." Most critics have taken "thanne at erst" to mean "at first, for the first time"; but in every one of the seven other instances in which Chaucer used the phrase it means "not until then."[6] Thus the fourth line of the Prologue to "Sir Thopas" means "And not until then [that is, after he has dispelled the gravity by joking] did the Host look at me." There is no justification for the interpretation "And then he looked at me as the first butt for his jokes." *The Canterbury Tales* is, above all else, the record of a storytelling game in which, after one story ends, the Host usually selects the next teller. By means of the fourth line in this passage, Chaucer the poet intends simply to inform the reader that the Pilgrim Chaucer has been selected to tell the next tale.

In the succeeding twelve lines the Host addresses Chaucer with a jesting condescension reminiscent of his remarks to the Parson, but Chaucer's reply seems to indicate that he has already decided to tell the highly skillful and entertaining "Sir Thopas" for the purpose of showing up Harry's affectation of literary critical ability. Harry first asks: "What sort of man are you?" Then he states: "Thou lookest as thou woldest fynde an hare,/For evere upon the ground I se thee stare." Here "evere" means no more than "steadily, fixedly at this moment";[7] therefore, in these two lines the Host simply remarks that at this time Chaucer is staring at the ground as if in search of a rabbit. Perhaps that statement suggests that Chaucer, who has just learned that his turn as storyteller has arrived, is staring at the ground in an effort to prevent the Host's seeing the merry twinkle which has come into his eyes at the prospect of the joke he plans. It may be that Harry, certainly not always quick at perceiving the finer shades of human feeling, mistakes the staring at the ground for an indication of Chaucer's being of a particularly contemplative nature, for he next commands Chaucer to approach and to look up merrily. One assumes that he carried out both commands. Then the Host, in his usual manner, makes a joke about the size of Chaucer's waistline, ironically suggesting that a lovely woman would be delighted to embrace a man with such a figure. Chaucer, forced to look up from the ground and to give the Host a clear view of his face, is unable to conceal the twinkle of anticipation in his eyes. Therefore, Harry calls him "elvyssh," that is, mischievous,

[6] J. P. Roppolo, *MLN*, LXIII (1948), 365–71.
[7] See Knott's article cited in n. 1 of this section.

in that Chaucer is obviously enjoying a private joke rather than making that joke generally known by doing "daliaunce" with the other Pilgrims.[8] Following these thrusts, the Host reminds Chaucer that it is his turn to tell a story, and, as usual, demands a "tale of myrthe." Certainly this demand from the Host for a merry tale is too typical a remark to bring about any violent emotional reaction in Chaucer at this point, as some critics have claimed it does.

In his reply to the Host's speech, Chaucer assumes an ironic mock humility. He expects and hopes that the Host will be disgusted by "Sir Thopas," in which the kind of literature that Harry likes is burlesqued. Chaucer therefore enjoys issuing a warning to the Host not to be "yvele apayd" and claims to know no other tale than "Sir Thopas." He implies, however, that his tale has the authority of age, suspecting that Harry will express enthusiastic approval at the prospect of such a story. Chaucer is not mistaken, for Harry cries: "Ye, that is good," and proclaims to the company that the Pilgrim Chaucer, now that he has consented to do "daliaunce," seems to be the kind of man who can tell a rare story.

If we have guessed the immediate intention of "Sir Thopas," no one can deny that the joke was highly successful. In "Sir Thopas" Chaucer presents, as one critic said, "a good-humored rollicking burlesque, a 'tour-de-force' of high spirits, the brilliance of which has hardly yet been fully recognized. In no other poem can we so plainly and clearly see Chaucer at play, having no end of fun with the romances and his readers and himself."[9] In a similar vein, another commentator wrote: "Genius is airily at play in 'Sir Thopas,' and the original combinations of old motifs, the unexpected grace of such lines as those describing the Fairy Queen, are not to be demonstrated. They illustrate Chaucer's unimpeded originality in the very midst of closest imitation."[10] But the Host, with whom I think the Pilgrim Chaucer is also having a great deal of fun, misses the point completely. He does not see the poetic ingenuity illustrated by "Sir Thopas," nor

[8] Compare Lawrence's interpretation of "elvyssh"; *PMLA*, L (1935), 85, 90.
[9] J. M. Manly, *MP*, VIII (1910–11), 144.
[10] See pp. 486–87 of the chapter by L. H. Loomis in *Sources and Analogues*.

does he appreciate the delightful burlesquing of the metrical romances in such scenes as the arming of Sir Thopas or the fight with the giant. The broad humor of the hero's name, of his search for an elf queen, and of his swearing by homely fare is lost for Harry, who emphatically interrupts:

> Namoore of this, for Goddes dignitee,
> . . . for thou makest me
> So wery of thy verray lewednesse
> That, also wisly God my soule blesse,
> Myne eres aken of thy drasty speche.
> Now swich a rym the devel I biteche!
> This may wel be rym dogerel. . . .   VII, 919–25

The Host sees only ignorance of creditable poetic practice in this performance and manages to exhibit his knowledge of a critical term, "rym dogerel." The subtle joke on the Host planned by the Pilgrim Chaucer is working without a hitch, but the latter keeps a perfectly straight face, for his exposé of the Host is only half-finished. His next remarks are accompanied by an injured tone:

> Why so? . . . why wiltow lette me
> Moore of my tale than another man,
> Syn that it is the beste rym I kan?   VII, 926–28

Harry is not slow to answer this question with a vulgar comparison and to state that since Chaucer is only wasting time, he will not be allowed to recite further in this sort of verse. However, not wishing to be unfair to a Pilgrim who apparently is making a sincere effort to please, the Host decides to give Chaucer another chance. But this time he must tell something in alliterative verse or in prose, and his tale must contain "som murthe or som doctryne."

Chaucer agrees with alacrity, for Harry continues to play right into his hand:

> Gladly, . . . by Goddes sweete pyne!
> I wol yow telle a litel thyng in prose
> That oghte liken yow, as I suppose,
> Or elles, certes, ye been to daungerous.
> It is a moral tale vertuous.   VII, 936–40

Now the burden of responsibility is shifted to the Host, for he is going to hear a moral tale "vertuous" in prose—just what he has demanded; if he is not pleased by such a performance, then certainly the fault lies with him, not with the teller. But Chaucer goes on in greater detail to make sure that Harry will have no grounds for complaint; by citing the authoritative example of the four Gospels, he protects himself from the possible charge that his version of the story varies somewhat from other versions. The accounts of Matthew, Mark, Luke, and John all carry the same "sentence," and similarly, despite the great number of proverbs included, his tale will not vary in meaning from his source.

Chaucer now feels that he has the necessary groundwork laid for the completion of his joke at the Host's expense: he has left Harry no defensible reason for interrupting the coming tale. To make this point absolutely clear, he closes his introductory remarks with a firm statement: "And therfore herkneth what that I shal seye,/And lat me tellen al my tale, I preye" (VII, 965–66). Then he sets forth on the lengthy journey through his prose tale, "Melibeus." To suggest the nature of his second performance, a brief summary of this story will be useful.

Melibeus returns home one day, after roaming pleasantly in the fields, and finds that his enemies have broken into his house in his absence and have beaten and wounded his wife and daughter. Almost insane with anger, he vows to revenge this act, but Prudence, his wife, urges him to be patient, to call together all his friends, to ask them whether he should make war or remain at peace, and to be guided by their counsel. Melibeus calls the assembly but receives contradictory advice. He is still determined to make war. Prudence then marshals her authorities and manages to win Melibeus' consent to a plan whereby she will hold a secret conference with his enemies. When these enemies meet with her, she stresses the advantages of peace and the righteousness of Melibeus' anger. Convinced, the enemies put their fate into her hands. Upon Prudence's return home, Melibeus accepts the confession of guilt from his enemies in the spirit in which it is offered. Prudence at once summons all her relatives and old friends to hear the case. They decide for peace.

The enemies place themselves wholly at the mercy of Melibeus, who accepts his wife's advice and forgives them.

This tale is not, of course, original with Chaucer.[11] It was written by an Italian judge named Albertano of Brescia, who had the rather heavy-handed habit, as his three sons came of age, of presenting each with a moral treatise as a guide for his actions. This piece, entitled *Liber Consolationis et Consilii*, was given to the third son, Giovanni, in 1246. But Chaucer's "Melibeus" is a close translation of an Old French condensed paraphrase of Albertano's Latin, done by Renaud de Louens sometime after 1336. The tale is obviously an allegory: "Melibeus" means "honeydrinker," that is, a sensuous man; Prudence's name explains itself; and the daughter, given the name Sophie by Chaucer, represents wisdom or right-living. The three "olde foes" (VII, 970), who stand for the world, the flesh, and the devil (VII, 1421), wound Sophie in five places, her five senses. In other words, Melibeus' sensuousness damages his soul; he is saved only by taking his wife's advice, that is, by becoming prudent.

Such moralizing allegory was very common in Chaucer's day, and there can be no doubt, as various critics have maintained, that he and his audience looked upon the "Melibeus" with a great deal less disfavor than do most modern readers.[12] Several other points have been brought forward by these critics in answer to the modern reader, who, bewildered at finding such a long, dull piece, stuffed full of commonplace axioms, included in the *Canterbury* collection, asks: Did Chaucer really consider this a good story, comparable, say, to the Nun's Priest's Tale? Or is it that he was simply trying to represent by his collection every type of literature popular in his day? It is very doubtful that either of these possibilities leads to a satisfactory answer. More pertinent are the facts that the medieval audience "found mental stimulus in very obvious truths, and a perpetual relish in the gnomic style"; and that in this tale the themes of peace as pref-

[11] See the chapter by J. B. Severs in *Sources and Analogues*, 560–614.

[12] W. P. Ker, "Chaucer," *English Prose* (ed. Henry Craik), I, 40; J. S. P. Tatlock, *The Development and Chronology of Chaucer's Works*, 188–97; Leslie Hotson, *SP*, XVIII (1921), 429–52; the essay by W. W. Lawrence and that by R. S. Loomis in *Essays and Studies in Honor of Carleton Brown*, 100–10, 129–48; Gardiner Stillwell, *Speculum*, XIX (1944), 433–44.

erable to war, of the necessity for selection of wise counselors, and of the excellence of woman as counselor, would have had especial significance for Chaucer and his audience because of the contemporary political situation, in which the English people were tired of unnecessary war, very desirous of able advisers for the young and unstable King Richard, and well aware of such wise women in high place as Queen Anne, Queen Philippa, and Joan of Kent. Such facts make more understandable the presence in the *Canterbury Tales* of "Melibeus."

But we see a far more cogent reason for the Pilgrim Chaucer's relating the "Melibeus" after the Host has put an end to "Sir Thopas" when we read it in its dramatic context. Granted that Chaucer was of his time rather than of ours in regard to such extended moralizing, we still could not urge that he lacked the literary discrimination necessary to see the difference in kind and degree between the "Melibeus" and the Nun's Priest's Tale, or the contrast between the didactic story and its forerunner, "Sir Thopas." The "Melibeus," whatever else it is, certainly is the second half of the joke used by the Pilgrim Chaucer to make evident the Host's lack of literary taste.

Harry neither interrupts nor complains in the course of "Melibeus." In delivering this lengthy moralistic tale, with a proverb for every possible need, the Pilgrim Chaucer has presented the most routine sort of literary fare, in direct contrast to the highly original "Sir Thopas," which the Host rejected. Thereby, Harry's lack of any real qualifications for his job as literary critic on this pilgrimage has been revealed for anyone whose taste runs to material of a less strictly hortative nature than the "Melibeus." And this jest is all the better by virtue of the fact that "Juge" Bailly does not realize what has happened to him.

We have only to look again at the lines quoted from Chaucer's remarks introducing this tale to see the fun he rightly expected to derive from the Host's reaction. There he spoke of the story he would tell as "a little thing in prose" (VII, 937), "this little treatise" (VII, 957, 963), and "this pleasant [murye] tale" (VII, 964). We may argue that since "murye" usually means "pleasant" in Middle English rather than "gay" as now,[13] and since the

13 W. W. Lawrence, *Chaucer and the Canterbury Tales*, 153–54.

medieval audience did not find moralizing unpleasant, no irony is intended by the third of the phrases; but there is no escaping the humorous contrast between the first two of these phrases and the length of "Melibeus."

There is a second important aspect to this joke which the Pilgrim Chaucer is playing upon the Host. It almost seems that the Narrator took for granted that the Host would miss the allegorical meaning of "Melibeus" and would accept it as a straightforward story. For, somehow or other, our inquisitive Narrator had found out that Harry Bailly is a henpecked husband. Immediately following the "Melibeus," the Host launches a lengthy lament about his life at home (VII, 1889–1923). Here he regrets that his wife, Goodelief, was not present to hear this tale. Then he reveals her great impatience with him and concludes that someday she will make it necessary for him to leave home. Nor does he conceal his fear of her "byg armes."

We see that the Pilgrim Chaucer has maneuvered Harry into the position of finding a moral applicable to his own marital situation in a story preaching mastery for the wife, a state which the Host would hardly favor. Indeed, although Melibeus first refuses to give over sovereignty to his wife (VII, 1055–63), he later says to her: "Dame, . . . dooth youre wil and youre likynge;/For I putte me hoolly in youre disposicioun and ordinaunce" (VII, 1724–25); and all consequently turns out well. One suspects that if the formidable Goodelief had heard the "Melibeus," as her husband pathetically wishes, she would have led him a sadder life than that which he reports.

In many ways Harry deserves this double-edged joke at his expense, for by his pompous yet inadequate criticisms of the various tales, as well as by his ready use of his authority over the Pilgrims—a sharp contrast to his position at home—he has furnished more than enough motivation for the treatment he receives from the Pilgrim Chaucer.

A manly man, to been an abbot able

9. THE MONK

To banish his melancholy reflections about his wife, the Host briskly calls upon the Monk for merriment. He, however, is not eager to please Harry Bailly and purposely inflicts upon him a series of dull tragedies that do nothing to relieve the Host's gloom. Two questions in connection with this performance by Chaucer's Monk have given rise to sharp difference of opinion: Is the Monk a Benedictine or an Augustinian?[1] and: Is the Monk who now tells the tragedies consistent with the Monk of the General Prologue?[2] The first of these questions need not particularly concern us here, but arriving at a defensible answer to the second is, of course, vital to an analysis of the dramatic interplay involved. I hold, with Professor Tatlock and others, that the Monk is consistent throughout and that his recital is quite suitable, in the light of the antagonistic feeling which the Host arouses in him.

The most striking fact about the Monk as described in the General Prologue (I, 165–207) is his sensuous love of luxury and creature comforts. This monk has nothing to do with the asceticism usually associated with monastic life. He is an outdoor man, loves hunting, and spares no cost in providing himself with the finest horses and dogs for that sport: "He yaf nat of that text a pulled hen,/That seith that hunters ben nat hooly men."[3] To the ears of the Monk the bells which hang from his horse's bridle jingle much louder than does the bell of his chapel, for his interests do not center about the chapel. His sleeves are

---

[1] See Ramona Bressie, *MLN*, LIV (1939), 477–90, and LVI (1941), 161–62; J. S. P. Tatlock, *MLN*, LV (1940), 350–54, and LVI (1941), 80; E. P. Kuhl, *MLN*, LV (1940), 480.

[2] See Manly, *New Light*, 161, and *Canterbury Tales by Geoffrey Chaucer*, 572, 636; Ramona Bressie, *MLN*, LIV (1939), 489; J. S. P. Tatlock, *MLN*, LV (1940), 350–54.

[3] Concerning this "text," see O. F. Emerson, *MP*, I (1903–1904), 105–15; Rudolph Willard, University of Texas *Studies in English*, XXVI (1947), 209–51.

trimmed with the finest fur, he wears a valuable golden pin, his boots are of the best, and his brown horse is expensively equipped. Furtherfore, the Monk loves to eat, especially when the main dish is a roasted swan, and his appearance reflects this fondness: "He was not pale as a forpyned goost"; rather, "He was a lord ful fat and in good poynt," whose face and bald head shine as if he had been anointed. There is an unmistakable aptness in the Narrator's choice of a "pulled" hen—that is, a hen of little value as food—as the commodity which the Monk is unwilling to exchange for the religious rule against hunting.

The Monk is by no means hesitant to defend the way of life which he practices, and it appears that he expressed himself vigorously in this vein to our Narrator during the evening at the Tabard Inn before the pilgrimage starts (I, 173–76, 183–88). Such talk does not fit well with our ideas of what a monk should be. Yet we should not censure Chaucer's Monk too severely, for he is an "outridere"; that is, he has been appointed by his abbot to manage the estates and to conduct the outside business of the monastery. Some of the blame, at least, for the Monk's likes and dislikes must rest upon the institution, the Church, which allotted to an individual who presumably had decided to withdraw from the world work which necessitated his taking an active part in the business of that world. I am not saying, of course, that the Monk in any way objected to the job assigned him—far from it. But the great number of contemporary worldly monks,[4] in perfectly good professional standing, indicates that the Narrator's remarks about the Monk should not be read as direct satire and suggests that his statement "And I seyde his opinion was good" probably refers to his approval of the Monk's making his way in the world. In fact, the Monk seems well on his way to high place in monastic circles: he is already prior of a dependent monastery, and we are told that he is fit "to been an abbot."

A further point is to be noted from the sketch in the General Prologue. Although the Monk certainly does not respect his vow of poverty, no comment occurs here to indicate that he is licentious or otherwise guilty of sexual infractions of his rules. Granted that to suspect the worldly Monk of licentious conduct

[4] Bowden, *Commentary*, 109–15.

puts no great strain on credulity, nevertheless, this worthy "kepere of the celle" has, for all we know, good reason to take offense at such a charge.

The Monk, of course, along with the Prioress, is next in rank after the Knight among the members of the company. And the Host, ever mindful of "degree," calls upon the Monk to perform when the Knight has finished his tale: "Now telleth ye, sir Monk, if that ye konne,/Somwhat to quite with the Knyghtes tale" (I, 3118–19). We note here, beneath the surface of Harry Bailly's respectful "sir Monk" and his use of the formal pronoun "ye" rather than the familiar "thou," just a trace of belligerence towards the Monk in the phrase "if that ye konne." It would seem that Harry personally doubts the ability of this hunting Monk to tell a story equal to the Knight's. But this situation is not developed, since Robin the Miller, drunk on ale of Southwark, disregards rank and successfully demands the stage. After this setback, Harry is less punctilious in his effort to arrange the order of storytelling and does not do the Monk the courtesy of calling on him again until after the Pilgrim Chaucer has finished "Melibeus."

In the meanwhile, as we have seen, there are two reflections upon the worldly Monk. First, he is very like Don John in the Shipman's Tale, who is an outrider (VII, 65), loves food and good living generally (VII, 73–74), and apparently has sufficient connection with hunting to bring a present of wild fowl (VII, 72) and to use a simile based on a hare worn out and frightened by the pursuing dogs (VII, 104–105). Of course, Don John is not an exact replica of the Monk: for one thing, the former seems much younger (VII, 26); and, more importantly, he is eager for, and expert in, amorous intrigue. Nevertheless, sufficient similarity is suggested to give the Monk reason for some displeasure at the Shipman's Tale. Then, right after that story, the Prioress makes a remark (VII, 642–43) probably aimed at him; and there is perhaps a repetition of this thrust in her later comment: "This hooly monk, this abbot, hym meene I,/His tonge out caughte, and took awey the greyn" (VII, 670–71). But the greatest insult to the Monk's dignity comes in the Host's words when the latter for the second time calls upon him for a tale (VII, 1924–90).

After his lengthy description of the difficulties his wife causes at home, and with a possible reference to the Miller's having earlier prevented the Monk from performing, Harry says: "My lord, the Monk, be cheerful, for [this time] you shall actually tell a tale." Perhaps also from this statement we are to infer that the Monk's facial expression mirrors his justifiable displeasure at the treatment he has received so far on this pilgrimage; and, to make matters worse, instead of letting the Monk commence, the Host addresses him further, with very little show of respect:

> Ryde forth, myn owene lord, brek nat oure game.
> But, by my trouthe, I knowe nat youre name.
> Wher shal I calle yow my lord daun John,
> Or daun Thomas, or elles daun Albon?
> Of what hous be ye, by youre fader kyn?
> I vowe to God, thou hast a ful fair skyn;
> It is a gentil pasture ther thow goost.   VII, 1927–33

The tone of these lines is patronizing, and the fact that "Don John" is the first name suggested for the Monk calls forth unpleasant association with the sly monk in the Shipman's Tale. Also, the question as to the Monk's religious house implies that Harry's expectations of an untruthful reply lead him to require the Monk to swear "by youre fader kyn." The Host's overfamiliarity is particularly apparent in his shift from the formal to the familiar pronoun of address. But he is just beginning here his banter at the Monk's expense.

Without waiting for answers to his questions, the Host shifts to the Monk's physical appearance, commenting on his fair skin and obvious well-being, from which he concludes that the Monk is not a poor cloisterer but a "governour, wily and wys," with the stature befitting such office. Then with ironic sympathy[5] the Host laments the Church's rule of celibacy which prevents so able-bodied a man from begetting children:

> I pray to God, yeve hym confusioun
> That first thee broghte unto religioun!
> Thou woldest han been a tredefowel aright.
> Haddestow as greet a leeve, as thou hast myght,

[5] Robinson, *Works*, 852.

To parfoune al thy lust in engendrure,
Thou haddest bigeten ful many a creature.

VII, 1943–48

Needless to say, Harry's concern here with the desirability of increasing the population should not be taken seriously. He is manifestly making off-color jests because he takes for granted that a worldly monk, "in good poynt" and addicted to hunting and luxury, must inevitably be involved in frequent sexual activities. And we should note that Harry assumes sufficient familiarity with the Monk's supposed extramonastic exploits to continue his use of the intimate "thou," "thee," and "thy" with fluent ease.

Furthermore, the Host labors his point for eleven additional lines, in which he first proclaims that, if he were pope, the Monk and all professional religious men equally capable physically would have wives. This statement then leads him to the conclusion that "Religioun hath take up al the corn/Of tredyng, and we borel men been shrympes," in which there is the fairly obvious jocular and lewd comparison of the sexual organ of the secular male to a shrimp. This manner of satirizing the licentious practices of contemporary churchmen the Host carries to greater lengths by stating that "oure wyves" prefer sexual experience with churchmen, whose physical prowess makes them better able to meet "Venus' payment"; such, of course, was the case with Don John and the wife of the merchant of St. Denis. Then, to cap his attack, the Host repeats a device he had used earlier with the Cook: "But be nat wrooth, my lord, though that I pleye./Ful ofte in game a sooth I have herd seye!" Obviously, this is no apology at all; rather, it is a further attempt to arouse the Monk's wrath and to put him in the wrong for not being able to take a joke.

Surely the Monk had reason to be displeased at the Miller's rudeness, the Host's neglect, the Shipman's story, and the Prioress' passing comment. But the Host's lengthy and unveiled assumption that the Monk participates in sexual activities with willing wives might well have given rise to an explosion. Doubtless Harry is hoping for the entertainment that would be provided by just such an outburst. But the Monk was not born yesterday, and he has not made his way in the world without learning how to handle scoffers. He seems quickly to arrive at a shrewd estimate of the situation and realizes that his best move is to disregard completely the Host's provoking remarks, and to punish the Host for his vulgar familiarity by subjecting him to a dull, learned sermon. Therefore, we are told that "This worthy Monk took al in pacience"; and his first words are a refutation of Harry's suggestive implications: "I wol doon al my diligence,/ As fer as sowneth into honestee,/To telle yow a tale, or two, or three." Very likely the other members of the company are just as uneasy as the Host, who probably had expected a flustered defense from the Monk, at the prospect of his telling three "honest" tales.

The Monk does nothing to allay such uneasiness. On the contrary, he offers to tell the group the life of St. Edward the Confessor—a dreary suggestion, from the Host's point of view—or else first to relate some tragedies, of which he has a *hundred* in his cell. Here is indeed an alluring choice for entertainment while traveling—either the life of St. Edward, or a hundred tragedies plus the life of St. Edward! But the Monk seems determined on his revenge, and, giving the Pilgrims no time to choose, he starts right in with the latter alternative by defining tragedy in the medieval sense. This routine definition over, he apologizes beforehand for any error in chronology he might make. One surmises that this apology stems from the Monk's realization that time spent in hunting has made his learning a bit shaky.

There is no need here to examine in detail the material which makes up the Monk's Tale. Suffice it to recall that he delivers seventeen completely uninspired, brief narratives, in each of which a famous individual falls from high place to low. Seemingly in an antifeminist answer to the Host's implications that he has improper relations with women, the Monk commences his tragedies with Satan and moves next to Adam and Samson, who were betrayed by women, the agents of Satan.[6] The Monk's recital, in the true tradition of a medieval sermon,[7] serves to exemplify the moral that no man should trust in blind prosperity,

[6] D. W. Robertson, Jr., *ELH*, XIX (1952), 9–11.
[7] Claude Jones, *MLN*, LII (1937), 570–72.

for when Fortune decides to desert him he cannot halt her. Such material is thoroughly suited to a churchman, and we can see some point in a worldly monk's choosing to include the "Modern Instances" within his recital of standard tragedies. But here indeed is a performance in great contrast to the "myrie cheere" the Host requested earlier of the Monk; and we can easily imagine the agony Harry is experiencing at the thought of the Monk's continuing through his hundredth tragedy—and then telling the life of St. Edward. However, the Host, feeling that this is "proper" material, is unwilling to interrupt. Fortunately—for the reader as well as for the Host—the Knight halts the recital.

With the authority of the Knight to support him, the Host rushes in to attack by heaping scorn upon the Monk:

> Ye, . . . by seint Poules belle!
> Ye seye right sooth; this Monk he clappeth lowde.
> He spak how Fortune covered with a clowde
> I noot nevere what; and als of a tragedie
> Right now ye herde, and, pardee, no remedie
> It is for to biwaille ne compleyne
> That that is doon, and als it is a peyne,
> As ye han seyd, to heere of hevynesse.   VII, 2780–87

Whether or not Harry realizes that the Monk has repaid him for his earlier familiarity is not completely clear; but we do note that in this passage the Host mocks the Monk's style[8] (compare lines 2785 with 1991; and 2782 with 2766), and then goes on to say that the Monk's story is annoying everybody, for it is not worth a butterfly. This time, however, Harry is careful to use the formal "you" and "your," to return to his respectful "sire Monk," and to refrain from levity in connection with the Monk's name, Don Piers. Also, we find entertaining evidence of the success of the Monk's revenge in the sincerity with which the Host says that only the jingling of the bells on the bridle of the Monk's horse kept him from sleeping and falling off his horse during the recital. Then, regaining his usual largeness of manner, Harry uses a semiphilosophical tag about the waste of speech where there is no listener, again boasts about his ability to recognize a

[8] H. R. Patch, *MLR*, XXII (1927), 386–87.

good story when he hears one, and politely requests the Monk to relate a hunting story: "Sir, sey somwhat of huntyng, I yow preye." He feels that a request for such material cannot displease the Monk, and at the same time doctrinal matter will be avoided. The reference here to the bells and to hunting shows that we are dealing with the same Monk whom we met in the General Prologue.

But the Monk seems to have had his fill of Harry Bailly and feels that he has sufficiently repaid him for the former vulgar liberties. Don Piers therefore simply dismisses the Host with the statement: "Nay, . . . I have no lust to pleye./Now lat another telle, as I have toold." As effectively as did the drunken Miller, though in an entirely different fashion, the Monk has defied the Host's rule and yet run no risk of paying all the expenses for the trip. Here the Host seems to realize that he has been bested, for he turns quickly to the Nun's Priest, a Pilgrim whom he does not fear to browbeat, with "rude speche and boold."

In the controversy that we have been examining, it is the nature of the tale as a whole, rather than themes or characters or incidents within it, which bears the weight of the revenge. There can be no question here, I think, as to whether or not Chaucer and his contemporaries were fonder of brief tragedies used as *exempla* than is the modern reader. This recital serves a perfectly obvious dramatic function as a speech delivered by the Monk; as such it well deserves its place in the *Canterbury Tales*. We are fortunate, however, that Chaucer had the good sense to limit the use of similar literary-revenge pieces to two additional performances—the "Melibeus" and the Parson's Tale.

10. THE NUN'S PRIEST

To many readers, the Nun's Priest's tale of the regal Chanticleer and the lovely Dame Pertelote represents the high point of Chaucer's narrative art in the *Canterbury Tales;* and this delightful story gains much when it is considered within the carefully prepared dramatic interplay which surrounds it. As an *exemplum* and as a mock-heroic beast-fable making use of learned material, the tale is a suitable one for a cleric; and its subtle antifeminist theme makes it appropriate for a cleric under the "petticoat rule" of the Prioress. But, in addition, the tale almost certainly includes the thrusts by the Nun's Priest at the Host's two most recent attackers—the Pilgrim Chaucer and the Monk. In fact, Harry Bailly's reactions form the background against which the tale functions dramatically. First we shall consider the problem of the traits, both physical and intellectual, which Chaucer intended us to associate with the Nun's Priest.

Concerning the character of the Nun's Priest, the Narrator gives almost no explicit information. This Pilgrim appears in only one phrase of the General Prologue: "Another Nonne with hire hadde she [the Prioress]/That was hir chapeleyne, and preestes thre" (I, 163–64); many scholars feel that even this one phrase is not by Chaucer. Whatever characteristics we attribute to the Nun's Priest must therefore be derived from his part in the drama of the pilgrimage.

Recent criticism as to this cleric's physical make-up and manner holds that he is a vigorous, rosy-cheeked, fun-loving youngster, who serves as one of three brawny, two-fisted bodyguards for the Prioress.[1] Where so few facts are available, however, wide difference of opinion is permissible if it can be supported. The view to be advanced in detail here differs considerably from that

[1] Arthur Sherbo, *PMLA*, LXIV (1949), 236–46; M. P. Hamilton in *Philologica: The Malone Anniversary Studies*, 179–90.

This sweete preest, this goodly man sir John

stated above. I conceive of the Nun's Priest as a timid and frail person of indeterminate years, whom the Host is not afraid to address rudely and upon whom he vents the annoyance he feels primarily as a result of the Monk's behavior.

It will be useful to pause here for a review of the role which the Host has played in the sections of the *Canterbury Tales* preceding the Nun's Priest's performance. In the General Prologue, after a few moments of suspicion on the part of the company, he won the group's eager acceptance of his plan for the storytelling game and of his position of authority. But, after his pleasure arising from the Knight's Tale, he was successfully challenged by the Miller, somewhat annoyed by the Reeve's "sermonyng," and shortly thereafter threatened by the Cook. Then his satisfaction with the Lawyer's performance was quickly dampened by the Shipman's revolt against his authority. Although the Shipman's tale restored the Host's good spirits, he seemed not too pleased with the gravity resulting from the miracle related by the Prioress. Next, his patience was strained beyond its limits by the Pilgrim Chaucer's "Sir Thopas," and he was moved to a lengthy recollection of his domestic woes by the "Melibeus." In the succeeding instance, he was granted no relief by the Monk, whose tragedies he found exceedingly boring, and who calmly overthrew his authority by refusing to tell a tale of hunting.

Surely, up until the time he calls upon the Nun's Priest for a story, the Host has fared rather badly on the pilgrimage. Looked at in this fashion, the sequence and the nature of the performances in Fragments I, II, and VII seem to have been considerably influenced by Chaucer's desire to represent a regular rise and fall in the Host's spirits, with the humorous deflating of him as a steady aspect of the drama. So far, Harry has played an important role in connection with every Pilgrim's recital; we therefore may not be far wide of the mark if, in trying to derive an acceptable portrait of the Nun's Priest, we examine that Pilgrim and his tale as they reflect against, and fit with, the Host's recent behavior.

That, after the Monk's performance, Harry is in search of a Pilgrim upon whom he can relieve his pent-up irritation is borne out by the following lines:

> Thanne spak oure Hoost with rude speche and boold,
> And seyde unto the Nonnes Preest anon,
> "Com neer, thou preest, com hyder, thou sir John!
> Telle us swich thyng as may oure hertes glade.
> Be blithe, though thou ryde upon a jade.
> What thogh thyn hors be bothe foul and lene?
> If he wol serve thee, rekke nat a bene.
> Looke that thyn herte be murie everemo."   VII, 2808–15

Though not bold enough to express his annoyance openly to the high-ranking Monk until after the Knight had interrupted the recital, Harry has picked out another churchman to whom he feels free to speak patronizingly and rudely. Especially noteworthy in this respect are his use in six instances of the familiar pronouns of address—"thou," "thyn," and "thee"—and his choice of "sir John," a familiar and even contemptuous appellation for a priest.

Apparently the Host is not wrong in his estimate of the Nun's Priest; the latter is unctuously humble and emphatic in his willingness to obey Harry's command:

> "Yis, sir," quod he, "yis, Hoost, so moot I go,
> But I be myrie, ywis I wol be blamed."
> And right anon his tale he hath attamed,
> And thus he seyde unto us everichon,
> This sweete preest, this goodly man sir John.
>   VII, 2816–20

A considerable part of the unction in this speech rests in the echo in line 2817 of the Host's earlier unsuccessful command to the Monk to be merry (VII, 1924). The Nun's Priest says, in effect: "Even though the Monk would not do as you told him, *I will.*" One surmises that the impoverished Nun's Priest is far from sympathetic with his wealthy fellow churchman. In his answer here, the Nun's Priest is running no risk of incurring the Host's wrath; and the Narrator's calling him "sweete" and "goodly" serves to emphasize the accommodating haste with which he has just accepted Harry's orders.

In view of this interchange, I find it impossible to go along with those critics who visualize the Nun's Priest as brawny and

vigorous; logic as well as kindness demands that we think of anyone who lets the pompous Host "push him around" in this fashion as being possessed of timidity and meekness which result
from a lack of physical prowess. The phrase "this sweete preest"
in line 2820, with its suggestion of femininity, is also difficult to
align with a concept of a brawny, vigorous Nun's Priest. In addition, note the seemingly spineless agreement signified by the
repetition of the emphatic "yis," as well as the contrast between
the Nun's Priest's lean and foul nag and the Monk's brown-as-a-
berry palfrey (I, 207). From the two passages quoted above we
are surely safe in assuming that the Host looks upon the Nun's
Priest as one churchman to whom he can with impunity speak
"as lordly as a king." Further, from these passages can be observed the Nun's Priest's willingness to curry favor with the Host
by fulfilling the command for merriment which was refused by
the Monk, towards whom the Nun's Priest has no reason to be
favorably inclined. In no way do the lines examined so far suggest impressive physical stature for the Nun's Priest; rather, the
opposite is implied, for Harry Bailly would automatically extend
the same respect to a physically impressive Nun's Priest that he
proffered the Miller and the Shipman.

It is, however, in the much-discussed Epilogue to the Nun's
Priest's Tale that the Host finally purges his system of the an-
noyance which the Monk has most recently occasioned him.
There he speaks as follows:

> "Sire Nonnes Preest, . . .
> I-blessed be thy breche, and every stoon!
> This was a murie tale of Chauntecleer.
> But by my trouthe, if thou were seculer,
> Thou woldest ben a trede-foul aright.
> For if thou have corage as thou hast myght,
> Thee were nede of hennes, as I wene,
> Ya, moo than seven tymes seventene.
> See, whiche braunes hath this gentil preest,
> So gret a nekke, and swich a large breest!
> He loketh as a sperhauk with his yen;
> Him nedeth nat his colour for to dyen
> With brasile, ne with greyn of Portyngale.

Now, sire, faire falle yow for youre tale!"
And after that he, with ful merie chere,
Seide unto another, as ye shuln heere.   VII, 3447–62

It is immediately apparent that in these lines, present in only ten of the scribal copies that have come down to us, the Host reproduces the tone and a part of the contents of his earlier speech to the Monk (VII, 1932–61). For this reason, Professor Manly and some other editors of the *Canterbury Tales* have concluded that Chaucer probably canceled the passage quoted above when he later wrote the Host's speech to the Monk. However, other scholars have maintained that Chaucer meant this passage to stand as it is. The grounds for this latter view are simply that the manuscript situation is inconclusive, that the repetition here is not extensive, and that elsewhere, as in Harry Bailly's remarks about his wife, Chaucer did not cancel repetitive lines.[2] There is, it seems to me, an additional and equally cogent argument, based on internal evidence, against cancellation.

In this epilogue, Harry is in far better spirits than when he first called upon the Nun's Priest; consequently, he shows this Pilgrim the courtesy of twice calling him "sire," and finally even uses the respectful "yow" and "youre." But the Host is not yet entirely satisfied that he has wiped away all trace of the Monk's intractability toward him. Therefore, using "thy" and "thou," he repeats, in his remarks to the Nun's Priest, a part of the identical vulgar routine joke at which the Monk had earlier taken offense; the core of this joke is, of course, the suggestion that a churchman has great sexual powers. But this time we should not take the routine jest at face value, as have those critics who base their claim for the Nun's Priest's brawn on these lines. Harry is speaking ironically here, and the intent of the passage is the opposite of its literal meaning. The Host is contemptuous towards the Nun's Priest because this churchman is under the supervision of a woman, the Prioress; note the emphasis in line 3447 which Harry places on the cleric's position by his use of the title "Sire *Nonnes* Preest." That we know the Host to be a henpecked husband makes his contempt for the Nun's Priest's situation the

---

[2] Manly and Rickert, *The Text of the Canterbury Tales*, II, 422–23, and IV, 517; J. S. P. Tatlock, *PMLA*, L (1935), 100–39.

more readily understandable. Furthermore, Harry feels that, by virtue of his unimposing physical stature, the Nun's Priest is well suited for supervision by a female and for a job that keeps him in a nunnery.[3] These are the two aspects of the Nun's Priest which led the Host earlier to select him as the churchman upon whom his irritation at the imposing and powerful Monk could be vented safely. Now, the tale over, Harry wishes to demonstrate to the company that he can successfully apply to another churchman the vulgar joke which the Monk earlier caused to fall flat.

A careful look at the Epilogue reveals three additional details to support a reading of this passage as irony. The Host here omits completely the remarks, present in his similar speech to the Monk, on the Church's folly in not permitting the clergy to marry in order to beget healthy children to populate the world; the physique of the Nun's Priest receives the entire emphasis here. I take it that this churchman's pallor, extreme slenderness, skinny neck, narrow breast, and dull eyes would make too far-fetched even an ironic argument from Harry that such men were needed to populate the earth. Also, there is the ring of irony about lines 3450–54, where the Host says that if the Nun's Priest were secular he would be a "trede-foul aright" and have need of many "hennes." His position does cause him to be surrounded by many women—the nuns—and it was generally taken for granted that a churchman stationed in a nunnery indulged in sexual license.[4] But the Nun's Priest's physical appearance is not such as to suggest that he is a source of temptation to the nuns. Finally, there is the appearance of ironic exaggeration in the line "Ya, moo than seven tymes seventene." When so industrious a servant of Venus as Chanticleer seems content with only 7 "hennes," and when more than 119 seems beyond the desires of even the mightiest Eastern potentate, we can suspect at least that Harry's statement means that the Nun's Priest appears too weakly to have any need at all for "hennes."

Having delivered this ironic speech on the Nun's Priest's physique, the Host is thoroughly satisfied with himself and returns to his usual jovial frame of mind, gone all thoughts of his diffi-

[3] Eileen Power, *Medieval English Nunneries c. 1275 to 1535*, p. 144–45.
[4] *Ibid.*, chap. xi.

culties with the Monk. The Narrator tells us that Harry turns to the next storyteller "with ful merie chere," an attitude in striking contrast to the "rude speche and boold" with which he called upon the Nun's Priest after the Monk's rebuff (VII, 2808). Rather than concluding that Chaucer canceled the Epilogue to the Nun's Priest's Tale when he wrote, perhaps later, the Prologue to the Monk's Tale, I find in the Host's remarks every indication of Chaucer's skillful use of a repetitive tone and partially repetitive lines to convey the dramatic situation surrounding the Host's dealings with the Monk and the Nun's Priest. For an editor to cancel this epilogue is to ruin one of the most carefully developed scenes in the whole pilgrimage. The high comedy of this scene, for the reader and for Chaucer the poet, lies in the Host's missing the subtler points of the tale and holding up to ridicule the meek little priest who superbly defends him.

For if we have found that the Nun's Priest's physical stature leaves much to be desired, there is nothing at all wrong with his intellectual powers. The tale that Chaucer assigned him is the most charming and one of the most expert in the *Canterbury* collection. Also, in this story the frail Nun's Priest manages to please the Host, to offer rebuttal for the theme of "Melibeus," to laugh at the Monk, and to express his dissatisfaction at working under the Prioress' direction. In order to comprehend these matters fully, we need a brief summary of the tale.

A poor widow has in her barnyard a gallant and imposing rooster, Chanticleer, and his favorite hen, Pertelote. One night in the chicken house Chanticleer dreams that he will meet with disaster from a yellowish-red beast if he flies down into the yard the next morning. He believes that this dream is an omen, but Pertelote maintains that it results from indigestion. Chanticleer wins the ensuing argument on the cause of dreams, but the depth of his amorous feeling for Pertelote leads him to disregard his conclusion by going down into the barnyard. Nearby lurks Don Russell, the evil fox; with elaborate flattery he maneuvers Chanticleer into a vulnerable position, snatches him up, and starts for home. The screams of Pertelote and Chanticleer's six other wives bring the entire household, human and animal, to give chase.

But Chanticleer can take care of himself: he tricks the fox into opening his mouth and then flies to safety in a tree. The fox tries to lure him down, but Chanticleer has learned a lesson from his experience.

Such a bare outline does far less than justice to the humor, the charm, and the skill of this tale. No critical exposition can hope to indicate the first two of these characteristics half so convincingly as will a reading of the story itself; but several critics have turned the full light of scholarship on the expertness with which Chaucer handled his materials in this instance. And, as we would expect, his manipulation of these materials appears to have been dictated by his concern for the dramatic function which the tale, as spoken by the frail and impoverished but witty Nun's Priest, fulfills.

The exact source which Chaucer used for this tale, if any, is not known, but there are two closely analogous stories that can be taken as representative of the materials he had at his disposal; one is the French *Roman de Renart*, the other is the German *Reinhart Fuchs*.[5] There is no need here to examine these pieces in detail, but we can profit from a brief statement of the major alterations Chaucer made in the narrative elements of the story, for these alterations play a crucial part in effecting the theme of Chaucer's version. Most importantly, whereas the two analogues are stories in which the cock is an egotistical fool, "who, repeatedly warned, refuses to heed and suffers in consequence," in the Nun's Priest's recital Chanticleer comes to grief because his amorous interest in Pertelote leads him to put aside his correct interpretation of his dream. Chaucer establishes this difference by shifting the reactions of the two main characters to the dream. In the analogues, the hen considers it an omen, and the proud cock disregards her warnings; in the Nun's Priest's version, it is Pertelote who scoffs at the dream's significance, and the theme of the story thus becomes "the baleful influence of woman's counsel."

Another change Chaucer makes in this narrative is to diminish the role of the fox. Whereas the fox is the one character whose

[5] J. B. Severs, *SP*, XLIII (1946), 22–41.

name appears in the titles of the two analogues, the manuscripts of the *Canterbury Tales* have for this performance the rubric "The Nonnes Preestes Tale of the Cok and the Hen." This alteration serves, of course, to place emphasis on the husband-wife relationship, the core of Chaucer's story, and helps clear the way for the theme, the ill effects of accepting a wife's advice.

This theme places the Nun's Priest's Tale in the large body of antifeminist literature of the late Middle Ages and thus puts it in exact contrast with the preceding "Melibeus," related by the Pilgrim Chaucer, in which all turns out well because of the acceptance of the wise counsel that Prudence gives her husband. Harry may not have realized that the Pilgrim Chaucer maneuvered him into approving the "Melibeus," the theme of which is in entertaining contrast with Harry's immediately succeeding revelations about his own wife. But the shrewd Nun's Priest saw this point at once, and now in his tale defends the Host by showing that a husband is not always wise in following his wife's counsel. There is, of course, perfect appropriateness in the assignment of an antifeminist piece to the Nun's Priest, since the clergy was especially prolific in producing treatments of this theme. But this particular story is further suited to its teller because he is under "petticoat rule" from the Prioress.[6] Yet his position prevents his risking a head-on attack similar to those used by the Friar, the Summoner, the Miller, and the Reeve; besides, what we have already seen of his nature shows that he is not the sort of man to become involved in a straightforward controversy. Rather, he will employ subtlety in making his point.

Thus it is that we find in the concluding lines of his tale a statement of what at first glance seems to be his "moralite": "Lo, swich it is for to be recchelees/And necligent, and truste on flaterye" (VII, 3436–37). But the primary point which he wants to illustrate has been plainly stated earlier:

> My tale is of a cok, as ye may heere,
> That tok his conseil of his wyf, with sorwe,
> To walken in the yerd upon that morwe
> That he hadde met that dreem that I yow tolde.
> Wommennes conseils been ful ofte colde;

[6] W. W. Lawrence, *Chaucer and the Canterbury Tales*, 134–36.

> Wommannes conseil broghte us first to wo,
> And made Adam fro Paradys to go,
> Ther as he was ful myrie and wel at ese. VII, 3252–59

We can be sure that if we had the Nun's Priest to explicate his line "Taketh the fruyt, and lat the chaf be stille" (VII, 3443), somewhere beyond the Prioress' overhearing, he would classify the first of the passages quoted above as bordering on the "chaf," and point to the second as the "fruyt." But in his tale he is not out of earshot of the Prioress, and he does not want to offend her. Therefore he hastens to add the following lines:

> But for I noot to whom it myght displese,
> If I conseil of wommen wolde blame,
> Passe over, for I seyde it in my game.
> Rede auctours, where they trete of swich mateere,
> And what they seyn of wommen ye may heere.
> Thise been the cokkes wordes, and nat myne;
> I kan noon harm of no womman divyne.
>
> VII, 3260–66

Even so, the Nun's Priest has not completely drawn the teeth from his attack, for the "auctours" to whom he refers his audience spoke with force and at length in an antifeminist vein.

In addition to answering the Pilgrim Chaucer and to implying his dissatisfaction with the Prioress' rule, the Nun's Priest manages to accomplish two other aims in his performance. The general merriment of his mock epic, the antifeminist theme itself, and the avoidance of a tragic ending similar to the *exempla* recounted by the Monk are aimed at pleasing the Host, whose good humor when the tale is finished we have already noted. Then, too, there is a possible application of several elements in the tale to the Monk.[7] That worthy's confidence and general affluence are in as great contrast to the Nun's Priest's timidity and poverty as is his fine palfrey to the latter's nag. It would not be unnatural for the Nun's Priest to feel a few twinges of antagonistic jealousy, and we saw that he did appear to say, in answering the Host: "The Monk wouldn't do as you wished, but *I will*." Then in his tale he puts into Chanticleer's mouth one of the tragedies which

---

[7] S. B. Hemingway, *MLN*, XXXI (1916), 479–83.

the Monk has just related, that of Croesus (VII, 3138–40); some readers have felt that the Nun's Priest is thereby ridiculing the Monk and is trying to call his audience's attention to the similar strutting manner of both the outrider and the cock.

But there is more certain ridicule in the following lines by the Nun's Priest:

> For evere the latter ende of joye is wo.
> God woot that worldly joye is soone ago;
> And if a rethor koude faire endite,
> He in a cronycle saufly myghte it write
> As for a sovereyn notabilitee.   VII, 3205–3209

The Monk's oft-repeated point in his performance is that worldly happiness soon passes away, as commonplace a remark at the time as one might hope to find. When the Nun's Priest applies this same routine point to Chanticleer's near disaster with the fox, and then calls it a "sovereyn notabilitee" which an expert rhetorician might well include in a chronicle, the satire on the Monk's dull sententiousness is easy to see. One other passage by the Nun's Priest seems also to apply unfavorably to the Monk. In his account of Samson, the Monk says:

> Beth war by this ensample oold and playn
> That no men telle hir conseil til hir wyves
> Of swich thyng as they wolde han secree fayn,
> If that it touche hir lymes or hir lyves.   VII, 2091–94

Here is, of course, a typical antifeminist statement, which a careful listener might happen to recall upon hearing the Nun's Priest's apology for speaking ill of women. And the Nun's Priest seems eager to help his audience arrive at such a recollection; he illogically shifts in his remarks from "reading" to "hearing" authors who have treated the woman question: "Read authors where they treat of such material, and you may *hear* what they say about women." Once again he equates the Monk with Chanticleer, this time pointing to their similar views about women.

There are aspects of this performance other than its antifeminist theme that make it apposite for the Nun's Priest. The rhetorical skill necessary for turning a beast-fable into a mock epic, as well as the learning that makes possible the inclusion of the debate on dreams, the many references to literary material, and the statement of the free will-foreordination problem, is not surprising in an individual who has the training given the clergy. Furthermore, the *exemplum* technique and other sermon devices in the performance come naturally from a priest. But our next actor-Pilgrim, the Wife of Bath, will submit views in sharp variance with those we have been considering. She is now introduced by means of six lines which have only recently[8] been accorded a place in the accepted text of the *Tales:*

> "Madame, and y durst, y wold you pray
> To telle us a tale y furtheryng of our way;
> Then myght ye do unto us gret ease."
> "Gladly," quod she, "so that y myght you please,
> You and this wurthy company."
> And began hir tale ryght thus full sobyrly.[9]

11. THE WIFE OF BATH

Many of the finest Chaucerian critics have commented at some length upon the sections of the *Canterbury Tales* devoted to the Wife of Bath.[1] Although most of these critics have been sympathetic towards the Wife, the analysis presented here will emphasize certain fundamental flaws in her character. In the section devoted to the Shipman, we considered the tale which Chaucer originally assigned to the Wife; her controversy with the Friar will receive attention in the section treating the worthy Hubert; and her interruption by the Pardoner will be analyzed when we come to his performance. Here we are concerned primarily with the Wife's character as it appears from the Narra-

---

[8] R. F. Gibbons, *SP*, LI (1954), 21–33.   [9] See Robinson, *Works*, 1013.
[1] See, for example, W. E. Mead, *PMLA*, XVI (1901), 388–404; G. L. Kittredge, *MP*, IX (1911–12), 435–67; Curry, *Sciences*, 91–118; H. R. Patch, *On Rereading Chaucer*, 161–65.

In felaweshipe wel koude she laughe and carpe

tor's sketch of her in the General Prologue (I, 445–76) and from her own autobiographical prologue (III, 1–856), and with the dramatic motivation and implications of the tale which she tells the company (III, 857–1264). From consideration of these parts of the *Canterbury Tales*, we shall find that the Wife's outstanding traits are aggressiveness and amorousness, and that the two combine to produce her militant feminism, which leads her to argue strongly for female sovereignty. Obviously, the tale she tells is aimed at illustrating this tenet; and her tale fits into the context of her antagonism towards antifeminist clerics, such as the Nun's Priest, who has just completed his tale, and towards recalcitrant husbands, such as Harry Bailly. But we shall also see that in the course of her performance Chaucer causes her to make clear certain unfavorable aspects of her character which she does not intend to reveal; she no doubt would look upon such revelation as a source of embarrassment.

At the opening of the portrait the Narrator states that there was in the company "A good Wyf . . . of biside Bathe." In Middle English, "wyf" had a more generalized meaning than it carries today in that it could apply to any woman, married or not. In Alice's case, however, the specialized meaning is also particularly apt, since she has had five husbands. This lady is immediately individualized for us by the Narrator's statement that she is partially deaf. The reason for this infirmity is later made vividly memorable when in her prologue she tells of her exchange of blows with her fifth husband (III, 788–96). The Wife does not live in Bath proper; she is from "biside Bathe." Apparently this means that she inhabited the parish of St. Michael-without-the-North-Gate, a small community just outside the town walls, in which weaving was the chief occupation.[2] It is fitting, therefore, that the Narrator should next point out that in clothmaking the Wife surpassed even the inhabitants of Ypres and Ghent, two cities in Flanders noted for the finest weaving. Some readers have seen irony in this statement, suspecting that Chaucer meant us to understand that the Wife thinks better of her own skill than it deserves; but such a view fails to take into account the Wife's highly developed competitive urge in any en-

[2] Manly, *New Light*, 231–32, and *Canterbury Tales by Geoffrey Chaucer*, 527.

deavor she might undertake. We can feel fairly confident that she successfully exerted every effort to produce weaving which would rank with the best. This aspect of her character is evident in her reaction to any other woman's preceding her to "the offrynge": if another woman does so, the Wife is so angry that she is "out of alle charitee." The size and quality of her Sunday "coverchiefs," the quality and arrangement of her red stockings, and her shoes "ful moyste and newe" also show her determination not to allow any other woman to outshine her. And her face—bold, fair, and "reed of hewe"—is that of an aggressive competitor.

But the Wife's care for her appearance doubtless also springs from another competitive motive: her desire to attract male attention. Here there can be no question of her standing, for she has had five husbands, not to mention "oother compaignye in youthe." Her account of these five husbands will form the main portion of her prologue, and "thereof nedeth nat to speke as nowthe." The Narrator feels it sufficient in the sketch to note that the Wife, as an expert in love, knows both its cures and its rules.

It is easily apparent that the Wife must have been a valuable member of the Canterbury company because of her wide experience with pilgrimages—three times to Jerusalem, to Rome, to Boulogne, to St. James's in Galicia, and to Cologne—and because of her gay sociability "in felaweshipe." The General Prologue presents no more striking picture than that of the Wife, laughing and talking as she rides along easily on her "amblere," on her head a hat as broad as a shield, on her heels a pair of sharp spurs, and about her "hipes large" a cloth to protect her skirt from dust and mud. But we hear nothing from her until she begins her prologue, though we can be sure that she has noted with interest both the pictures of married life and the implications concerning dominance in marriage which have appeared in the various preceding recitals.

The Wife of Bath's Prologue, whatever else it may be, is primarily a masterful piece of dialectic, a purposeful attempt at vigorous argumentation. The Wife, aggressive competitor that we have seen her to be, will discuss matrimony, the field of competition which to her is most important. And, chiefly in answer to the Nun's Priest, she is going to use the opportunity afforded by her turn in the center of the movable stage on the road to Canterbury for as strong a presentation of her central view as she can muster, namely, that unhappiness in marriage can be avoided only when the husband grants sovereignty to the wife. When this prologue is examined carefully as such a piece of dialectic, it is perfectly unified and extremely close-knit. We are misled when we maintain, as do some readers, that the Wife's Prologue is divided into two sharply distinct portions by the Pardoner's interruption (III, 163–87), and that the first part (III, 1–162) treats the question of chastity, while the second (III, 188–828) alone concerns sovereignty in marriage. Rather, the matter uppermost in the Wife's mind throughout is female sovereignty, and the lines preceding the Pardoner's interruption represent what she considers necessary and pertinent introductory argument.

The Wife wastes no time in preliminary amenities; she leaps at once into a statement of her topic and of her right to discuss such a topic authoritatively:

> Experience, though noon auctoritee
> Were in this world, is right ynogh for me
> To speke of wo that is in mariage;
> For, lordynges, sith I twelve yeer was of age,
> Thonked be God that is eterne on lyve,
> Housbondes at chirche dore I have had fyve—
> If I so ofte myghte have ywedded bee,—
> And alle were worthy men in hir degree.   III, 1–8

The Wife's topic, then, is "the wo that is in mariage," and it is very important to notice here that the woe of which she will speak is that experienced by husbands who fail to grant their wives mastery, rather than any unhappiness which she herself may have undergone. The lines in which she thanks God for her five husbands, as well as the long segment of her prologue following the Pardoner's interruption, show that she intends this interpretation of "wo." Thus her whole attitude towards marital happiness is in a sense negative: she will show how to avoid misery, not how to be happy.

In the first eight lines of her prologue the Wife also reveals clearly her understanding that points in argumentation derive support from two kinds of evidence—personal experience and authorities; she hastens to indicate the extent of her experience, and she will soon quote authorities in great plenty. But her first aim in this discussion of marriage is to contravert two preliminary arguments which she considers fallacious: first, the idea that an individual should be married only once (III, 13); and, second, the claim that God commanded virginity (III, 62). Citing the Bible with easy familiarity—doubtless the result of her fifth husband's constant reading to her—she maintains that God, rather than forbidding more than one marriage, instructed us to multiply. Since Solomon, Lamech, Abraham, and Jacob had more than one wife and were still holy men, she can see no reason why she cannot have had five husbands; in fact, she will welcome the sixth when her present husband dies. Moreover, she is certain that God did not intend for everyone to be chaste, for "if ther were no seed ysowe,/Virginitee, thanne whereof sholde it growe?" (III, 71–72). She will grant that chastity is a higher state, but as for herself, she will freely enjoy the physical acts of marriage. In fact, she says:

> An housbonde I wol have, I wol nat lette,
> Which shal be bothe my dettour and my thral,
> And have his tribulacion withal
> Upon his flessh, whil that I am his wyf.
> I have the power durynge al my lyf
> Upon his propre body, and noght he.
> Right thus the Apostel tolde it unto me;
> And bad oure housbondes for to love us weel.
> Al this sentence me liketh every deel—   III, 154–62

The Wife here states her policy of completely subjugating her husband by exhausting his sexual potency, and, at this point, the Pardoner interrupts to say that though he is about to take a wife, if matters are as Alice of Bath describes them, he will not enter into marriage. But the Wife tells him to withhold his decision, for before she has finished her performance he will hear of more important troubles in marriage (III, 172–77). As in the opening lines of her prologue, the Wife here announces her main topic, "tribulacion in mariage"; and this time she makes fully clear that this tribulation has been felt not by her but by her husbands, since she has been the "whippe" or held the mastery. Having disposed of the two preliminary questions to her own satisfaction, now, to illustrate in detail her central theme that only unhappiness can result for husbands who refuse to give their wives mastery, she is ready to recount fully her five marital experiences. And she seems to feel confident that because of her preliminary discussion, no antifeminist cleric can halt her exposition to interpose arguments concerning either bigamy or chastity—matters which, in her opinion, she has shown to be irrelevant.

In her autobiographical account, the Wife of Bath groups together her first three husbands. All three were completely under her thumb, and she apparently can no longer remember their distinguishing traits. Each was aged and rich, and each, like old January in the Merchant's Tale, uxorious. With complete shamelessness the Wife tells the company just how she unscrupulously controlled these three old men (III, 197–451). As she says, "I hadde hem hoolly in myn hond" (III, 211), a situation which she preserved by withholding her body from them or by scolding them mercilessly. The result she desired—and obtained—was that they gave her all their many possessions and were happy only when they did not oppose her.

With her fourth husband the case was considerably different (III, 453–502), for "he hadde a paramour." But Alice claims that she brought him to heel by making him jealous. Yet she does not seem to have found much pleasure in this marriage; when he died she quickly buried him as cheaply as possible: "It nys but wast to burye hym preciously."

Although Jenkin, her fifth husband, was hardest of all to subjugate, of him the Wife seems most fond: "I trowe I loved hym best, for that he/Was of his love daungerous to me" (III, 513–14). Jenkin had been a student at Oxford, and came to board with the Wife's closest friend, Alisoun. One Lent, while her fourth husband was away in London, the Wife walked in the fields with Jenkin and told him that if she were a widow she would marry him. This situation soon developed, when her fourth husband died; within a month, forty-year-old Alice and twenty-year-old Jenkin were married. Before long, however, the Wife had reason to regret her action: Jenkin would do nothing to please her. He beat her and read aloud to her many clerical

stories from his antifeminist anthology about wives who were unfaithful and who brought their husbands to ruin. But the Wife of
Bath was not to be so easily outdone, and she continued to go
about visiting as she always had, even though Jenkin forbade it.
To her, Jenkin's antifeminist stories were far more infuriating
than instructive, for she has no high opinion of clerics who write
and tell such stories:

> Therfore no womman of no clerk is preysed.
> The clerk, whan he is oold, and may noght do
> Of Venus werkes worth his olde sho,
> Thanne sit he doun, and writ in his dotage
> That wommen kan nat kepe hir mariage!   III, 706–10

This state of open controversy reached a high point one night
when Jenkin read to her of Eve's bringing mankind to wretchedness, of Delilah's betrayal of Samson, of the trouble Deianira
caused Hercules, of Xanthippe's oppression of Socrates, of the
terrible lust of Pasiphaë, of Clytemnestra's infidelity to Aga-
memnon, of Eirphyle's treachery towards Amphiaraus, of the
poisoning of husbands by Livia and Lucilia, of how Arrius
wished to rid himself of his evil wife, and of many other treacherous wives who brought their husbands woe. When the Wife saw
that Jenkin intended to continue reading such material to her,
she tore three leaves from his book and knocked him into the fire.
Then he angrily hit her upon the head. At this, the Wife pretended to be unconscious for so long that he thought he had killed
her and started to flee. But the Wife spoke to him recriminat-
ingly, and he contritely leaned over her to be forgiven:

> And neer he cam, and kneled faire adoun,
> And seyde, "Deere suster Alisoun,
> As help me God! I shal thee nevere smyte.
> That I have doon, it is thyself to wyte.
> Foryeve it me, and that I thee biseke!"   III, 803–807

Taking advantage of his kneeling position, the Wife hit him
hard. But after long wrangling, the two patched up their differences, which is to say that Jenkin granted Alice complete
mastery:

124]

> He yaf me al the bridel in myn hond,
> To han the governance of hous and lond,
> And of his tonge, and of his hond also;
> And made hym brenne his book anon right tho.
> And whan that I hadde geten unto me,
> By maistrie, al the soveraynetee,
> And that he seyde, "Myn owene trewe wyf,
> Do as thee lust the terme of al thy lyf;
> Keep thyn honour, and keep eek myn estaat"—
> After that day we hadden never debaat.   III, 813–22

Since that day, says the Wife, she has been wonderfully kind and absolutely faithful to her husband.

The Wife of Bath's lengthy account of her relationships with her five husbands has served to illustrate her principal theme—that if a husband does not grant his wife sovereignty, he will suffer great woe. This was the topic she introduced in her opening lines and restated in her answer to the Pardoner, after she had disposed of the preliminary matters of bigamy and chastity. Now she is ready to go on to her tale of the punished knight and the ugly hag, and her purpose in telling this tale is exactly the same as that which she has had throughout.

Her story takes place in the days of King Arthur. A young knight of Arthur's court rapes a girl whom he chances to meet. There is great protest from the populace to the King, and the knight is sentenced to die. But the Queen and other ladies of the court beg so hard that mercy be shown him that the King finally gives the knight to the Queen, to choose whether he should live or die. The Queen tells him that he can save his life if, within a year and a day, he can tell her what it is that women most desire; if he cannot answer the question correctly, he must die. For almost a year the knight searches unsuccessfully for the answer. As he is sadly returning to the court, he meets an old hag, who tells him that she will give him the correct answer if he will promise to grant the next request she makes of him. The knight agrees and goes to the court, where he supplies the correct answer: Women desire most to have sovereignty. The knight is, of course, very happy at escaping death, but when the old hag demands that he fulfill his promise to her by making her his wife, he feels that death might have been preferable. Nevertheless, the two are married. When they are alone in the marriage bed, the knight turns his back upon his wife. She asks why this is so, and he tells her it is because she is so ugly, so old, and of such low birth. She replies that she can change these matters if he will do as she says, and then she preaches him a fine sermon on gentilesse. At the end of her sermon, she tells him that she will fulfill his "worldly appetit," and offers him the choice of having her ugly and old but faithful, or beautiful and young but possibly unfaithful. Faced with such a difficult choice, the knight answers that he will leave the choice to her. Then come the crucial lines:

> "Thanne have I gete of yow maistrie," quod she,
> "Syn I may chese and governe as me lest?"
> "Ye, certes, wyf," quod he, "I holde it best."
> "Kys me," quod she, "we be no lenger wrothe;
> For, by my trouthe, I wol be to yow bothe,
> This is to seyn, ye, bothe fair and good."   III, 1236–41

By granting his wife mastery, the unhappy knight has escaped all woe; in fact, "his herte bathed in a bath of blisse."

Both the answer to the question and the happy ending make it obvious that the Wife of Bath tells the company this story to illustrate the same point which she has had in mind since she first began her performance. She has kept steady emphasis on the theme that a husband can avoid unhappiness only by giving his wife mastery, a theme that quite naturally results from her combination of aggressiveness and amorousness, her two chief characteristics, which she herself explains astrologically (III, 603–26). Moreover, her performance, as if an answer to the Nun's Priest's Tale, has been delivered in a context of antagonism against husbands "That wol not be governed by hir wyves" (III, 1262), and against the antifeminist clerics who write only evil of women (III, 706–10).

But Chaucer does not permit this actor-Pilgrim to leave the stage with her performance so complete a success as she believes. As we shall see in discussing the Friar, "this worthy lymytour" takes pains to deflate the Wife of Bath in the eyes of the company (III, 1265–77). And, what is more to our point here, Chaucer has so constructed the Wife's performance that for the careful reader there are a number of evidences and implications therein that reveal the Wife in a less favorable light than she intends. Three such matters deserve attention.

First of all, she does not realize that from her account of her marriages a member of her audience can very easily equate her present situation with that of her first three husbands, whom she held up to such ridicule. She states that of her five husbands, three were good and two were bad. "Good," applying to the first three, she defines as rich and old and easy to manage; "bad," designating the fourth and fifth, means to her poor and young and difficult to manage. In the case of her first three marriages, the Wife is young, very attractive physically, and without money; hence her elderly husbands are so influenced by lust that they are willing to sign their possessions over to her in exchange for her physical favors. But by the time of her fourth marriage, though she has become a wealthy widow, her physical charms are fading, and, as her vehement protests suggest, her sexual powers must be supported by recourse to wine (III, 455–68). In this instance, physical attraction does not bind her husband to her; on the contrary, he takes a mistress. Although the Wife boasts that she subjugated him by making him jealous, we have reason to be a trifle dubious, for she later reveals that he was sufficiently independent of her to make a lengthy visit to London and leave her at home (III, 550). In the case of her fifth husband, the situation is exactly the reverse of her first three marriages. As she is well aware (III, 469–80), she is now old, while Jenkin is a handsome youth; and she, captivated by his physical charms and sexual potency, signs over her possessions to him. Although she finally manages to gain mastery over Jenkin, doubtless by unceasing nagging, we suspect at least that in the event of Jenkin's death she will fall easy prey to the first impoverished but attractive young man whose eye for her money leads him into wooing her.

Second, an important theme, of which she seems completely unaware, can be derived from the Wife of Bath's Tale. Even though she thinks that her story merely illustrates her argument that a husband should give his wife mastery in order to avoid misery, we can see that the knight in the story grows by virtue of his experiences and is converted from a callous lawbreaker into a courteous gentleman.[3] When we first meet the knight, he is an arrogant and lustful rapist (III, 882–88). Later he appears as a snobbish aristocrat when he berates and neglects his wife, though she has saved him from death, because of her lack of beauty, her advanced age, and her low rank. However, as a result of her sermon on gentilesse, in which she shows him the error of his attitude, he alters his manner completely and addresses her as she deserves. And this alteration comes before the knight knows that it will bring about his happiness. The knight wins happiness, not primarily because he granted his wife sovereignty, as the Wife of Bath thinks she is showing, but because, as a converted sinner, he has earned it.

Third, and perhaps most striking, is the sharp contrast between the Wife of Bath's completely unethical conduct towards her husbands, as described in her prologue, and the admirable rules of behavior set forth by the old hag in her sermon on gentilesse near the end of the Wife's story. There are many indications that the Wife identifies herself with the old hag in her tale. As we have seen, it is the hag who provides the answer to the effect that women most desire mastery and who demands mastery of her husband; female sovereignty is, of course, the central point which the Wife intends her tale to illustrate. Also, the situation between the hag and the knight—old, ugly wife and young, vigorous husband—bears close similarity to that existing between Alice of Bath and Clerk Jenkin; and, in view of the Wife's touching lament for her lost youth and beauty (III, 469–79), we might argue that the hag's magic transformation represents pertinent wishful thinking on the Wife's part and furnishes her with particularly satisfying vicarious pleasure. Furthermore, the climactic position of the bed scene in the tale, a theater of operations with which the Wife has been much concerned during most of her life, comes very naturally from this particular storyteller. But by no stretch of the imagination can we find any similarity between the rules of conduct laid down by the hag in her sermon and the principles of behavior practiced by the Wife of Bath.

[3] J. P. Roppolo, *College English*, XII (1950–51), 263–69.

This sermon seems to be Chaucer's deliberate addition to the tale; although we have no actual source for the Wife's story, the closest analogues—Gower's "Tale of Florent," "The Marriage of Sir Gawaine," and "The Weddynge of Sir Gawen and Dame Ragnell"—do not include such a sermon.[4] The old hag tells her husband that true gentilesse comes from God and is not inherent in noble birth; that both low rank and lack of wealth, rather than being disgraceful, may motivate virtue; that the young should be respectful towards the aged; and that lack of beauty may ensure fidelity. To none of these tenets has Alice of Bath subscribed in her relationships with her five husbands. And, most surprisingly, the Wife of Bath, in concluding her tale, is led to say that the knight's wife obeyed him in everything that might give him pleasure (III, 1255–56); such mastery the Wife herself would be willing to bestow upon no husband. Thus we find in this section of the *Canterbury Tales* not only the suiting of tale and teller within a context of dramatic antagonism, but also full-scale character revelation that goes beyond the intention of the storyteller.

12. THE FRIAR

Although it has been suggested that the Friar and the Summoner are enemies of long standing, perhaps having come in conflict in a district of Yorkshire, we have no proof of this.[1] Nor is such an assumption necessary to explain the obvious dislike which each of these Pilgrims feels for the other. As is well known, the open antagonism between them is sufficiently motivated by the clash of their professional interests. No two professions of the time were

---

[4] See the chapters by B. J. Whiting in *Sources and Analogues*, 207–68.
[1] Manly, *New Light*, 102–22.

An esy man to yeve penaunce

more often at variance.[2] The friars, much to the annoyance of the secular clergy and its subordinates, claimed that only the pope had supervision over them. The two types also clashed in their attempts to fleece the same victims. We should not be surprised, therefore, when during the Wife of Bath's performance, a quarrel breaks out between these Pilgrims, or when each uses his tale to discomfit the other. It is also important to note that the tale each tells is particularly suited to his character as presented in the General Prologue—a point too frequently overlooked in the commentaries—and that there is sharp contrast between the two Pilgrims and between their tales. The likable Friar keeps his temper and tells a good-humored story, while the repulsive Summoner is consumed with anger and includes two vulgar jests in his recital.

This quarrel begins when the Wife reaches the end of her autobiographical prologue. The Friar laughs and says: "Now dame, ... so have I joye or blis,/This is a long preamble of a tale!" (III, 829–31). There is nothing especially offensive about this remark, particularly in view of the Wife's preceding line, "Now wol I seye my tale, if ye wol heere," in which she seems to invite expressions of opinion from the group. True, we may be sure that the Friar does not look upon Alice of Bath as the sort of woman with whom he would seek an intimate relationship—she is far too strong-minded for him—and he is doubtless opposed to her arguments for sovereignty of women. But, in answer to her comment, he merely observes that her prologue has been lengthy, and thus perhaps hopes to keep her from telling an equally lengthy tale. Certainly his comment is far from belligerent. Yet the Summoner breaks in at once. It seems as if he has just been waiting for a chance to pick a fight with the Friar, and assuredly he, not the Friar, begins their quarrel. He insultingly compares friars to flies, in that they meddle with everything, and accuses the Friar of interrupting the Pilgrims' fun (III, 833–39).

The Friar does not lose his temper because of the Summoner's attack; however, he makes no effort to shrink from the quarrel and indicates the method he will use to ridicule his antagonist:

[2] Frederick Tupper, *Types of Society in Medieval Literature*, 56–57.

> Now, by my feith, I shal, er that I go,
> Telle of a somonour swich a tale or two,
> That alle the folk shall laughen in this place.
>
> III, 841–43

At this the wild Summoner erupts with a roar:

> Now elles, Frere, I bishrewe thy face,
> . . . and I bishrewe me,
> But if I telle tales two or thre
> Of freres, er I come to Sidyngborne,
> That I shal make thyn herte for to morne,
> For wel I woot thy pacience is gon.   III, 844–49

Note the irony in the Summoner's statement that the Friar's patience is gone; it is, rather, the former who has completely lost control of himself.

But the Host puts a temporary halt to this quarrel and asks the Wife of Bath to tell her tale. She feels a bit annoyed at the Friar and replies, with heavy sarcasm: "Al redy, sire, . . . right as yow lest,/If I have licence of this worthy Frere" (III, 854–55). The Friar is perfectly polite in his answer: "Yis, dame, . . . tel forth, and I wol heere." After a passing jibe at the ubiquity and licentiousness of friars, the Wife tells her story, following which the Friar proceeds to fulfill his promise to tell a tale about a summoner.

In the sketch of the Friar in the General Prologue (I, 208–69), one of the longest in the series, we are told that the Friar is called Hubert, a name, whether or not Chaucer realized it, which suits him extremely well, since etymologically it means "bright, lively, gay."[3] He is attractive and pleasant, and much given to sprightly and agreeable conversation. His musical accomplishments are considerable: he sings, and plays the fiddle, and is familiar with a large stock of ballads. He frolics like a puppy, and after he has sung, his eyes twinkle like stars on a frosty night.

Though appealing, these are hardly qualities of first importance in a professional religious; but the Friar has a number of far less admirable traits typical of his professional group at that time.[4] The four orders of friars had come to England in the thir-

---

[3] For a different view, see Bowden, *Commentary*, 119.

[4] G. G. Coulton, *Five Centuries of Religion*, presents much material concerning

teenth century, and in the beginning were made up of genuinely holy men, who begged for the few material things they required, tended the sick, helped the needy, and led generally exemplary lives. But by the fourteenth century corruption had set in, and the friars became the scourge of England. They were extremely numerous, primarily interested in gaining wealth and position, and much given to indulging in sins of the flesh, especially immoral relations with women. As a result, documents from the fourteenth century present an astounding number of diatribes against the friars; in fact, hardly a good word about them is to be found.[5] The Wife of Bath's passing thrust is typical of contemporary opinion:

> But now kan no man se none elves mo,
> For now the grete charitee and prayeres
> Of lymytours and othere hooly freres,
> That serchen every lond and every streem,
> As thikke as motes in the sonne-beem,
> Blessynge halles, chambres, kichenes, boures,
> Citees, burghes, castels, hye toures,
> Thropes, bernes, shipnes, dayeryes—
> This maketh that ther been no fayeryes.
> For ther as wont to walken was an elf,
> Ther walketh now the lymytour hymself
> In undermeles and in morwenynges,
> And seyth his matyns and his hooly thynges
> As he gooth in his lymytacioun.
> Wommen may go now saufly up and doun
> In every bussh or under every tree;
> Ther is noon oother incubus but he,
> And he ne wol doon hem but dishonour.   III, 864–81

Friar Hubert seems to practice the usual abuses of his class. He arranges marriages for young women with whom he has had sexual relations; he curries favor with wealthy landowners and their wives by hearing confession pleasantly and assigning easy penance in exchange for gifts; he seeks to please attractive women by presents of knives and pins, very valuable household

medieval friars; see especially II, 124, and chaps. viii and ix. See also Karl Young, *MLN*, L (1935), 83–85.

[5] Bowden, *Commentary*, 122–39.

items in his day; he frequents the taverns and feels that he is above helping the sick and needy, while he is courteous and humble to the wealthy; he leaves no stone unturned in making his begging profitable; he takes part in scandalous legal proceedings; and, finally, he dresses in a most expensive manner. Truly, this long list of nefarious activities bears witness to the corruption that had grown up among the four orders of friars in the 150 years since they reached England.

However, granted that Friar Hubert in his professional activities is no better than his colleagues, Chaucer, as usual widely tolerant, still seems to feel that this businessman of religion is not completely reprehensible, for Hubert's saving grace is that he is a likable fellow. As we have seen, he has numerous pleasing accomplishments and he works hard at making people like him. There is little that is mean, harsh, or bitter about Friar Hubert, and, though we should by no means overlook his matching his professional dealings to the current evil mode, we would not call him devious or malicious. In this respect, he differs greatly from his antagonist, the Summoner, and their two tales reflect this difference.

When the Wife finishes her tale, Chaucer reopens the Friar-Summoner controversy (III, 1265–85). To be sure, there is irony in the Narrator's words here, when he speaks of Hubert as "worthy" and "noble." Yet, despite his frowning at the Summoner, the Friar has courteously maintained silence during the Wife's tale. But before taking up this quarrel, the Friar settles his score with the Wife, cleverly repaying her for the jibes she made at friars. His device in this is subtle: he pretends to have missed completely the amusement value of her performance and places her in the position of usurping the function of her enemies, the clergy, by preaching. In addition, though he compliments her for treating many things well, he suggests that the company has found her material exceedingly boring. To my mind, there can be no doubt that the Friar comes out ahead in his secondary tiff with the Wife.[6] But he passes on immediately to the primary

[6] This point is usually overlooked by commentators; for example, J. E. Wells says: "The Wife . . . has her gibe at the limitors and other holy friars (D 866 ff.). The matter comes to nothing, however, for, at the end of her tale, the Friar is too

matter—discomfiting the Summoner—and in so doing implies that his chief concern is to relate a joke that will help the company to recover from the boredom brought on by the Wife. Here again the Friar refrains from an uncontrolled attack, but he effectively makes his point by seeming to apologize for the fact that his topic—a summoner—is one which permits no good to be said, since summoners incur everyone's hatred.

The Host appears afraid that the quarrel will get out of hand, for he very judiciously points out to the Friar that a man of his high position should not demean himself by bickering; instead, he should tell his tale and "lat the Somonour be" (III, 1286–89). But the irate Summoner does not want matters halted and cries out:

> Nay, . . . lat hym seye to me
> What so hym list; whan it comth to my lot,
> By God! I shal hym quiten every grot.
> I shal hym tellen which a greet honour
> It is to be a flaterynge lymytour;
> And eek of many another manere cryme
> Which nedeth nat rehercen at this tyme;
> And his office I shal hym telle, ywis.   III, 1290–97

Here again the Summoner's manner is vituperative, whereas the Friar is perfectly controlled. The Host seems to realize this difference, for he roughly silences the Summoner and courteously requests the Friar to continue (III, 1298–1300).

But order is not yet assured. The Friar opens his tale with what, so far as we know, is an accurate description of the abuses practiced in the ecclesiastical courts of the time.[7] He tells of an archdeacon "in my contree" who was excessively zealous in extracting fines from all sorts of sinners, but especially from lechers. This archdeacon employs a summoner as his spy—"a slyer boye nas noon in Engelond"—and this summoner's method is to let one or two lechers go free if they tell him where to find "foure and twenty mo." Then the Friar applies his introductory

---

preoccupied with the Summoner to follow up her challenge."—*A Manual of the Writings in Middle English 1050–1400*, p. 721.

[7] L. A. Haselmayer, *Speculum*, XII (1937), 43–57; J. A. Work, *PMLA*, XLVII (1932), 425.

comments directly to the Summoner on the pilgrimage, pointing out that summoners have no jurisdiction over friars (III, 1327–32). As usual, the Summoner's rebuttal is vulgar; he bluntly compares friars to licensed prostitutes. Again the Host calls for peace and again makes evident his disgust at the Summoner and his respect for the Friar. The latter now resumes his description of the summoner in his tale. That worthy employs bawds as his agents, extorts bribes from sinners, and does not hand over these bribes to his archdeacon; in short, his chief interest is to wring money from the people, whether they are guilty or not. This point established, the Friar commences his narrative proper.

The Friar's Tale, for which no definite source has been found,[8] represents Chaucer at his best as storyteller. Its expert economy, inevitable motivation, natural dialogue, climactic structure, and ironic characterization have frequently been commented upon. The Summoner, riding out to force a bribe from an old woman, meets a fiend disguised as a yeoman. Because of the summoner's greed, the yeoman, at the end of the story, takes him off to hell, that place where summoners "han hir heritage."

The Friar then says that he could describe in detail the pains of hell, but ironically concludes his performance by urging his audience to pray that summoners will repent of their misdeeds and become good men before the devil takes them. At the same time he manages to equate the Summoner with Satan, who lies in wait like a lion to slay the innocent. He has indeed entertained the company with extreme skill. The chief fact to notice here, however, is that, though the Friar has in no way sought to avoid open controversy with the Summoner, he has made his point by means of an entertaining, highly appropriate fabliau; and throughout, by maintaining good-humored control of his temper, he has kept his performance free of bitter and ugly vituperation. In so doing, he has evidenced the agreeable merriment emphasized by his sketch in the General Prologue. How widely the Summoner's nature and actions differ from his, we shall now see.

[8] See the chapter by Archer Taylor in *Sources and Analogues*, 269–74.

13. THE SUMMONER

Of the entire group of Canterbury Pilgrims, the Summoner seems to me the least attractive, both physically and spiritually. As Professor Curry has demonstrated, he has a kind of leprosy called *alopicia*.[1] The sketch in the General Prologue (I, 623–68) shows that his face is fiery-red, his eyes narrowed to slits, his brows black and scabby, his beard thin; and his cheeks are covered with suppurating "whelkes" and "knobbes," which no medicinal agent can dry up. Certainly there is good reason for Chaucer to say that children are afraid of the Summoner's appearance. We are also told why he is thus diseased: he loves to eat garlic and onions, to drink strong red wine, and to indulge in sexual license—the causes to which medical authorities of the time attribute *alopicia*. His love of wine is symbolized by the wreath he wears upon his head, his gluttony by the loaf he carries under his arm.

The Summoner's behavior is of a sort with his appearance. When drunk, he shouts out Latin tags that he has learned around the ecclesiastical court, but his learning goes no deeper. For a quart of wine as a bribe he will withhold his report on a man who is keeping a mistress; in fact, he keeps a concubine himself. Furthermore, he makes no bones about telling a rogue that he need not fear excommunication from the archdeacon if he can pay a fine, for "Purs is the ercedekenes helle." In connection with this view, the Narrator inserts a personal comment:

> But wel I woot he lyed right in dede;
> Of cursyng oghte ech gilty man him drede,
> For curs wol slee right as assoillyng savith,
> And also war hym of a *Significavit*.   I, 659–62

This comment, however, is not the simple negation of the Summoner's statement that it seems at first glance. Chaucer is

[1] Curry, *Sciences*, 37–47; see also H. B. Woolf, *MLN*, LXVIII (1953), 118–21.

Of his visage children were aferd

shrewdly pointing to the complete corruption of the Summoner and the whole ecclesiastical legal system of which he is a part. Thus he implies that, though the archdeacon's writ of excommunication is of equal value with his absolution, in such a corrupt system neither can be particularly meaningful.[2] One of the most unfortunate aspects of the system is that the young people in the diocese, in fear of the Summoner's spying on them and reporting their activities, place themselves under his control and seek his guidance. The Summoner's loudmouthed offensiveness is to be seen early on the pilgrimage when he joins with "his freend and his compeer," the Pardoner, in singing a lewd song.

We have already seen something of the contemporary ecclesiastical legal system; a few more details will fill out the picture.[3] The bishop turned over to the archdeacon the administration of the diocesan court, in which persons were tried for any crimes coming under Church jurisdiction—and such crimes were manifold. The archdeacon seems to have employed summoners not only to serve the summons which hailed such people in to court, but also to spy out prospective victims. The court had, of course, the power of excommunication, but it seems that both summoners and archdeacons were quite willing "to settle out of court" in exchange for a bribe. As a consequence, not the rich but the impoverished suffered excommunication. One can hardly imagine a more despicable field of endeavor than the Summoner's, or a less attractive individual in appearance and behavior than he is.

The Summoner's starting a quarrel with the Friar and his several disorderly outbursts are just what we should expect, in view of the description of him which Chaucer gave in the General Prologue. When the Friar completes his tale, the Summoner is so enraged that he is shaking "lyk an aspen leef." He makes only one request: that the company allow him to tell his tale without interruption. Then he says that the Friar should be qualified to describe hell, since "Freres and feendes been but lyte asonder" (III, 1674), and goes on to relate an anecdote, the point of which is that friars have their final dwelling place in Satan's anal tract.

[2] J. S. P. Tatlock, *MP*, XIV (1916–17), 261–62.
[3] L. A. Haselmayer, *Speculum*, XII (1937), 43–57; J. A. Work, *PMLA*, XLVII (1932), 419–30.

With that he concludes his prologue by saying: "God save yow alle, save this cursed Frere!/My prologe wol I ende in this manere." Both the vulgarity of the anecdote and the free expression of animosity towards the Friar come naturally from the mouth of this diseased and embittered scoundrel, and they continue the same sort of behavior he has exhibited earlier.

The tale which the Summoner now relates, and for which there is no direct source,[4] is on a par with that told by the Friar, in so far as structure, characterization, and dialogue are concerned. In it is a most detailed account of the unholy methods of the begging friars in the fourteenth century, and we can surmise the pertinency of this attack by noticing that the Friar loses control of his temper for the only time when the Summoner says that the begging friar of whom he is telling irresponsibly erases the names of donors for whom he has promised to pray: " 'Nay, ther thou lixt, thou Somonour!' quod the Frere" (III, 1761). There is, however, about this tale, in which old Thomas bestows the unwelcome gift upon Friar John, the same ugly air that surrounds the Summoner himself. Even the humorous device suggested by the lord's squire at the end of the tale has its unattractive aspects. Moreover, a close parallel exists between the wrath which Thomas feels toward Friar John and that which the Summoner exhibits towards Friar Hubert.

An attempt to decide who won the Friar-Summoner controversy would be fruitless. Each has openly attacked the other with a skillful story suited to its teller's character and filled with detailed elements applicable to the profession which the other practices. In the exchange, however, the Friar proved far less harshly acrimonious than the Summoner, a difference stemming perhaps from the different demands of their professions.

[4] See the chapter by W. M. Hart in *Sources and Analogues*, 275–87.

14. THE CLERK

Following the Friar-Summoner controversy, the Clerk relates the admirably suited tale of patient Griselda, which illustrates the moral that every individual should be steadfast in adversity (IV, 1145–46). The dramatic technique in this performance combines the realization of subtle personal application present in the narrations by the Nun's Priest and the Pilgrim Chaucer with something of the open debate evidenced in the Miller-Reeve and Friar-Summoner antagonisms. The Clerk, in a disguised answer to Alice of Bath's contention that in any well-run marriage mastery must be in the hands of the wife, tells a tale in which the chief figure, Griselda, is a wife whose guiding tenet is obedience to her husband; then, when his tale is over, he makes the direct application of his story to the Wife of Bath's argument.

The Clerk of Oxford, in his disregard for material gain and in his devotion to learning and teaching, is one of the most inspiring members of the company; and the sincere praise evident in the last line of his sketch—"And gladly wolde he lerne and gladly teche"—bears witness to Chaucer's appreciation for, and understanding of, contemplative, humanistic, intellectual, and spiritual values, despite—or perhaps as a result of—his own lifetime of immersion in the active affairs of court and market place. Chaucer's attitude is the clearer when we note that the portrait of the Clerk in the General Prologue (I, 285–308) immediately follows that of the Merchant, in whom such values are manifestly lacking and who there receives brief and unsympathetic handling.

The Clerk, we are first told, is well advanced in his study of the medieval curriculum, having long ago progressed to logic. The less pleasant consequences from his choice of a scholarly career are at once apparent: his horse is lean as a rake; he himself is by no means fat but looks hollow; and his clothing is thread-

Of studie took he moost cure and moost heede

bare. Contrast the Clerk in these respects with the well-fed Monk, with his expensive clothes, sleek horse, and discriminating palate. Further, the Clerk's chances for adequate income are diminished by his not being worldly enough to get and hold a secular job while he waits for a benefice, for he prefers owning books of philosophy to enjoying the usual luxuries. But, says Chaucer with a good-natured pun involving alchemy, the Clerk cannot make even philosophy pay by discovering the philosophers' stone to turn baser metals to gold. Instead, he spends all the money he can obtain from his friends "on bookes and on lernynge," and dutifully prays for the souls of his benefactors. The Clerk's chief interest is clearly stated in the line "Of studie took he moost cure and moost heede"; his reticence and the moral content of his few remarks reflect this interest (I, 304–307). We conclude that the Clerk's presence on this pilgrimage is motivated by sincere devotion and that he is not the man to contribute a great deal to the merry dalliance with which the Host is eager to surround the trip. But, as we shall see, he is sufficiently experienced as a teacher to lighten his "hy sentence" with a flash of raillery, for his austere reserve is delightfully accompanied by a sense of humor. Moreover, we should note that in contrast to Chaucer's usual method of combining expected and unexpected traits in the sketches of his Pilgrims, his presentation of this man seems completely typical of the contemporary picture of a good clerk.[1]

The Host does not share the admiration for the Clerk's way of life which the Narrator expressed in the General Prologue. When Harry calls upon the Clerk to perform, he patronizingly twits him for his silence, comparing him to a newly married girl, tells him to give up his contemplative manner, and demands a cheerful tale. But the Host wants to make sure that the Clerk will not deliver a boring sermon (IV, 2–14). As in his remarks to other professional men, Harry takes pains in addressing the learned Clerk to show that he is able to use the proper professional vocabulary. He now produces a series of rhetorical terms: he thinks the Clerk is pondering over some subtle point in dialectic ("sophyme"), and the Clerk must not use his "termes," his "col-

[1] See A. W. Green, *ELH*, XVIII (1951), 1–6; H. S. V. Jones, *PMLA*, XXVII (1912), 106–15.

ours," and his "figures" until he has occasion to write in the "heigh style." Such an attitude on the Host's part does not disturb the Clerk, and he agreeably replies that he will do as the Host demands. He will tell a tale that he learned from Francis Petrarch, the worthy Italian poet, now deceased, God rest his soul! In keeping with Harry's instructions, the Clerk further states that, though Petrarch graced his version of the story with a lengthy geographical prologue done in the high style, he will avoid length and rhetorical intricacies by omitting this prologue.

In the tale which follows we find that Walter, the young Marquis of Saluzzo in Italy, arranges a series of tests to prove the obedience of his wife, Griselda. In no instance does she question her husband's authority; as a result, the story ends happily. His narrative over, the Clerk draws his moral (IV, 1142–62): he has told this story, not to encourage wives to attempt the impossible imitation of Griselda's humility, but to show that every individual should be, like Griselda, steadfast in adversity. For, if a woman exhibited such constancy when tested by a mortal man, then we all should receive even more steadfastly the difficulties which God sends us, since God does not, like Walter, test people unnecessarily; indeed, He places hardships in our paths in order to strengthen us, for all His plans work toward our own good. Consequently, we should live in "vertuous suffraunce."

This moral, coming at the end of the Clerk's story, is supported throughout his performance by the emphasis he places on the beneficent results from cheerful obedience to constituted authority, even when such obedience entails hardship. This theme is evident as early as the Clerk's own expression of agreement to tell a "murie thyng of aventures" (IV, 15). He says:

> Hooste, . . . I am under youre yerde;
> Ye han of us as now the governance,
> And therfore wol I do yow obeisance,
> As fer as resoun axeth, hardily.   IV, 22–25

The Clerk is under the Host's management and will therefore obey him in any reasonable request. When the tale opens, we learn that the people of Saluzzo are "obeisant" and ever ready to do their lord's bidding (IV, 66–67); consequently, life in this

noble country is happy and prosperous. When Griselda is introduced, she is praised for according to her father "everich obeisaunce" (IV, 230), and Janicula himself, when Walter asks for
Griselda's hand, expresses his absolute obedience to his lord's will
(IV, 319–22). Later, the officer whom Walter sends to take away
Griselda's daughter voices the need for obedience to a ruler's
commands (IV, 528–32), and Griselda herself, accepting this
opinion, asks that he bury the daughter's body carefully only if
Walter does not forbid it (IV, 570–72).

The necessity for a wife's exhibiting unquestioning obedience
to her husband is, of course, a major concept in the body of the
Clerk's Tale. This view, an established part of Church doctrine,
is not surprising on the part of the Clerk. Walter first states that
he wishes to ask Griselda whether she will "be my wyf, and reule
hire after me" (IV, 327), and then he emphatically sets absolute wifely obedience as the condition upon which he will
marry her (IV, 351–57). She, with equal emphasis, accepts this
condition: "In werk ne thoght, I nyl yow disobeye" (IV, 363).

In the course of the story, as Walter carries out his cruel tests,
Griselda repeatedly restates her determination to obey his every
wish. When he says that their daughter must be killed, she replies: "My child and I, with hertely obeisaunce,/Been youres
al . . ." (IV, 502–503); when he repeats the same argument with
reference to their son, she says: "Dooth youre pleasaunce, I wol
youre lust obeye" (IV, 658); when news comes of Walter's plan
to take another wife, she does not question his desires (IV, 757–
59); when he tells her she must return to her former home, she
simply says: ". . . I wol goon whan yow leste" (IV, 847); and
when he asks her to take charge of the preparations in the palace
for the new wife, she states: ". . . I am glad . . ./To doon youre
lust . . ." (IV, 967–68).

Walter realizes how well Griselda has fulfilled the condition
which he set for their marriage, and speaks of the pleasure he
has had in her "obeisaunce" (IV, 794); particularly concerning
this point, the Clerk himself, in giving his audience advance information as to the happy outcome of his narrative, observes that
all will come out for the best because Griselda exhibited clearly
that no wife should desire anything except what her husband

wishes (IV, 718–21). It seems clear, then, that the Clerk's concluding moral of steadfastness in adversity is founded throughout on the concept of cheerful obedience to constituted authority, and that this concept is chiefly illustrated in his story by Griselda's unquestioning obedience to Walter's unnatural demands. In presenting an *exemplum* characterized by "hy sentence" and in illustrating the Church's teaching of wifely obedience, the Clerk is consistent with the impression we gained of him from the sketch in the General Prologue.

It is likely that the more attentive and intelligent Pilgrims realized long before the Clerk had finished his tale that the theme and action of the story are in direct contrast with the Wife of Bath's argument for supremacy of a wife over her husband.[2] Certainly the obedient steadfastness in adversity which brings happiness to the household of Walter and Griselda bears little similarity to the methods whereby the Wife claims to have established happy relationships with her five husbands. An observant member of the Clerk's audience would also recall that, since the Wife's view is opposed to the established teachings of the Church and since in answer to the Nun's Priest she went out of her way to satirize clerics for their licentiousness and antifeminism, the Clerk has more than enough motivation for using his performance to answer her. In fact, the Wife even maintained that it is impossible for any clerk to speak well of a woman, except in a saint's life (III, 688–91). But it is not until the last six stanzas of his performance that the Clerk indicates clearly that he has just such a purpose. Indeed, there is some evidence in his narrative that he is trying to keep this purpose subtly concealed until he is ready to attack the Wife straight on.

This evidence consists of the efforts the Clerk seems to make to keep his audience in some doubt as to just what is the chief lesson it should draw from his tale. Alongside the steady emphasis on Griselda's obedient constancy in adversity, he offers recurring jibes at Walter's unnatural cruelty. When Walter first plans to test his wife, the Clerk says:

> Nedelees, God woot, he thoghte hire for t'affraye.

---

[2] This interplay was discussed by G. L. Kittredge, *MP*, IX (1911–12), 435–67.

> He hadde assayed hire ynogh bifore,
> And foond hire evere good; what neded it
> Hire for to tempte, and alwey moore and moore,
> Though som men preise it for a subtil wit?
> But as for me, I seye that yvele it sit
> To assaye a wyf whan that it is no nede,
> And putten hire in angwyssh and in drede.   IV, 455–62

The last four lines here are Chaucer's original addition to his two sources, Petrarch's Latin and a fairly literal French translation of Petrarch's story.[3] Again, when Walter decides to take the son from Griselda, the Clerk comments on the needlessness of the test:

> O nedelees was she tempted in assay!
> But wedded men ne knowe no mesure,
> Whan that they fynde a pacient creature.
>
> IV, 621–23

And again the passage is original with Chaucer.

The Clerk's lengthiest remarks of this nature come when Walter conceives the idea of announcing his intention of taking a new wife:

> But now of wommen wolde I axen fayn
> If thise assayes myghte nat suffise?
> What koude a sturdy housbonde moore devyse
> To preeve hir wyfhod and hir stedefastnesse,
> And he continuynge evere in sturdinesse?
>
> But ther been folk of swich condicion
> That whan they have a certein purpos take,
> They kan nat stynte of hire entencion,
> But, right as they were bounden to a stake,
> They wol nat of that firste purpos slake.
> Right so this markys fulliche hath purposed
> To tempte his wyf as he was first disposed.   IV, 696–707

A few lines later, in stating the reaction of the populace to Walter's behavior, the Clerk once more stresses his unnecessary cruelty:

> The sclaundre of Walter ofte and wyde spradde,
> That of a crueel herte he wikkedly,

[3] For a comparison of this tale with its sources, see J. B. Severs, *The Literary Relationships of Chaucer's Clerkes Tale.*

> For he a povre womman wedded hadde,
> Hath mordred bothe his children prively.
> Swich murmur was among hem comunly.
> No wonder is, for to the peples ere
> Ther cam no word, but that they mordred were.
>
> For which, where as his peple therbifore
> Hadde loved hym wel, the sclaundre of his diffame
> Made hem that they hym hatede therfore.
> To been a mordrere is an hateful name;
> But nathelees, for ernest ne for game,
> He of his crueel purpos nolde stente;
> To tempte his wyf was set al his entente.   IV, 722–35

Although we know here that all will turn out happily for Griselda (IV, 718–21), the important point is that Griselda is not aware of this and has every reason to consider Walter's actions beyond what she should endure. The Clerk's final adverse comment about Walter is simply to mention his "wikke usage" (IV, 785).

These passages might easily lead one to conclude that the Clerk's story is aimed at attacking unnecessary cruelty in husbands rather than at showing the benefits of wifely obedience and patience; to such a theme the Wife of Bath would certainly not object. True, she would probably have noted some slight contradiction of her statement on the subject when the Clerk said:

> Men speke of Job, and moost for his humblesse,
> As clerkes, whan hem list, konne wel endite,
> Namely of men, but as in soothfastnesse,
> Though clerkes preise wommen but a lite,
> Ther kan no man in humblesse hym acquite
> As womman kan, ne kan been half so trewe
> As wommen been, but it be falle of newe.   IV, 932–38

But such a half-hearted and inoffensive rebuttal would certainly not disturb her.

As if he plans to continue the disguise of his real intention, which he has maintained throughout his tale, the Clerk, after delivering his three-stanza moral (IV, 1142–62), seems about to pay an agreeable compliment to Alice of Bath, whom he even mentions by name, as a kind of postscript to his story:

> But o word, lordynges, herkneth er I go:
> It were ful hard to fynde now-a-dayes
> In al a toun Grisildis thre or two;
> For if that they were put to swiche assayes,
> The gold of hem hath now so badde alayes
> With bras, that thogh the coyne be fair at ye,
> It wolde rather breste a-two than plye.
>
> For which heere, for the Wyves love of Bathe—
> Whos lyf and al hire secte God mayntene
> In heigh maistrie, and elles were it scathe—
> I wol with lusty herte, fressh and grene,
> Seyn yow a song to glade yow, I wene;
> And lat us stynte of ernestful matere.
> Herkneth my song that seith in this manere.
>
> IV, 1163–76

This passage amplifies the Clerk's earlier remark in explaining why Walter's son did not test his wife: "This world is nat so strong, it is no nay,/As it hath been in olde tymes yoore" (IV, 1139–40), for which reason Petrarch said that it would be impossible for modern wives to imitate Griselda, even if they wished to do so. Until he reaches his envoy, the Clerk gives the impression that he accepts philosophically this deterioration in wives and that he bears no grudge against the Wife of Bath.

This envoy, with which the Clerk ends his performance and which we shall examine shortly, is marked in the manuscripts "Lenvoy de Chaucer," but the title does not mean that the stanzas are spoken by the Narrator rather than by the Clerk. It does mean that the scribes copying the manuscripts recognized and indicated that these stanzas are original with Chaucer and are not to be found in his sources. The Clerk's continuity from his narrative to the Envoy is perfectly effected.

Another point worth noticing here is that the word "secte" in line 1171, quoted above, can apparently either mean "sex" or refer to a heretical religious group.[4] Arguments have been ad-

---

[4] See Helge Kökeritz, PQ, XXVI (1947), 147–51, and NED, "secte," sense 1. **d.** (initial entry "sect").

vanced for each of these readings; that is, the Clerk here prays either that God will preserve the Wife of Bath and *all other women* in high mastery, or that God will preserve in high mastery the Wife and *all heretics* who share her views. The point at issue is whether or not the Clerk is calling the Wife a heretic. It seems to me that the Clerk here intends both meanings for the attentive listener in his audience but feels sure that the Wife of Bath will choose to understand his words as a compliment to herself and all women. This interpretation is in accord with the view that the Clerk wants to keep his satiric intent more or less under cover until he reaches his envoy.

But if until his envoy the Clerk appears desirous of disguising his intention of settling a score with the Wife, his six final stanzas (IV, 1177–1212) constitute an extremely skillful burlesque attack which gives him a clear victory in this debate concerning the status of a wife in the home. The first of these stanzas is harmless enough; in fact, except for the last line, the Clerk here expresses once more the moral against cruelty in husbands which, as we have seen, he prepared for throughout the tale; and in that last line he merely restates his point about deterioration in wives. Then the blow falls—in his last five stanzas. Here, with broad exaggeration and unveiled irony, the Clerk advises wives not to follow Griselda's example in patient obedience; instead, they should emulate Echo, whose tongue is never still. Wives should not be so innocent as to accept their husbands' commands, but, for common profit, should take over complete mastery in the home. Strong wives can accomplish this by main strength; weak wives should bring it about by constant complaining. Husbands are not to be feared, for wives can put them in their places by "the arwes of thy crabbed eloquence" and by causing them to be jealous of their wives' "freendes." In sum, a wise wife will let her husband "care, and wepe, and wrynge, and waille."

By thus exaggerating the point of view advanced earlier by the Wife of Bath, the Clerk has made glaringly evident the ridiculousness of any possibility for a happy home in which her theories are practiced; and at the same time he has managed to avoid advocating the opposite extreme, as represented by Griselda's unbelievable patience in the face of Walter's cruelty.

Furthermore, the Clerk has accomplished these aims without involving himself in any unbecoming bickering. Truly, the long years of study have not been wasted on this clerk, and Harry Bailly was correct in thinking that he was pondering "som sophyme" as he rode along before his performance, for that "sophyme" was his brilliant refutation of the Wife's arguments.

The Host's comment upon the Clerk's Tale furnishes a concrete example of the validity of the Clerk's contention. Harry says that he wishes his wife at home could have heard this story of patient Griselda. He restrains himself here from giving the details of his home life, but we earlier learned that Goodelief, his wife, behaves in accord with the Wife of Bath's theories and with the Clerk's exaggerated advice to both "archewyves" and "sklendre wyves" in his envoy. Later Harry will disclose that he wishes he were not tied to her (IV, 1226). So much for the possibility of a happy home where the wife exercises the mastery!

In addition to being motivated by the Clerk's antagonism towards the Wife's views on marriage, this tale includes "hy sentence" and "moral vertu" which suit it and its teller, as he was described in the General Prologue. In fact, there may be a real possibility that the unusual typicality, noted earlier in the Clerk's portrait and continued in his conversation with the Host, is a part of Chaucer's intentional dramatic plan to keep the Clerk's unexpected, individualizing traits—his sense of humor and his ability at controversy—hidden until the end of his performance, and thus to heighten the effect of his burlesque refutation of the Wife's arguments.

15. THE MERCHANT

For some reason that will probably never be fully clear, Chaucer's sketch of the Merchant in the General Prologue (I, 270–84) is characterized by such cautious disinterestedness and evident lack of sympathy that it stands unique among the series of portraits. By remarking that this Pilgrim sits "hye on horse" and speaks his opinions "ful solempnely," Chaucer conveys the impression of a pompous individual who thinks very well of himself; and the Merchant's beard, forked in the prevailing fashion, as well as his expensive boots and beaver hat from Flanders, shows that he takes unusual care with his appearance. In his description of the Merchant's business dealings, Chaucer indicates clearly that this man practices illegal methods prevalent among merchants at the time.[1] He sells French gold coins in "eschaunge," despite the laws prohibiting traffic in foreign money; he engages in "chevyssaunce," or usury, and thereby breaks the laws of both Church and State; and he keeps his wits about him in order never to disclose his own indebtedness, thus misleading those with whom he deals. Also the Merchant is loud in his demand for governmental help in maintaining favorable business conditions: he wants the sea kept free from pirates between the Dutch and English trading ports, Middelburg and Orwell. But the Merchant's greatest sin, in a social sense at least, is that he is a terrible bore, "Sownynge alwey th' encrees of his wynnyng"; he subjects anyone who will listen to detailed accounts of his own business acumen. Evidently the Narrator prudently avoided such torture by staying out of the Merchant's way, for he says: "But, sooth to seyn, I noot how men hym calle"; despite the close sociability among this group of travelers, the Narrator did not even take the trouble to learn the Merchant's name.

Although the traits mentioned in the preceding paragraph

[1] Bowden, *Commentary*, 146–53; T. A. Knott, *PQ*, I (1922), 1–16.

Sownynge alwey th' encrees of his wynnyng

build up a far from attractive picture of the Merchant, both as a person and as a business man, the Narrator makes some small effort to cover up his own seemingly negative attitude. He says: "For sothe he was a worthy man with alle": in spite of being a pompous bore who breaks laws in an unprincipled fashion, he is a "worthy" man. The choice of such a noncommittal word as "worthy" is certainly meaningful, for it does little more than pay lip service to offsetting the Merchant's unattractiveness.

It has been suggested that the attempted restraint in expressing disapproval of the Merchant, and the decision not to give him a name, result from Chaucer's unwillingness to run the risk of having some powerful London merchant think himself the subject here for ridicule.[2] In fact, a particular merchant named Gilbert Maghfeld has been pointed out as a possible model for this sketch, and it seems that Chaucer actually had borrowed money from this man. But we can only speculate about such an identification and about Chaucer's personal reasons for seeming eager to cover up his real feelings. It takes no speculation, however, to conclude that the tone and manner in Chaucer's presentation of the Merchant differ markedly from those used with any other Pilgrim. Usually, whether the individual under discussion is the righteous Parson or the rascally Pardoner, the Narrator seems to say to us: "Here is a person whom I was glad to meet and whom I think you will like to know. We don't have to pass any judgment on this Pilgrim; we can simply enjoy the interesting aspects of his character." This attitude is present even in the section treating the evil Summoner; and there is good-natured joviality in the Narrator's ridiculing the Sergeant of the Law. But in the case of the Merchant, Chaucer shows his own lack of sympathy, makes no effort to interest us in him, and says, in effect: "I am sorry that this man was a member of our group." As we shall see, this uniqueness of tone in the Merchant's sketch is matched by the uniqueness in atmosphere of the tale he tells.

We hear nothing from the Merchant until the Clerk has finished his story of Griselda and the henpecked Host has made brief practical application of that tale to his own married life. Then, without being called on, the Merchant breaks in with a

---

[2] Manly, *New Light*, 181–200.

vigorously bitter statement of his own unhappy marital situation:

> Wepyng and waylyng, care and oother sorwe
> I knowe ynogh, on even and a-morwe,
> . . . and so doon other mo
> That wedded been. I trowe that it be so,
> For wel I woot it fareth so with me.
> I have a wyf, the worste that may be;
> For thogh the feend to hire ycoupled were,
> She wolde hym overmacche, I dar wel swere.
> What sholde I yow reherce in special
> Hir hye malice? She is a shrewe at al.   IV, 1213–22

At first glance, it is surprising for a man so closemouthed about his financial difficulties as is the Merchant to deliver uninvited this frank disclosure of his marital troubles. But the answer is not far to seek: he has been angered by the Wife of Bath's account of her treatment of her husbands, and the effect upon him of the Clerk's narrative is such that he is moved to forget, for once, his customary restraint. His first words are more or less an echo of the Clerk's last line (IV, 1212), and in giving further details of his miserable state, the Merchant explicitly indicates the Clerk's story as the immediate occasion for his outburst (IV, 1223–39). Indeed, he gives a far from pretty picture of wedded bliss. Married but two months, he can only curse his state and that of most married men. Certainly his careful shrewdness in matters financial was not duplicated two months ago by an equally expert judgment of women. And it is hard to refrain from the suggestion that the Narrator, whose dislike of the Merchant was apparent in the General Prologue, enjoys greatly the latter's revelation of his unhappy choice of a wife. In any event, the Host is quick in his attempt to turn this outburst to the benefit of the storytelling game. Instead of asking the Merchant the question which must have been uppermost in everyone's mind—"Why did you marry such a woman?"—Harry says, with unusual brevity: "Now, . . . Marchaunt, so God yow blesse,/Syn ye so muchel knowen of that art,/Ful hertely I pray yow telle us part" (IV, 1240–42).

The Host likes nothing better than to draw personal revelations from the Pilgrims, and in this case he is hopeful of hearing the confessions of a fellow sufferer in wedlock. But the Merchant seems to regain some of his usual cautious poise, and, in agreeing to Harry's request, states that he will talk no more of his own situation: "Gladly, . . . but of myn owene soore,/For soory herte, I telle may namoore" (IV, 1243–44). Such attempted restraint about personal matters is in keeping with what we know of the Merchant from the General Prologue, but, considering the bitterness of his preceding remarks about his wife, it is almost beyond belief that the Merchant could relate a story treating marital misfortunes without there being some connection between that story and the "cursednesse" of his own wife. The point is, I think, that by his disavowal he is simply trying to cover up his own stupidity in his selection of a wife. But, as we shall see, he thereby misleads only himself, for in his tale he inadvertently sheds a great deal of light as to the cause for his present "sorwe." I am not saying that the Merchant's Tale is pure autobiography, or that January in the tale is the Merchant. But I am saying that because of the wide discrepancy between what the Merchant thinks is the "moral" to be drawn from his tale, on the one hand, and the inevitable conclusion to which that tale leads, on the other, the Merchant unwittingly gives considerable grounds upon which to base speculations about the reason for his own marital situation.[3]

There is nothing at all appealing or cheerful about the Merchant's story. In its cold intellectualism, its lack of genial raillery or healthy animal enjoyment, and in its piling up of sharply satiric details, it conveys a bitter irony unique in Chaucer's writings. Neither of the chief characters arouses the least sympathy in the reader, and a dirtily obscene atmosphere is ever present. Why this is so, we cannot say. Perhaps Chaucer felt very strongly against the not infrequent marriages of old men to young girls, which probably occurred among his associates at court and in the city. Or maybe, as Professor Tatlock has suggested, he looked upon the Merchant's Tale as an exercise in a literary method other than that he regularly practiced.[4] Whatever the explanation, it is particularly striking that the uniquely unsympathetic

[3] G. G. Sedgewick, *UTQ*, XVII (1947-48), 337–45.
[4] J. S. P. Tatlock, *MP*, XXXIII (1935–36), 367–81.

portrait of the Merchant in the General Prologue is matched by this uniquely bitter irony in his tale. We thereby return to our original tantalizing conclusion: for some reason, Chaucer did not like his Merchant; an analysis of the dramatic implications of the tale as they reflect upon its teller will bear out this conclusion.

We saw that the Merchant, at the Host's request, sets out to tell a story that will illustrate the sorrow which most husbands experience as a result of their wives' "cursednesse," and which will thereby imply that marriage is inevitably a thoroughly miserable state for almost any husband. And, when this story is ended, the Host's sympathy is with January, and his interpretation centers on the perfidious wife; for him, May is the sole villain, and in his mind the tale shows only that wives are always trying to deceive their husbands, just as May by her treachery deceived January. Here is Harry's comment:

> Ey! Goddes mercy! . . .
> Now swich a wyf I pray God kepe me fro!
> Lo, whiche sleightes and subtilitees
> In wommen been! for ay as bisy as bees
> Been they, us sely men for to deceyve,
> And from the soothe evere wol they weyve;
> By this Marchauntes tale it preveth weel.
>
> IV, 2419–25

But we should observe, I think, that the Host's simple interpretation is considerably narrower than the Merchant's intention as to how his tale should be understood. For the Merchant, there must be two villains: May, automatically, but particularly January. The Merchant, like the Host, certainly considers May's treachery typical; yet he seems to attach greater blame to January on two accounts: for thinking that marriage could possibly be a happy state, and for accepting May's farfetched lie at the end of the story. In the mind of the Merchant, the probable twofold moral of his tale is, first, that few marriages are likely to work because most women are faithless; and, second, that any husband is both stupid to feel certain that a marriage will turn out well and foolish to allow his wife to lie successfully about her perfidy. Only by assuming that the Merchant takes such a view of his story can we explain why he as teller expresses such angry

[157

disgust with January's words and actions; this disgust appears in a steady stream of bitter, caustic irony, woven into every section of this tale.

The Merchant uses only the opening four lines of his story to establish the narrative situation in which January is the central figure:

> Whilom ther was dwellynge in Lumbardye
> A worthy knyght, that born was of Pavye,
> In which he lyved in greet prosperitee;
> And sixty yeer a wyflees man was hee.   IV, 1245–48

Then immediately we begin to get indications of this knight's folly and of the Merchant's vitriolic attitude towards that folly (IV, 1249–66). January has in the past satisfied his lust with a variety of women, as do fools who are "seculeer," that is, laymen, who are not protected by religion from sin, as are the clergy.[5] But now in old age he decides to enter into the holy estate of matrimony, where he will be able to satisfy his lust regularly and will also have the protection of religion; and he hypocritically prays to God that he may enter into the "holy bond" of wedlock, in which the "blissful life" is a paradise on earth. This passage introduces one of the most important themes running through the story up to the scene of the wedding: January, wanting at sixty to make peace with the Church, figures out that he can by marriage accomplish this peace and still satisfy his lust. Thus all his talk about the holiness of marriage in this passage and in the following 130 lines represents his use of religion as protection for his doing just what he wants to do, namely, indulge in "bodily delyt." Two lines of the passage show clearly the Merchant's attitude toward January's rationalizing: first, by immediately stating "Were it for hoolynesse or for dotage,/I kan nat seye," the Merchant sets up a choice for us; then by the final ironic line, "Thus seyde this olde knyght, that was so wys," he indicates to us which alternative to choose: "dotage"—senile lechery—is January's motivation, not "hoolynesse." Consequently, we are sure from the very beginning of what is to come, for we know that, given his present motivation, January's marriage will not be either "esy" or "clene." The first twenty-two lines of the Mer-

[5] J. C. McGalliard, *PQ*, XXV (1946), 193–220.

chant's Tale, by their revelation of the rationalizing whereby January is using religion as an attempted disguise for his lecherous intent, inform us that the final cuckolding in the pear tree is already inevitable.

Perhaps the most skillful touch in these introductory lines comes in the clause "but swich a greet corage/Hadde this knyght to been a wedded man"—where the word "corage" can refer to both sides of January's double-talk. As in line 22 of the General Prologue, this word can indicate religious piety: the Narrator is there ready to go on the pilgrimage with "ful devout corage"; but, as in the Host's jesting words to the Nun's Priest—"For if thou have corage as thou hast myght,/Thee were nede of hennes" (VII, 3452–53)—the word can connote sexual potency.

The Merchant, in the second segment of his tale, devotes 130 lines (IV, 1267–1396) to presenting the reasoning—or better, false reasoning—whereby January arrives at his decision to take a wife. These lines come forth as musings which pass through January's mind, and in them the evidence that he convinces himself by a process of rationalization builds upon that apparent in the introductory section, but takes shape here in much bolder outlines. The Merchant now discloses January's folly with broad and unmistakable strokes. The core of January's argument here with himself is the ironic idea already introduced: marriage is pleasing to God. But, we are told, this fact is especially true when an old man takes a young wife with whom he can produce an heir. Bachelors, in their irregular licentiousness, are like beasts, while a wedded man experiences orderly happiness. His wife will faithfully obey and attend him, in sickness or in health, and writers like Theophrastus are completely wrong when they say that a wife is mercenary and easily unfaithful.

Theophrastus' comment foreshadows, of course, exactly the point of view and the conduct which May will illustrate. But January is sure that a wife is God's gift and that "Mariage is a ful greet sacrement." God intended a wife as man's helpmate and his terrestrial paradise; any man without a wife cannot hope for bliss. As January's thoughts about marriage progress, his conclusions are expressed with increasing certainty and vigor: "A wyf! a, Seinte Marie, *benedicite!*/How myghte a man han any adversitee/That hath a wyf? Certes, I kan nat seye." A married man will be so happy and his wife so thoroughly admirable that he can in no way be deceived; therefore, says January, "Do alwey so as wommen wol thee rede," if you wish to act wisely. To illustrate this point, he cites the examples of Rebecca, Judith, Abigail, and Esther; and we note that, ironically, the husband involved in each of these stories suffers. But old January is oblivious to such possibilities, for he has had no trouble in convincing himself that he should marry, and his musings conclude with a lyric statement of the ideal relationship experienced by husband and wife. The Merchant has now shown us conclusively that January's decision is the result not of "hoolynesse" but of "dotage." Yet the degree to which the Merchant hates this old knight's folly is even more fully illustrated in the coming section of the tale, where January acts upon his decision to take a wife (IV, 1397–1767).

January's first move is to send for his friends, to whom he delivers a long speech informing them of his purpose and asking that they find him a suitable wife. In this speech his argument is based on a paradox which plainly indicates his rationalizing. On the one hand, he says that he is old and near the grave and must marry in order to avoid punishment after death for his many years of lechery; on the other hand, he claims that despite his advanced years he is still possessed of sufficient virility to enter into the duties of marriage fully. He insists, therefore, that he will marry a young girl not over twenty, whom he can mold like wax, and we get an unpleasant glimpse into his filthy mind when he dwells expectantly on the prospect of his sexual relations with such a wife, while maintaining that his actions will honor God. January states emphatically: "I dote nat, I woot the cause why/ Men sholde wedde"; but the Merchant has made it abundantly clear that this old and lecherous knight knows nothing of the more admirable reasons for a marriage.

January's friends are divided in their reaction to his decisions, and two sharply differing opinions are presented by his two brothers, Placebo and Justinus. Placebo, a sycophantic courtier, says that January must have good judgment because he is a wealthy knight and should therefore carry out his plan. Justinus, a wise and experienced man with no illusions, urges January to exercise great caution in selecting a wife in order to avoid making a regrettable mistake. Obviously, the names of the brothers are allegorical for the purpose of irony: "Placebo" means "I shall please" and aptly describes a "yes man"; Justinus, whose name means "the just man," is the only clear-thinking individual in the whole story, thereby representing a sharp contrast with the Merchant himself, as well as with January.

But, as we expect, January rejects Justinus' wise warnings. He exclaims:

> Wel, . . . and hastow sayd?
> Straw for thy Senek, and for thy proverbes!
> I counte nat a panyer ful of herbes
> Of scole-termes. Wyser men than thow,
> As thou hast herd, assenteden right now
> To my purpos. Placebo, what sey ye?   IV, 1566–71

Notice that January addresses Placebo with the formal, polite "ye," while for Justinus he has only the familiar "thou." Placebo is ready with a pleasing answer: "I seye it is a cursed man . . ./ That letteth matrimoigne, sikerly." And the Merchant thus shows that January's request for advice is merely a gesture, since he intends to take a young wife, whatever his advisers say. This situation is even more apparent in his next move: Although he has asked his friends to find him a wife, he makes the selection himself. Here again the Merchant gives us a whiff of the old knight's malodorous mind, for in reviewing the advantages and disadvantages of all the young girls he knows, January uses criteria that do not include the important aspects of disposition and character stressed earlier by Justinus; rather, his interest is primarily in matters physical, and, after making his selection, he lies in bed gloating over May's bodily charms. It is also a part of the Merchant's ironic treatment that January has selected a girl of no wealth and station, whose family will agree to an immediate marriage.

Now January calls his friends together to tell them that they need search on his behalf no longer. He is certain that he has made the wisest possible choice, and asks them not to argue against it, since his "purpos was plesant to God" (IV, 1621). Again, in what has become a regular habit for him, he uses religious talk as a cover for his lustful intent. This time his rationalizing is such that it would be laughable if it were not surrounded by lecherous implications. He tells his friends that he has only one worry: he has heard that an individual cannot have "parfite blisses two" (IV, 1638); a man cannot hope for heavenly bliss if he experiences such pleasure on earth "As alle wedded men doon with hire wyvys." The Merchant has Justinus give the fitting answer to this ridiculous problem. Using the religious contexts which January has hypocritically chosen, Justinus tells him not to worry too much over this question, for it may happen that January's wife will turn out to be his purgatory, and then his soul can skip up to heaven unimpeded. But for January such a possibility is beyond consideration, and the marriage preparations are quickly carried out.

The Merchant's description of the wedding contains numerous mordant touches which continue his ironic treatment of January's lustful stupidity. He says that he will not go into detail, for it would take too long to recount "every scrit and bond/By which that she was feffed in his lond" (IV, 1697–98), and we thereby see clearly May's mercenary intent, of which January pretends to be oblivious. As she stands before the priest, May is compared to Sarah and Rebecca for wisdom and fidelity—certainly an ironic comparison. The priest makes "al siker ynogh with hoolynesse" (IV, 1708), but we are forcibly reminded that there is nothing holy about January's desires. The wedding feast is a splendid affair, provided with the finest of everything that Italy can furnish; but Venus laughs at, not smiles with, every person present, "For Januarie was bicome hir knyght" (IV, 1724); and Martianus could not adequately describe this marriage, for "Whan tendre youthe hath wedded stoupyng age,/ Ther is swich *myrthe* that it may nat be writen" (IV, 1738–39). It is not hard to believe that the Merchant means for "myrthe" in this sentence to signify more than just "pleasure." Then May's glances at January are likened to those Esther cast upon Ahasuerus, whom she hated; and we are told that January sits at the table thinking constantly of the physical pleasures of the wedding night, which he will enjoy after the feast; and he does all he can to hasten the guests away. He has but one regret: that so tender a creature as May must endure the fury of his sexual powers; and he vows to restrain himself out of consideration for her. This whole passage is characterized by the savage irony with which the Merchant regularly portrays January, but the old knight's lecherous rationalizing so well deserves such treatment that we feel no sympathy for him. The entire situation is inherent, of course, in the allegorical names of the two chief characters: January (old age) and May (youth).

The complication from which January's deserved cuckolding will come is not long in developing. Throughout the next section of the tale (IV, 1768–2155), the Merchant does not in the least diminish the ferocity or the frequency of his thrusts at January; if anything, the view of this aged lecher becomes increasingly repellent. During the dancing and drinking which follow the wedding feast, everyone is gay except the squire Damian, who, in true courtly-love fashion, falls in love with his lord's wife at first sight and retires to his bed, suffering severely from the malady of love. But there will be little else of a courtly nature about this affair as it progresses towards its consummation in the pear tree.[6] Meanwhile, the impatient January, naturally unaware of Damian's situation, manages to get rid of his wedding guests and prepares for bed. He now plies himself with many aphrodisiacs, such as are listed in the book *De Coitu* by the Arab Constantinus Afer; thus the Merchant exposes the emptiness of January's earlier boastful thoughts about his inexhaustible virility. May is led to the marriage bed "as stille as stoon" (IV, 1818), for she looks forward to the night's activities with far less enthusiasm than does her husband. The hypocrisy of this union is again underlined by the Merchant's mention at this point of the priest's blessing the marriage bed. But at last the newly wed couple are alone.

Nowhere in the tale is the atmosphere more nauseatingly unpleasant than in the account of January's love-making on his wedding night. He is now experiencing the situation for which he has longed and for which he has paid handsomely. He mouths a sophistical apology to May for the leisure with which he plans to enjoy this night, and he rejoices in his certainty that now "in trewe wedlock" his lechery is not sinful. But the Merchant pre-

[6] Margaret Schlauch, *ELH*, IV (1937) 201–12.

sents this ardent lover to us through the eyes of his young wife, and the picture is not appealing. May finds January's thick whiskers as sharp as the "skyn of houndfyssh," and she considers his antics when morning comes thoroughly ridiculous:

> Thus laboureth he til that the day gan dawe;
> And thanne he taketh a sop in fyn clarree,
> And upright in his bed thanne sitteth he,
> And after that he sang ful loude and cleere,
> And kiste his wyf, and made wantown cheere.
> He was al coltissh, ful of ragerye,
> And ful of jargon as a flekked pye.
> The slakke skyn aboute his nekke shaketh,
> Whil that he sang, so chaunteth he and craketh.
> But God woot what that May thoughte in hir herte,
> Whan she hym saugh up sittynge in his sherte,
> In his nyght-cappe, and with his nekke lene;
> She preyseth nat his pleyyng worth a bene.

IV, 1842–54

The Merchant could hardly have devised a more devastating description of this ridiculous newlywed.

After resting from his amorous labors, January rises and goes happily about his palace, but custom demands that May remain in her room until the fourth day after the wedding. Meanwhile Damian, sick unto death with love for her, decides to write out his feelings in a letter, which he places over his heart. Three days later, when January and May sit eating in the main hall, January notices his squire's absence, and is told that Damian is ill. With pompous concern, seemingly motivated by a desire to appear magnanimous before his wife, he instructs May to pay Damian a comforting visit after the meal. Here the Merchant is showing us the old husband sending his young wife into the eager arms of his squire, and the expected result comes about. While January waits in bed for her return, May visits Damian; pleading for mercy, he slips her his letter, which she hides in her bosom until she can read and dispose of it in the privy. The locale in which this love missive is read by May sets the tone for her subsequent relationship with Damian. May returns to bed, and, when coughing brought on by old age and his years of licentious living arouses January from sleep, she submits to her husband's amorousness. But while January makes love to her, she is thinking hard about Damian, and the Merchant for a second time suggests her negative reaction to the old knight:

And she obeyeth, be hire lief or looth.
But lest that precious folk be with me wrooth,
How that he wroghte, I dar nat to yow telle;
Or wheither hire thoughte it paradys or helle.
But heere I lete hem werken in hir wyse
Til evensong rong, and that they moste aryse.

IV, 1961–66

May's unpleasant afternoon with January is preparation for her decision concerning Damian. Although the Merchant says with heavy irony that the astrological situation at this time led May to accept Damian, we know very well that disgust with January as a lover is primarily responsible for the following conclusion on her part:

Certeyn . . . whom that this thyng displese,
I rekke noght, for heere I hym assure
To love hym best of any creature,
Though he namoore hadde than his sherte.

IV, 1982–85

Then in the very next line Chaucer gives his favorite remark to the Merchant for use in this ironic context: "Lo, pitee renneth soone in gentil herte!" May has been said to illustrate by her acceptance of Damian the courtly ideal of "pitee," but, without any trace of the usual courtly hesitation, she visits the sick Damian a second time and slips a note under his pillow, informing him that she will give herself to him as soon as possible. Damian at once recovers and pleases everyone with his charming behavior; but he is not here experiencing the ennobling effects of his lady's grace; he is simply looking forward gaily to the consummation of his desire for May. The Merchant is now beginning to make clear the results of January's folly.

Seeking to increase his sexual pleasures with May, January has had made a walled garden, the only key to which he keeps himself. That the beauty of this garden is to be put to unwholesome use is suggested when the Merchant remarks that Priapus, the phallic god, could not describe its beauty, and that Pluto and Proserpine, from the world of fairy, often frolicked there. We shall soon find these last two in January's garden, taking a hand in his marital affairs; there is, of course, an apt parallel in their presence there, for they are from the underworld, and Proserpine handles her husband with as great ease as that with which May will later control January.

For a time the garden is all that January had hoped it would be, "And thynges whiche that were nat doon abedde,/He in the gardyn parfourned hem and spedde" (IV, 2051–52); but, as every medieval person realized, "worldly joye may nat alwey dure." Fickle Fortune, like a scorpion, flatters him whom she will deceive; in short, she dampens January's lecherous joy by depriving him of his eyesight. And now he greatly fears that he will be cuckolded. For once, January has arrived at a sound conclusion, but the Merchant hastens to show that even this conclusion stems from the old knight's usual hypocrisy. January knows in his heart, of course, that his attractions for May, other than his wealth, are few; and he consequently expects, now that he cannot watch her closely, that she will be unfaithful to him. The thought of her loving or marrying another, even after his own death, fills him with burning jealousy, and, unwilling to admit his shortcomings in May's eyes, he evolves a protective system: he keeps his hand upon her at all times so that she cannot betray him.

This precaution drives both May and Damian to the depths of despair; she is consumed by a yearning for the squire, and he is "the sorwefulleste man" that ever was. But by writing to each other, they arrange to satisfy their desires. May makes an impression of the garden key in wax, and Damian prepares a copy from it. Unavoidably, as the Merchant intends, our thoughts here go back to January's statement to his friends that a young girl can be molded like wax by her husband; but now May makes wax literally the key to January's cuckolding.

With all her arrangements in readiness, May one day purposefully excites January's lust for her; he leads her to the garden, and she sends Damian in ahead, by means of the second key, to wait for her. The Merchant here points up the grossness of the May-Damian relationship by ironically comparing it to the sincere and tragic love affair of Pyramus and Thisbe, and by exhibiting Damian to us as he crouches in ignoble fashion under a bush, awaiting May's directions. But January is still the chief recipient of the Merchant's irony, and once again we find the old dotard expressing his lust in the terms of religion, when he paraphrases the Song of Solomon to invite May to the garden:

> Rys up, my wyf, my love, my lady free!
> The turtles voys is herd, my dowve sweete;
> The wynter is goon with alle his reynes weete.
> Com forth now, with thyne eyen columbyn!
> How fairer been thy brestes than is wyn!
> The gardyn is enclosed al aboute;
> Com forth, my white spouse! out of doute
> Thou hast me wounded in myn herte, O wyf!
> No spot of thee ne knew I al my lyf.
> Com forth, and lat us taken oure disport;
> I chees thee for my wyf and my confort.   IV, 2138–48

Of this speech the Merchant can only say: "Swiche olde lewed wordes used he."

As we have seen at considerable length, the Merchant has built up his narrative situation with detail after detail of savage irony. Now, in the last section of his tale (IV, 2156–2418), comes the inevitable conclusion, in which the lustful old knight gets his just deserts. But before presenting the conclusion to his story, the Merchant takes time to give a further example of January's complete hypocrisy. Having led May into the garden, January in his jealousy sanctimoniously says:

> For Goddes sake, thenk how I thee chees,
> Noght for no coveitise, doutelees,
> But oonly for the love I had to thee.
> And though that I be oold, and may nat see,
> Beth to me trewe, and I wol telle yow why.
>
> IV, 2165–69

We recall very well how January chose May for his wife, and there has been reason to suspect strongly throughout the story that he always realized clearly that her interest was primarily in his wealth; we are therefore not surprised at this point to find him advancing the fact that he will assign to her all his property as the chief reason why May should not make him a cuckold. But May is more than a match for him, and, by means of her first speech in the story, puts on a fine example of play acting. She weeps, claims to be "a gentil womman and no wenche," and forcefully declares her faithfulness to her husband. Then, at the finish of this fine speech, she signals Damian to climb the pear tree, where she will later join him and make January a cuckold. We should note in passing that the Merchant's not having May speak until so late in the story is a part of his effort to keep attention and interest focused upon the dotard January.

The climax of the Merchant's Tale is also accompanied by sharp thrusts at January. May claims that she has a great hunger for fruit, and January puffs with pride as he remembers that hunger for a specific thing indicates pregnancy; now, he thinks, his earlier boasts to his friends will be fulfilled and he will have an heir. May also plays upon his jealousy when she gets him to encircle the pear tree with his arms, as she goes to meet Damian in the tree by climbing up on her husband's back. As when he sent her to visit the sick Damian, January is once more helping his wife to reach the arms of her lover. And, most pointedly, the intervention of Pluto and Proserpine reduces January to a completely ridiculous position. When Pluto restores his eyesight, the old knight realizes fully what May is doing, but his lust—and perhaps his unwillingness to have Justinus say "I told you so"—cause him to accept the preposterous answer which Proserpine furnishes May, and to treat his wife as if nothing has happened.

Truly, the Merchant throughout his tale treats January with such frequent and concentrated bitterness that one wonders how the Host could have selected May as the sole bearer of guilt. In some ways the most effective device the Merchant employs in satirizing January is his extended use of physical blindness as a symbol for mental blindness. This idea is introduced when January selects May as the girl he wishes to marry. Using a proverb, the Merchant says at this point,

> But nathelees, bitwixe ernest and game,
> He atte laste apoynted hym on oon,
> And leet alle othere from his herte goon,
> And chees hire of his owene auctoritee;
> For love is blynd alday, and may not see.   IV, 1594–98

The reader, having seen at length the hypocritical bases for January's choice, is already fully able to guess that the Merchant's comment as to the blindness of January's love is prophetic. Then, as the plot unfolds, January's glaring lack of insight and the constant blearing of his judgment by rationalizing prepare us for the loss of his physical sight. The Merchant announces the blindness in the following words: "Allas! this noble Januarie free,/Amydde his lust and his prosperitee,/Is woxen blynd, and that al sodeynly" (IV, 2069–71). The words "noble," "free," and "lust" carry marked ironic implications; January is neither noble nor generous, and his "lust" is more a matter of lecherous pleasure than real happiness. Moreover, he has not gone blind "al sodeynly"; he has exhibited a startling lack of mental sight from the very beginning. Certainly January could never see the point of the Canon's Yeoman's wise remark: "If that youre eyen kan nat seen aright,/Looke that youre mynde lakke noght his sight" (VIII, 1418–19).

Some lines later the Merchant very clearly makes the point that January's vision was much impaired even before he lost the use of his eyes: "O Januarie, what myghte it thee availle,/Thogh thou myghte se as fer as shippes saille?/For as good is blynd deceyved be/As to be deceyved whan a man may se" (IV, 2107–10). The suggestion is that physical blindness for January is a fortunate thing, since he would have been just as easily cuckolded had he retained his eyesight. For, says the Merchant, Argus was deceived despite his hundred eyes, and so are many others who, like January, think deception cannot happen to them. Then the Merchant makes a subtle foreshadowing remark: "Passe over is an ese, I sey namoore" (IV, 2115). When mental insight is lacking, deception will come, whether or not an individual has physical sight; in such a situation the best "ese" (comfort) is simply to "passe over" (overlook) the deception. And that is exactly what

January will do at the end of the story when he accepts May's lame explanations.

Blindness figures largely in the section of the story involving Pluto and Proserpine. Pluto, in his jaundiced antifeminism, is as misguided as the Host later shows himself to be in his sympathy for January. Pluto says:

> Ne se ye nat this honurable knyght,
> By cause, allas! that he is blynd and old,
> His owene man shal make hym cokewold.
> Lo, where he sit, the lechour, in the tree!
> Now wol I graunten, of my magestee,
> Unto this olde, blynde, worthy knyght
> That he shal have ayeyn his eyen syght,
> Whan that his wyf wold doon hym vileynye.
> Thanne shal he knowen al hire harlotrye,
> Bothe in repreve of hire and othere mo.   IV, 2254–63

Pluto seems not to realize here that "lechour" better fits January than Damian, or that the restoration of his eyesight will not improve his judgment. Proserpine knows, however, that though a man sees a thing with both eyes, he can still remain "as lewed as gees" (IV, 2275). She therefore is determined to illustrate her point by giving May a successful lying answer. Pluto has long ago learned the folly of trying to outargue his wife, but to maintain his prestige he must carry out his promise to restore to January the use of his eyes. As soon as this happens, January jealously looks up into the tree to see what May is doing. And he undoubtedly sees.

In the remainder of the story—the debate between January and May—the Merchant very carefully shows us that regaining physical sight has done nothing to improve January's insight; for though Pluto gave him back the use of his eyes, he rejects what he sees and willfully remains blind. This process is presented in three stages, each more damaging than the preceding to our estimate of January. First, when May, in reply to his angry question as to what she is doing, says that she is struggling with a man in a tree because she was told that this act would cure January's blindness, the old knight bluntly and correctly states: "He swyved thee, I saugh it with myne yen" (IV, 2378). But, second,

when May says that he is in error because his sight is not yet perfectly restored, January weakens his accusation: "And by my
trouthe, me thoughte he dide thee so" (IV, 2386). Then, third,
when she repeats that he is mistaken and upbraids him for not
appreciating her kindness towards him, he gives up altogether
and apologetically says:

> Now, dame, . . . lat al passe out of mynde.
> Com doun, my lief, and if I have myssayd,
> God helpe me so, as I am yvele apayd.
> But, by my fader soule, I wende han seyn
> How that this Damyan hadde by thee leyn,
> And that thy smok hadde leyn upon thy brest.
>
> IV, 2390–95

With full knowledge that January is still blinding himself as
much as ever, May shamelessly and exultingly taunts him. "Ye,
sire," she says, "ye may wene as yow lest." And knowing that she
has January completely under her thumb, she concludes:

> Beth war, I prey yow; for, by hevene kyng,
> Ful many a man weneth to seen a thyng,
> And it is al another than it semeth.
> He that mysconceyveth, he mysdemeth.   IV, 2407–10

January first *saw* her unfaithful act, then *it seemed* to him that
he had seen it, and finally he *thought* that he saw it. By these
steps, the old man relinquishes the sight that Pluto has restored
to him. Then he happily embraces and kisses his wife—"on hire
wombe he stroketh hire ful softe"—and he leads her home. With
ruthless bitterness the Merchant has shown that January cannot
attain clear vision, no matter what he sees, for his lustful rationalization prevents his accepting reality.

The Merchant's purpose in the tale, then, is far wider than the
Host realizes, for the Merchant's emphasis is steadily upon January's libidinous rationalizing and its inevitable results. But, as
numerous critics have remarked, the dramatic texture of this
performance is extremely tight, and there is a still wider third
application of the story, which Chaucer as author seems to have
intended and which we as readers can perceive. For us there
should be three "villains" of the piece: May, incidentally; Jan-

uary; but especially the Merchant himself. Although the Merchant, unlike the Host, realizes that January is responsible for his own difficulties and heaps bitter satire on him for his folly, he unintentionally reveals in the telling of his story that he has not been willing or able to transfer his understanding of January's flaw to his own unhappy marital situation, which he described so vigorously in his prologue. The real moral of the Merchant's Tale is not that most wives deceive their husbands, or that most men are foolish even to consider marriage; it is, as the Merchant realizes, that this particular marriage between January and May is doomed from the start because of January's sinful false reasoning. The point to keep in mind is that Chaucer has the Merchant tell a tale with a moral applicable to his own situation, and then shows us that the Merchant lacks the wisdom and humility to make that application.

As a result of the performances by the Wife of Bath and the Clerk, marriage is the topic uppermost in the Merchant's mind as he addresses the Host in his prologue. He includes many general remarks on this topic as he angrily illustrates his point of view by a tale which bears similarity to his own two months of married life. But the Merchant apparently feels that there is one important difference between the two situations: his eyes have been opened to his wife, while January remains blind to May. Thus, in his tale, with a feeling of immeasurable superiority, he vents his anger on January with pitiless irony for swallowing May's lies. But the Merchant's foolish certainty in his prologue that most wives are bad and that any single man knows less of sorrow than a married man, shows that his own eyes have not really been fully opened, for he is not willing to admit that his particular marriage is unsuccessful for the same reason as January's; namely, his own lustful false reasoning led him to an unwise choice of a wife. In this way, the Merchant's Prologue and Tale, without his realizing it, reveal his pompous dishonesty as clearly as does his sketch in the General Prologue. He feels that he is to be praised for drawing from his marital experience the only feasible conclusion about marriage; but we suspect that from that experience he has not gained any insight into his own fallacious motivation.

That the Merchant approached his marriage two months ago with the same hypocritical line of reasoning that January uses is evident, I think, in the section of the tale in which January's musings are presented (IV, 1267–1396). There the personal pronoun "I" designates both January now and the Merchant two months ago; but the Merchant lets his present feeling of superiority over January seep through these musings by occasional negative remarks which would be otherwise inconsistent. Thus, as January reflects that a wife will outlast other transitory blessings, such as riches, the Merchant tartly observes that she may last "Wel lenger than thee list, paraventure" (IV, 1318). Again, when January reminds himself that a man and his wife are so closely united that no harm can come to either of them, the Merchant's dry comment is "And namely upon the wyves syde" (IV, 1392).

The Merchant's identifying the preliminaries to his own marriage with those which January goes through is nowhere clearer than in the otherwise puzzling reference by Justinus to the Wife of Bath:

> But lat us waden out of this mateere.
> The Wyf of Bathe, if ye han understonde,
> Of mariage, which ye have on honde,
> Declared hath ful wel in litel space.
> Fareth now wel, God have yow in his grace.
>
> IV, 1684–88

It is the Merchant, of course, who has heard the Wife on the subject of marriage, and not Justinus, just a character in this story. But so exactly is Justinus at this moment the spokesman for the Merchant's point of view that the Merchant puts into his mouth the most telling satire he can recall against January's folly: the Wife of Bath's treatment of her husbands.

Yet there is a difference between Justinus' general point of view about marriage and the Merchant's; that the Merchant does not realize this difference contributes largely to his unwitting self-revelation in his tale. The Merchant does give Justinus his "own power of attorney," as one critic put it, to attack January's stupidity. But Justinus, though disillusioned in his own marriage, is a wise man who has attained inner peace and who is re-

As fressh as is the month of May

signed to his lot. His unhappy marriage does not lead him to condemn the whole system; he simply cautions January that the trick of a successful marriage lies in making a wise selection of a wife. The proud Merchant is as far from this sensible conclusion as his bitter anger is from Justinus' inner peace and resignation. Consequently, despite the distasteful atmosphere of this tale, the Merchant's amazingly tight-woven performance stands as an illustration of Chaucer's use of his dramatic principle with highly skillful complexity.

16. THE SQUIRE

We have had plentiful evidence that the unhappy marital situation of the Host is kept as a background against which are projected the views of marriage presented by the various Pilgrims. Now, following the Merchant's Tale, Harry again makes a comparison between the central female character and his wife (IV, 2419–40). This time the comparison begins favorably for Goodelief: unlike May, she is "trewe as any steel," though she is poor. However, the thought of his wife immediately leads the Host to recall her "heep of vices," such as her being a "labbyng shrewe," and he admits openly that he wishes he were not tied to her. Apparently, in Harry's opinion, a wife can have faults more annoying to her husband than infidelity; but, since making public his many complaints against Goodelief, he has heard Alice of Bath's views concerning a woman's right to deal dishonestly with a man, and he feels that he would now be foolish indeed to list his domestic grievances, for "it sholde reported be/And toold to hire [Goodelief] of somme of this meynee." The implication is here directed against the Wife of Bath. Therefore, he ends his personal reflections and calls upon the Squire for a tale of love (V. 1–8).

Numerous commentators have pointed out that in the succession of stories which make up the *Canterbury Tales* Chaucer followed a principle of contrast in the type and content of contiguous tales. What seems a more fundamental observation, however, is that this contrast derives from a principle of contrast in the personalities of the successive storytellers. Thus, the rough Shipman follows the proper Lawyer; the devout Second Nun appears after the impious Pardoner; the prosperous bourgeois Merchant, in what is an exact and perhaps purposeful reversal of the order of their sketches in the General Prologue, succeeds the impoverished and scholarly Clerk; and the witty Nun's Priest follows the sententious Monk. But nowhere in the book is the contrast between storytellers more immediately apparent than when the fresh young lover, the Squire, is called forward to banish the atmosphere which the bitter Merchant created by means of his unpleasant portrayal of old January. Harry Bailly is guilty of obtuse moments at times, but in this instance he certainly has his wits about him.

The most striking fact about the Squire as he appears in the General Prologue (I, 79–100) is his youthful happiness and zest for living: "Syngynge he was, or floytynge, al the day;/He was as fressh as is the month of May." He is a "lusty bacheler," who gives careful attention to his hair and to his clothing, and "So hoote he lovede that by nyghtertale/He sleep namoore than dooth a nyghtyngale." Not only is this squire the ideal of his type—well-developed physically, impressive "as of so litel space" in the 1383 campaign, properly educated in courtly love, horsemanship, musical composition, dancing, drawing, writing, jousting, carving, courtesy, and humility—but he also has an active interest in the world and the people who inhabit it. And although Miss Hadow thought the Squire notable for a kind of joyous naïveté, this young man has considerable learning and experience for his twenty years.[1]

---

[1] Grace Hadow, *Chaucer and His Times*, 81. Both Miss Hadow and Nevill Coghill (*The Poet Chaucer*, 167) state that the Franklin purposely interrupts and cuts off the Squire's story, because he realizes that the Squire is likely to run on at considerable length. I see no evidence for this view; certainly the Franklin's words to him (V, 673–94) suggest that the "worthy vavasour" would have listened happily until the Squire finished. See also E. P. Kuhl and H. J. Webb, *ELH*, VI (1939), 282–84.

The story that the Squire delivers, for which no source has been found,[2] presents a difficult problem as to why Chaucer left it "half-told,"[3] but there is considerable evidence for the dramatic suitability of the tale and its teller.[4] First of all, the Squire's Tale is a love story, and, as Harry Bailly said, certainly the Squire knows "theron as muche as any man" (V, 3); in fact, the first thing that we learned in the General Prologue about the Squire was that he is "a lovyere" (I, 80). Furthermore, it is perfectly in keeping with his station and interests for him to recite romance materials dealing with kings and court life. There are, however, two particular aspects of the Squire's Tale which make even clearer Chaucer's probable efforts to suit it and its teller: first, numerous expository comments in the course of the tale match surprisingly well with the qualities attributed to the Squire in the General Prologue; and, second, a number of passages in the tale echo materials to be found in the story told by the Squire's father, the Knight, with whom the Squire has been closely associated during a particularly impressionable period of his life.

When he introduces Canacee, shortly after the opening of his story, the Squire says:

> But for to telle yow al hir beautee,
> It lyth nat in my tonge, n'yn my konnyng;
> I dar nat undertake so heigh a thyng.
> Myn Englissh eek is insufficient.
> It moste been a rethor excellent,
> That koude his colours longynge for that art,
> If he sholde hire discryven every part.
> I am noon swich, I moot speke as I kan.   V, 34–41

Somewhat later, as he comments upon, and prepares to report,

---

[2] See the chapter by H. S. V. Jones in *Sources and Analogues,* 357–76.

[3] Gardiner Stillwell has set forth in detail the argument that Chaucer left the Squire's Tale incomplete because romance materials did not fit his realistic interests and abilities; see *RES,* XXIV (1948), 177–88. Stillwell regards the realistic passages in the Squire's Tale (e.g., V, 347–56) as comments by Chaucer, whereas I take them to be placed by Chaucer in the mouth of the Squire. As such, they do no great violence to dramatic suitability, for there is nothing in the sketch of the Squire which demands that he should show disregard for realistic people and human reactions. In fact, he has had opportunity to learn a great deal from his widely traveled, philosophical father, who, as Stillwell observes, "introduced humour and realism" into his tale.

[4] Marie Neville, *JEGP,* L (1951), 167–79.

the speech of the knight who rides into Cambuscan's court with gifts, the Squire says:

> And, for his tale sholde seme the bettre,
> Accordant to his wordes was his cheere,
> As techeth art of speche hem that it leere.
> Al be it that I kan nat sowne his stile,
> Ne kan nat clymben over so heigh a style,
> Yet seye I this, as to commune entente,
> Thus muche amounteth al that evere he mente,
> If it so be that I have it in mynde.   V, 102–109

In these remarks we see reflected several facets of the Squire's personality as it appeared in the General Prologue. His proper humility (I, 109) is apparent in his disclaimer of ability to describe Canacee's beauty or to equal the visiting knight's flights of oratory. Of course, he manages thereby to convey Canacee's excellent appearance far more forcibly than if he had tried to describe it. We also see in these passages his familiarity with formal rhetoric, which held a place in the training he had received (I, 96), and his general gaiety is probably to be observed in the pun on the word "stile."

The Squire's earlier reference to the "swerd of wynter, keene and coold" (V, 57) may well reflect his personal experience in the field, even though his "somtyme in chyvachie" seems to have covered warmer months.[5] But almost certainly his training in horsemanship (I, 94) lies behind his professional comment on the horse presented to Cambuscan by the visiting knight:

> For it so heigh was, and so brood and long,
> So wel proporcioned for to been strong,
> Right as it were a steede of Lumbardye;
> Therwith so horsly, and so quyk of ye,
> As it a gentil Poilleys courser were.   V, 191–95

The Squire's interest in courtesy makes thoroughly appropriate his comments on the visiting knight's manners, which could not have been improved by Gawain "Though he were comen ayeyn out of Fairye" (V, 96). And the respect which the Squire

---

[5] J. S. P. Tatlock, *The Development and Chronology of Chaucer's Works*, 148.

shows his superiors, the "knyghtes olde" (V, 69), in his reference to the stories they have told him of the strange customs existing in foreign lands, is to be expected from his respectful attitude toward his father (I, 101–102). Again, in the passage on sleep and hang-overs (V, 347–67), matters in which a gay young man like the Squire might be expected to have had some experience, we see the same humorous turn which was probably apparent in the pun on "stile." Then, in the description of the "lusty seson soote" on which Canacee takes her morning walk (V, 388–400), can be seen the Squire's zest for nature. Finally, when he speaks of the revelry following the banquet in Cambuscan's court (V, 278–90), we feel from knowledge gained in the General Prologue that he is fully familiar with the "forme of daunces" and the "subtil lookyng and dissymulynges/For drede of jalouse mennes aperceyvynges," even though he says that "no man but Launcelot" could describe them—for the Squire is not a "dul man." In short, all these expository remarks are quite in keeping with such a person as was described in the Squire's sketch in the General Prologue.

The other pertinent point here is that a significant number of passages in his story either echo or show connection with materials in the tale told by his father. The Knight is quite insistent on narrative economy and wishes to "Lat every felawe telle his tale aboute" (I, 890); the Squire seems to share this feeling and says: "I wol nat taryen yow, for it is pryme,/And for it is no fruyt, but los of tyme" (V, 73–74). Later on, he makes a similar point against "prolixitee" (V, 401–408). Note, too, that his laudatory description of Cambuscan (V, 9–27) gives to that worthy king many of the virtues which characterized Theseus in the Knight's Tale. Closer parallels, however, can be seen in the Squire's repetition of two of the Knight's central comments: "pitee renneth soone in gentil herte" (I, 1761; V, 479), and make "vertu of necessitee" (I, 3042; V, 593). There is also a familiar ring about the Squire's "Though al the world the contrarie hadde yswore" (V, 325), when we recall the Knight's "although we hadde it sworn" (I, 1089). And it is perhaps noteworthy that the Squire's passage concerning the desire that birds feel to escape from cages

(V, 607–20) occurs in *Boece* almost immediately after the section from which the Knight takes Arcite's speech on the folly of desiring things we do not have.[6]

It is true that a number of the matters discussed in the last three paragraphs are often characteristic of Chaucer in his other writings. For example, many of his storytellers stress narrative economy, and "pitee renneth soone in gentil herte" occurs in the Merchant's Tale (IV, 1986) and in the Prologue to the *Legend of Good Women* (F, 503), as well as in the stories of the Knight and the Squire. But the fact remains that we do find in the Squire's performance specific details which reflect his training and personality as presented in the General Prologue, and which echo the sentiments of the Knight, under whom the Squire is serving his apprenticeship. Such details bear witness to the dramatic suitability of the tale and its teller, and we can at least hazard a guess that if other business had not prevented Chaucer's completing the story—to my mind the best explanation for its unfinished state—there would have been numerous other such details. For one can well believe that the young Squire must have brought to Chaucer many pleasant memories of his own youth.[7]

17. THE FRANKLIN

When we examine carefully the critical comment on the Franklin's Tale, we find a difficult state of affairs with regard to the suitability of this story and its teller. Earlier scholars, though they analyzed the Franklin and his performance from varying points of view, agreed that the tale was admirably suited to him;[1]

---

[6] *Boece*, Bk. III, pr. 2, m. 2, as presented in Robinson, *Works*, 400.
[7] Bowden, *Commentary*, 74–75.
[1] E.g., R. K. Root, *The Poetry of Chaucer* (rev. ed.), 271–77; G. L. Kittredge, *Chaucer and His Poetry*, 205–10, and *MP*, IX (1911–12), 435–67; G. H. Gerould, *PMLA*, LXI (1926), 262–79.

Epicurus owene sone

more recent writers, however, find it impossible to imagine the "son of Epicurus" as the teller of the story of Dorigen, Arveragus, and the black rocks of Brittany.[2]

Such sharp difference of opinion makes necessary a re-examination of the question in some detail. In the course of this re-examination I shall suggest (1) that Chaucer presents the Franklin as a man whose knowledge of, and regard for, the practical, everyday world are joined with a strong desire for social advancement; (2) that each of the Franklin's appearances in the *Canterbury Tales* bears out this appraisal of him; and (3) that this appraisal not only accounts for certain incongruities in the Franklin's Tale, but also makes apparent the suitability of this tale and its teller.

Before considering the sections of the *Canterbury Tales* pertinent to these three conclusions, we should review briefly the information set forth by Professor Manly in connection with Chaucer's Franklin.[3] A franklin named John Bussy was a close neighbor and associate in Lincolnshire of Thomas Pynchbek, whom Manly suggested as the possible model for Chaucer's Sergeant of the Law. Pynchbek was on the opposite side politically from Chaucer, offended Chaucer's friend William Beauchamp, and signed a writ for Chaucer's arrest. It may be, Manly argued, that the Franklin, as companion of the Lawyer, is modeled after Bussy. Chaucerian scholarship, after almost twenty-five years, is apparently willing—if we judge from Miss Bowden's *Commentary on the General Prologue*—to grant Manly all but certainty in the identification of Pynchbek, and a high degree of likelihood in the case of Bussy.[4] Thus, Chaucer's satiric treatment of the Lawyer presumably should be read in the light of Pynchbek's activities. Bussy seems to have been regarded as a man who sought to imitate the ways of the nobility, and the Franklin's conversation with the Squire indicates his ambitions for his family to join the ranks of the nobility (V, 673–94). Of course, neither the identification of Bussy as model nor the interpreta-

[2] E.g., J. R. Hulbert, *SP*, XLV (1948), 574; Nevill Coghill, *The Poet Chaucer*, 165–66.

[3] Manly, *New Light*, 157–68. A different view is held by K. L. Wood-Legh, *RES*, IV (1928), 145–51.

[4] Bowden, *Commentary*, 172, 177.

tion stressing the Franklin's social aspirations can be proved absolutely. But the two points match surprisingly well and in my opinion afford sufficient reason for attempting to determine the extent to which Chaucer's Franklin exhibits his social aspirations alongside his practical concern for the everyday world.

To return to the re-examination of the Franklin, we find in Chaucer's text that four sections of the *Canterbury Tales* are concerned with him: the thirty-line sketch in the General Prologue; the conversation of the Franklin, the Squire, and the Host; the Franklin's Prologue; and the tale of Dorigen and Arveragus. These four sections present us with the following materials:

1. The Franklin accompanies the Sergeant of Law, loves food and drink, entertains lavishly, and has often held high public office (I, 331–60).

2. The Franklin is impressed with the Squire's gentilesse, in contrast with his own son's irresponsibility. But the Host says: "A straw for your gentilesse!" and the Franklin readily placates and flatters him (V, 673–708).

3. The Franklin says he will tell a Breton lay and introduces it with a "modesty prologue" (V, 709–28).

4. The Franklin's so-called "Breton lay," which includes proper names and rocks from Geoffrey of Monmouth, is concerned with generosity in marriage and sets forth a *demande d'amour* based on a section of Boccaccio's *Filocolo* (V, 729–1624).

There is one striking point about the sketch of the Franklin in the General Prologue: he is very wealthy and has epicurean tastes which he satisfies by luxurious living for pure pleasure; yet he also has often held important public offices, offices which beyond doubt were regularly held in Chaucer's day by men of outstanding ability and industry.[5] There may be many epicureans with ability, but an epicurean noted for industry is rare, especially when he has the money with which to indulge his tastes. Thus, it is possible that good hard work is more important to Chaucer's Franklin than his love of food, drink, and pleasure; if so, his lavish hospitality becomes in some respects play acting. In addition to the public offices he has earned, we find that the

---

[5] See the article by Gerould cited in n. 1 of this section.

Franklin is a "worthy vavasour." Although "worthy" is one of the most difficult of Chaucer's words to pin down, when we see it coming right after a list of deserved public offices a man has held, we are justified in taking it as a compliment to that man. There is also emphasis here on accomplishments, and industry is one of the Franklin's recommendations to the Squire. He says: "Fie on possessions, unless a man is also capable" (V, 686–87)—hardly a remark one would expect from the usual epicurean. Perhaps the Franklin acts the part of St. Julian in his country in an effort to imitate conduct he thinks suitable for great nobles, whose ranks he is eager to join. But before accepting or rejecting this idea, we must see how the Franklin's performance in the body of the *Canterbury Tales* fits with it.

In complimenting the Squire on his excellent performance, the Franklin expresses regret that his own son wastes his time and money and prefers to talk with a page rather than with gentle folk from whom he could learn gentilesse correctly. As noted earlier, these comments seem to indicate the Franklin's social aspirations. Professor Kittredge says:

He is . . . a rich freeholder, often sheriff in his country. Socially, he is not quite within the pale of the gentry, but he is the kind of man that may hope to found a family, the kind of man from whose ranks the English nobility has been constantly recruited. And that such is his ambition comes out naively and with a certain pathos in what he goes on to say: "I wish my son were like you. . . ."

This interpretation obviously complements the view of the Franklin as a man who has understanding of, and ability in, the routine world, and who strives to carry out his idea of noble conduct. There is further support for this argument in the Host's conversation with the Franklin.

When the Franklin states that his son will not learn gentilesse, the Host breaks in roughly:

> Straw for youre gentillesse! . . .
> What, Frankeleyn! pardee, sire, wel thou woost
> That ech of yow moot tellen atte leste
> A tale or two, or breken his beheste.   V, 695–98

Note that it is at the word "gentillesse" that the Host interrupts.

And he does not say "a straw for gentilesse"; he says "a straw for *your* gentilesse." It is not that Harry is impatient with the idea of gentilesse; he simply has no patience with *the Franklin's* holding forth on the subject. Harry Bailly, as an innkeeper, is an experienced man where questions of rank are concerned (witness his treatment of the Knight) and in his estimation, at any rate, the Franklin's station in life does not warrant such concern for gentilesse. Harry seems to feel that the Franklin is giving himself airs, and he takes immediate action to put an end to it. The Franklin's reaction to the Host's interruption also fits this reading. He meekly apologizes to the Host, as if he realizes that he has been somewhat presumptuous. Then the Host bluntly orders him to "Telle on thy tale withouten wordes mo" (V, 702), after which the Franklin shamelessly flatters Harry by saying: "I prey to God that it may plesen yow;/Thanne woot I wel that it is good ynow" (V, 708–709).

This brings us to a consideration of the Franklin's Prologue, in which he announces that his story will be a Breton lay, and apologizes for his ignorance of rhetoric. In this prologue are two points of importance to an interpretation of the dramatic interplay involved. First, the Franklin indicates immediately that he is not going to give up his interest in gentilesse just because of the Host's abrupt remarks. In fact, in the first line of his prologue he speaks of "thise olde *gentil* Britouns" and the kind of literature they liked, namely, Breton lays (V, 709–13). Such stories fit the Franklin's idea of propriety, and he points out that he is going to tell one.

The second point in this passage of interest here concerns the so-called "modesty prologue." One writer in 1927 commented on numerous parallels to this passage, showing that in the late Middle Ages, as now, it was not unusual for a speaker to begin by saying "unaccustomed as I am to public speaking," and then to talk for two hours.[6] But, as numerous eminent Chaucerians have observed, one of Chaucer's distinctive devices is putting conventional elements to functional uses; and that, I think, applies

[6] E. P. Hammond, *English Verse Between Chaucer and Surrey*, 392 ff. On the Franklin's inconsistency here, see B. S. Harrison, *SP*, XXXII (1935), 55–61; and C. S. Baldwin, *PMLA*, XLII (1927), 106–12.

also to the Franklin's "modesty prologue." Rather than thinking this passage accounted for by simply noting many parallels to it, we must explain it satisfactorily in its dramatic context; and the context in the present instance is furnished by the Host's preceding attack on the Franklin's interest in gentilesse, and by the succeeding Breton lay which the Franklin tells, a story in which gentilesse figures largely.

Despite the Host's attack, the Franklin indicates his determination to retell a lay made by the "gentle Bretons in their days." But he also seems eager to combat any inclination on the part of those of his listeners who are not interested in the behavior of the nobility to think that he is giving himself airs, as Harry has implied. He therefore ends his prologue with a fourteen-line section in which he states as plainly as possible that he is a "burel" man, who speaks crudely and who is ignorant of rhetoric. For the same purpose he even gets off a rather clumsy pun involving rhetorical colors and the colors of flowers and dies. But for those in his audience capable of appreciating it and of being properly impressed, he includes mention of Cicero and Mount Parnassus. He does exactly the same thing in his tale when he describes the magician's astrological preparations (V, 1261–84). He starts using technical terms, breaks off abruptly to say "I ne kan no termes of astrologye," and then proceeds to give a detailed account of the magician's activities, in which the Franklin displays impressive learning. Another similar instance is his well-known comment: "The horizon has reft the sun of his light—this is as much to say it was night" (V, 1017–18). Such remarks give evidence of his double interest: in gentilesse and the high style, but also in less elevated matters.

In each instance so far, the two sides of the Franklin's nature are apparent: on the one hand, his knowledge of, and regard for, the ordinary, practical world; on the other, his social aspirations, which lead him to conduct himself as he thinks befits the nobility. We come now to the discussion of how his tale fits into this interpretation. As preparation for this discussion we should rule out two matters: first, the idea that Chaucer had an actual Breton lay as his exact source for the Franklin's Tale, an idea in support of which one hundred years of intensive scholarship has

186]

found not the least evidence; and, second, the theory that Chaucer used the Franklin's Tale as a means of setting forth his own view of the perfect marriage. As replacement for these views, I shall attempt to show that the story Chaucer prepared especially for his Franklin evidences great originality, in that it presents an attempted combination of the two then current systems for relationships between men and women—courtly love and marriage. Further, I think that the impossibilities of such a combination cause incongruities which make evident the unworkable aspects of the Franklin's attempt to concern himself with the gentilesse he thinks proper for the nobility. These incongruities stem from the same dichotomy in the Franklin's make-up already observed. Thus his tale is not "an entirely harmonious whole": it is at the same time a courtly-love *demande d'amour* stressing gentilesse, and an attempt at defining the ideal marital situation. That such an uneasy combination does not come off successfully should surprise no one; neither should the assigning of this sort of failure to the Franklin surprise anyone who bears in mind the dramatic principle which Chaucer employed regularly in the *Canterbury Tales*. For we can be sure that Chaucer intended this tale to be read as a dramatic performance by the Franklin. In no other section of the *Tales* does a teller exhibit greater awareness of his listeners. This awareness can be observed not only in the Franklin's Prologue and at the end of his story, but also at regular intervals within the body of his tale.

Chaucer probably took the bare outline for this tale from a story told by Menedon in Boccaccio's *Filocolo*, and added to it many details similar to those used in the so-called Breton lays.[7] But although these sources contribute the atmosphere of courtly love which makes appropriate the emphasis on gentilesse, they by no means account for the Franklin's extended treatment of a happy marriage. In this connection, the opening of the Italian tale deserves attention:

In the land where I was born, I remember there being an extremely rich and a noble cavalier, who, loving a noble lady of that land with a most perfect love, took her for wife. Of which lady another cavalier,

---

[7] See the chapter by Germaine Dempster and J. S. P. Tatlock in *Sources and Analogues*, 377–97.

named Tarolfo, became enamored; and he loved her with so great love that he did not see anything except her, nor did he desire anything more. And in many ways, either by often passing in front of her house, or by tilting or by jousting or by other acts, he contrived to have her love. . . .

Although this story opens with immediate emphasis on the love triangle, at the beginning of the Franklin's Tale we have seventy-six lines devoted to Arveragus' winning Dorigen as his wife and to the arrangements they make to insure a happy marriage. The endings of the two stories also show widely differing emphasis. In the *Filocolo* we merely have each character's release of the other and then the *demande d'amour:* Who was the most generous? Near the end of the Franklin's Tale, however, Aurelius draws a moral for all wives—"every wife should be careful in her promises" (V, 1541)—and we have the Franklin's lengthy description of the happy reunion between Dorigen and Arveragus (V, 1551–56), in addition to the competition for the prize in noble conduct and the concluding question. Neither in Menedon's story nor in the Breton lays is there the constant attention which the Franklin devotes to marriage.

The details of the Franklin's attempt to combine a relationship exemplifying courtly love with an ideal marital situation can be most clearly seen from an analysis of the two chief characters in the tale—Dorigen and Arveragus—and of the asides which the Franklin inserts into their story. We learn at the opening of the tale that a knight does his "payne" to serve a lady, to please whom he carries out many a great undertaking. Because this lady is of a nobler family he scarcely dares tell her of his love. But finally she is moved by his abject humility to take pity upon him. Here is the typical courtly-love situation, described in the customary terminology. Then the knight and the lady marry, and the courtly-love relationship, in which the lady is properly supreme and the knight her servant, is replaced by the marital situation, in which the wife is considered subordinate to the husband. But the newly wed couple do not proceed according to the rules: they attempt to retain in their marital state certain aspects of their courtly-love relationship. And the passage (V, 744–52) from which we learn of this is full of a strange combination of terms from the two systems: alongside "mastery," "sovereignty," and "humble true wife," we find "obey her and follow her will, as should any lover to his lady." Dorigen and Arveragus love each other sincerely and have all the requirements for a highly successful marriage and a happy life. Yet into their marriage they carry attitudes and actions from the system of courtly love.

At this point in the story the Franklin digresses from the narrative to comment at length on the wisdom of this arrangement. He feels that he is accomplishing both his aims: he is portraying a workable marriage acceptable to those of his listeners for whom courtly love holds no charms; and also he can still tell a tale of gentilesse and magic, ending with a *demande d'amour*. Accordingly, his comments here reveal his double interests. First he points out that "love will not be constrained by mastery; for when mastery appears, the God of Love at once beats his wings, and, farewell, he is gone (V, 764–65). Then he enters his common-sense plea for tolerance in marriage. Finally he caps his digression with a fine example of double-talk:

> Thus hath she take hir servant and hir lord,
> Servant in love and lord in mariage.
> Thanne was he bothe in lordshipe and servage.
> Servage? nay, but in lordshipe above,
> Sith he hath bothe his lady and his love;
> His lady, certes, and his wyf also,
> The which that lawe of love acordeth to.   V, 792–98

Arveragus now takes his wife home to Pedmark and they live in great happiness. Here the Franklin in his more matter-of-fact role interrupts the story to say:

> Who koude telle, but he hadde wedded be,
> The joye, the ese, and the prosperitee
> That is bitwixe an housbonde and his wyf?   V, 803–805

This excellent state of affairs lasts more than a year until Arveragus goes to England for two years to seek worship and honor in arms, "For al his lust he sette in swich labour" (V, 812). A happy marriage is fine, but Arveragus has remembered that he is a courtly knight and he must go away to win honor in the tournaments. From this knightly act will stem the trouble which almost wrecks the happy marriage of Dorigen and Arveragus. We should also not overlook the fact that his leaving home is Chaucer's addition to his source; the cavalier in the *Filocolo* does not go away.

Dorigen grieves mightily over her absent husband, and her grief becomes symbolized for her in the black rocks along the coast. Thus it is that when the squire Aurelius pleads for her love, she assigns him the seemingly impossible task of removing the black rocks. But here Dorigen is not exactly the haughty lady of the courtly romances, though the way is paved for the approaching difficulties by her shifting momentarily into a courtly-love situation. She first says firmly that she will never be an unfaithful wife. Then, in jest and in the language of courtly love, she assigns the task and promises her love if Aurelius can remove the rocks. But immediately she shifts back to practical, down-to-earth considerations and tells him to put such matters out of his mind, for a man can have no pleasure in loving another man's wife (V, 1002–1005).

With Aurelius, however, the Franklin's sense of literary propriety can be indulged fully. His description of this squire includes all the conventional details: Aurelius suffers the malady of love for more than two years and utters a complaint to Apollo that would do justice to Troilus. But even with Aurelius, the Franklin is not altogether comfortable; he leaves the lovesick squire with the matter-of-fact remark: "Let him choose for me whether he will live or die" (V, 1086).

Arveragus returns, and the emphasis is placed on the happiness of the reunited husband and wife. Although Arveragus suspects nothing, the elements of courtly love which he and Dorigen have brought into their marriage—his interest in winning honor in the tournaments, and her assigning the task to Aurelius—will soon threaten their happiness.

Meanwhile, Aurelius, who has properly observed secrecy, learns from his brother that there are magicians in Orleans. He goes to Orleans, meets the magician, and strikes a bargain for the removal of the black rocks. Returning with Aurelius, the magician in due time makes the rocks disappear. Throughout this long section of his tale (V, 1101–1296), the Franklin is dealing with the kind of romance material which he thinks proper for people of breeding; yet we find injected here the same sort of matter-of-fact comments noticed earlier. When the subject of magic is introduced, the Franklin speaks of it as "such folly as in our days is not worth a fly—for our faith in Holy Church does not permit illusions to grieve us" (V, 1131–34). And later the acts of magicians are spoken of as japes, wretchedness, superstitious cursedness, and illusions which heathen folk used in those days (V, 1271–72, 1292–93). Even though magic was standard material in the Breton lays and the romances, the Franklin's practical sense prevents his acceptance of it.

When Aurelius tells Dorigen of the disappearance of the rocks, she is stunned. Arveragus is away, and she grieves alone at home. At this point in the story we have the much-debated "Complaint of Dorigen," which Chaucer took from Jerome against Jovinian, and in which Dorigen calls up as models many famous ladies of the past who chose death rather than dishonor (V, 1355–1456). Although the artistic function of this complaint has recently been skillfully defended on other grounds,[8] I feel that the presence of this lengthy passage, which so many critics have found objectionable, is most convincingly explained by reference to Dorigen's carrying over into her marriage aspects of the rules of conduct she followed when, at the beginning of the story, she was a courtly-love heroine. The "complaint" itself is a courtly-love device, as is the noble choice of suicide rather than dishonor. And the *exempla* which Dorigen cites are part and parcel of elevated literature in the Middle Ages. But even though Dorigen concludes that she should commit suicide, the tone and exaggerated nature of her complaint convince the reader that she is not going to do so. Rather, as soon as Arveragus returns, she tells him her difficulty in true wifely fashion. In other words, the "complaint" represents her testing of one aspect of courtly behavior, her discarding it, and then her adopting a more realistic and practical solution. In this connection we should note that the lady in Menedon's story in the *Filocolo* does not immediately tell her husband the cause of her grief. He has to force the facts from her.

---

[8] James Sledd, *MP*, XLV (1947–48), 36–45.

But Dorigen unburdens herself to her husband as soon as he **asks** why she weeps. In her actions here we see that, for the moment at least, the Franklin's understanding of a workable marriage overcomes his interest in what he thinks the proper behavior for noble folk.

Arveragus, however, has not yet given up the courtly principles that he brought to his marriage. Although he comforts his wife in husbandly fashion, he proclaims that she must give herself to Aurelius because "Trouthe is the hyeste thyng that man may kepe" (V, 1479). Then he instructs two servants to conduct her to Aurelius. That the Franklin realizes how strange this decision must sound to those of his listeners who put no stock in the courtly code is evident in his next comment:

> Paraventure an heep of yow, ywis,
> Wol holden hym a lewed man in this
> That he wol putte his wyf in jupartie.
> Herkneth the tale er ye upon hire crie.
> She may have bettre fortune than yow semeth;
> And whan that ye han herd the tale, demeth.
>
> V, 1493–98

The everyday listener or reader is now assured of a happy ending to the story, despite Arveragus' strange behavior, and the Franklin can proceed with his illustrations of gentilesse and the concluding *demande d'amour*. Dorigen encounters Aurelius, who asks where she is going. "To the garden, as my husband bade," she replies (V, 1512). Notice that she is here no courtly lady; she is the conventional, obedient wife. Aurelius is filled with pity and decides that to hold her to her promise would not be in accord with gentilesse. He therefore releases her, but we have difficulty praising Aurelius for noble actions when we recall that he did not hesitate to use trickery to make the rocks disappear. Even he, however, seems to realize now that the principles of courtly love do not fit well in the marital situation, and he calls Dorigen "the truest and best wife I ever knew in all my life" (V, 1539–40). Dorigen "goes home to her *husband*," not to her lord or to her knight, and they live happily ever after. If my analysis of this story is correct, we can readily suppose that their marriage was not again threatened by behavior in accord with the code of courtly love, and we note that at this point the Franklin speaks of them as "Arveragus and Dorigen his *wife*," not "Arveragus and Dorigen his *lady*," as in the earlier section of the tale.

The Franklin now presents the magician's releasing Aurelius from the debt of a thousand pounds, whereby the magician shows that he can in his actions illustrate gentilesse as well as can a knight or a squire. Then comes the Franklin's concluding question to his listeners: "Who was the most generous?" (V, 1622). It is important to observe here that whereas in the *Filocolo* the question is "Which of the three men—the cavalier, Tarolfo, or Tebano—was the most generous?" the Franklin simply asks who was the most generous. This alteration throws the competition open to Dorigen, as well as to the three men, and to my way of thinking she would win the prize by virtue of her giving up, through the immediate confession to her husband of her foolish promise, the attitudes from courtly love that she brought into her marriage.

Even so, the *demande d'amour* seems strangely out of place at the end of the Franklin's Tale. This results, I think, from the fact that the Franklin's frequent comments on the happy workability of the marriage between Dorigen and Arveragus build up a pattern which is in opposition to courtly-love elements. Thus we cannot quite accept Arveragus, whose counterpart in the *Filocolo* is judged the most generous, as a noble husband, for we have seen him send his wife to another man.

In his tale and elsewhere the Franklin tries to satisfy his two fields of interest and to appeal to his listeners of both types—the "gentils" and the less elevated folk. So far as we know, since we have no epilogue to the Franklin's Tale, his device was successful on the Canterbury pilgrimage, but most critics have been struck by the incongruities in his tale, incongruities which I think result from the ambivalence of this "worthy vavasour" so greatly concerned with gentilesse.

For gold in phisik is a cordial

18. THE PHYSICIAN

The suitability of the Physician's Tale and its teller is much debated. As I see it, there is evidence that Chaucer provided this Pilgrim with material that fits the two primary aspects of his character. The Physician is presented in the General Prologue as a "society doctor," who attempts to impress his public with his learning and skill, though he is mainly interested in collecting fat fees; in other words, he is primarily concerned with putting on an impressive show to cover his real motives. Similarly, when he performs before the Pilgrims, he tries through an allegory directed against lust to impress them with his noble defense of chastity. But Harry Bailly shrewdly explodes the bubble of his pomposity by pointed reference to the Physician's activities toward corrupting chastity.

From the sketch in the General Prologue (I, 411–44), we learn that the Physician is thoroughly familiar with the medical authorities of his time—Esculapius, Dioscorides, Rufus of Ephesus, Hippocrates, Hali, Galen, Serapion, Rhazes, Avicenna, Averroës, Constantinus Afer, Damascenus (?), Bernard Gordon, John Gaddesden, and Gilbertus Anglius. However, the numerous ironic touches in the portrait make it almost certain that Chaucer aimed at pointing up lapses in the character of this doctor, despite his learning and financial success. As early as the opening lines of the sketch, Chaucer seems to strike this satiric note. He says:

> With us ther was a Doctour of Phisik;
> In al this world ne was ther noon hym lik,
> To speke of phisik and of surgerye,
> For he was grounded in astronomye.   I, 411–14

The crucial words here are "to speke." According to one possibility, the lines mean: "If we speak generally of members of the medical profession, in all the world there was no one equal to him." The second possible reading would be: "In all the world there was no one equal to him for talking about medical matters." In my opinion, this doctor is not necessarily the world's leading practitioner of "phisik and of surgerye"; he leads the world in *speaking about* medicine.[1] In line 411 the general subject of medicine is introduced by mention of the "Doctour of Phisik" as the individual now under discussion. It would therefore seem unnecessary and clumsily out of place for Chaucer again to indicate the subject being discussed, when only one line has intervened. Moreover, although we do not know with certainty just what was Chaucer's view of astronomy as a serious part of medical science, we do know that some of his contemporaries were very dubious about it.[2] With that fact in mind, I find difficulty in accepting "For he was grounded in astronomye" as anything other than a part of a jibe at the Physician. The introductory "for" shows that we can expect to be told the reason for the Physician's pre-eminence in *talking about* medicine; and the reason is that he knew "astronomye" thoroughly.

If there is room for doubt about the presence of satire in the lines just treated, certainly in the mention of the Physician's "arrangement" with the apothecaries Chaucer is plain enough. "For ech of hem made oother for to wynne—/Hir frendshipe nas nat newe to bigynne." The same certainty is to be felt in connection with the line "His studie was but litel on the Bible." Nowadays we hardly notice that certain scientists may care little for formal religion, but that was not the case in Chaucer's day.[3]

There is one other important satiric thrust at the Physician in the portrait: he is extremely tight-fisted. Although he will spend money on fine clothes, he will use it for very little else. Indeed, one suspects that his moderate diet was dictated more by concern for expense than by considerations of health. Further, a good bit of this money which he hoards he made during times of plague— times when a doctor should have thought more of helping in an emergency than of collecting his fees. The sketch ends with an

---

[1] Curry (*Sciences*, 28) advanced this view; Manly (*Canterbury Tales by Geoffrey Chaucer*, 524) differed sharply.

[2] Bowden, *Commentary*, 204–205.

[3] G. G. Coulton, *Medieval Panorama*, 445 ff.

apt pun on "goldwasser": "For gold in phisik is a cordial,/There-fore he lovede gold in special." All in all, the Physician is not a particularly appealing individual, in that his superficial show of professional expertness is aimed principally at making money.

The story told by this fashionable medical man[4] concerns the beautiful and innocent Virginia, whose father kills her to prevent her falling victim to the lust of an evil judge. Even though in the first line of his story the Physician refers to Livy as his source, it seems that Chaucer used the skeleton of this narra-tive as he found it in Jean de Meun's *Romance of the Rose*, adding to it material from Livy's Latin version.[5] One point in connection with Chaucer's use of source materials for this tale is of particular importance here. Whereas in the account of De Meun, the evil judge is the center of interest, in the Physician's Tale, Virginia is made the central figure,[6] and as such represents the ideal of virginity. The judge, Appius, on the other hand, Chaucer con-trives as little more than a threat to Virginia's chastity.

The idea that the Physician intends his performance as a moral story primarily in praise of chastity is also supported by examina-tion of the first hundred-odd lines of the tale. With the narra-tive economy usual in the *Canterbury Tales*, we are first intro-duced to a worthy knight, Virginius, who had an only daughter. But then we find a thirty-four-line description of Virginia's phys-ical beauty; and the method of this personal description differs greatly from that employed for the sketches in the General Pro-logue or for such descriptions as those of Nicholas, Alison, and Absolon in the Miller's Tale. Here we have no easy, natural, gos-sipy, conversational tone; rather, there is the somewhat stilted, semilearned device of having Nature proudly speak of Virginia as one of her finest creations. This method seems well suited to the pompous Physician, who apparently stresses Virginia's phys-ical beauty in order to increase his emphasis on her inner purity. In fact, he says: "And if that excellent was hire beautee,/A thou-sand foold moore vertuous was she" (VI, 39–40).

This statement introduces a lengthy passage in detailed praise

---

[4] The term is Miss Bowden's; see *Commentary*, 199.
[5] See the chapter by E. F. Shannon in *Sources and Analogues*, 398–408.
[6] R. K. Root, *The Poetry of Chaucer* (rev. ed.), 222.

of Virginia's admirable conduct, for "As wel in goost as body chast was she" (VI, 43); also she avoided all occasions which make young people "to soone rype and boold" (VI, 68). The Physician now inserts a long plea addressed to governesses and to parents, urging them to guard well the virtue of their young charges. Then he calls attention to the wide fame which Virginia won, both for her beauty and her virtuous behavior. At last, after 116 lines, the Physician is ready to begin his narrative, which he closes with the noble advice "Forsaketh synne, er synne yow forsake" (VI, 286).

This story is a strangely moral one for a man whose study is but little on the Bible, whose arrangements with his apothecaries are suspect, and whose main interest is in collecting and holding on to as much money as possible. The Host, in commenting on the tale, first expresses his reaction to the false judge and to the piteous death of the "sely mayde," and sententiously concludes that "Men han ful ofte moore for harm than prow" from the gifts of Nature and Fortune (VI, 287–300). Then Harry seems to be struck by the incongruity between the theme of the tale and the real character of its teller. He says:

> But trewely, myn owene maister deere,
> This is a pitous tale for to heere.
> But nathelees, passe over, is no fors.
> I pray to God so save thy gentil cors,
> And eek thyne urynals and thy jurdones,
> Thyn ypocras, and eek thy galiones,
> And every boyste ful of thy letuarie;
> God blesse hem, and oure lady Seinte Marie!
> So moot I theen, thou art a propre man,
> And lyk a prelat, by Seint Ronyan!
> Seyde I nat wel? I kan nat speke in terme;
> But wel I woot thou doost myn herte to erme,
> That I almoost have caught a cardynacle.   VI, 301–13

It seems to me that the Host is in this passage making fun of the Physician by none-too-veiled allusions to his hypocrisy in telling a story so out of keeping with his real character.[7] First, we note that Harry calls this doctor "myn owene maister deere,"

[7] This view was advanced by Frederick Tupper, *JEGP*, XV (1916), 61–67.

the same exaggeratedly polite title that he used in addressing the Friar (III, 1337; see also III, 1300); and we can be sure that Harry was well aware of the hypocritical practices of the "worthy lymytour." Then the Host comments again on the piteous nature of the story, but now says: "However, forget that; it doesn't matter." It is almost as if Harry is a bit ashamed of himself at this point for having been so disturbed by a story of innocence betrayed, when he reflects that this story came from the lips of a man himself not above suspicion as a betrayer in various kinds of activities. Whether or not this guess at Harry's reaction here is sound, the fact remains that he does dismiss the tale as of no importance and turns his attention to the teller.

His opening prayer for the Physician's body would seem to indicate something more than literal meaning for the line, especially when we recall how general in Chaucer's day was the assumption that doctors regularly indulged in questionable practices.[8] But Harry's ironic intent here is most clearly seen in his mention of "ypocras" and "galiones," two currently well-known love-philters widely purveyed by doctors.[9] No great interpretative straining is needed to find irony in the Host's asking God to save the aphrodisiacs sold by a man who has just completed a tale in praise of virginity. Then Harry goes on to call down the blessings of the Virgin Mary on these same items. Even this does not complete the Host's jest at the Physician's expense. He next tells the doctor that he is "a proper man, and like a prelate." The reputation of fourteenth-century prelates makes this comparison a dubious honor,[10] and Harry seems to underscore his meaning here by a lewd pun on the nickname of St. Ninian.[11]

Certainly a partial explanation for this passage is the pride the Host takes in being sufficiently learned as to address a professional man in high-sounding technical terms relating to that man's profession. We have seen this same motivation in Harry's using legal terms when addressing the Lawyer and rhetorical terms in speaking to the Clerk. Thus it is that he now proudly

[8] Bowden, *Commentary*, 209–11.

[9] See the article by Tupper cited in n. 7 of this section.

[10] See Robinson, *Works*, *CT*, VII, 1924–64, for the Host's views of the clergy's behavior.

[11] See Tupper's article cited in n. 7 of this section and Robinson, *Works*, 833.

asks the Physician: "Seyde I nat wel?" and adds with mock modesty: "I kan nat speke in terme." But, in making his transition to calling on the next storyteller, he takes one parting shot at the Physician: "But I know very well that you have caused my heart to grieve, so that I have almost caught a 'cardynacle.' "[12] Notice that it is not the sad story of Virginia which causes the Host's pain around the heart; the Physician (*thou*) causes it. In the light of Harry's preceding ironic remarks to the Physician, we have reason for suspecting that he here means that his ailment is caused by the Physician's hypocrisy in telling a moral tale which his own practices rob of any sincerity.

In conclusion, if the foregoing interpretation of the Physician's performance is tenable, the piteous story of Virginia must be regarded as his bold attempt to perpetrate on the Pilgrims a bit of moral virtuosity. When the tale is so understood, the pompous and exaggeratedly noble tone of the long introductory passage on Virginia's purity, the so-called "digressive" plea to governesses and parents, and the concluding moral do not cause baffling difficulties in the drama of this section of the *Canterbury Tales*, for they represent a part of the Physician's dramatic purpose. That the Host, in his comments upon the performance, does not allow the Physician to carry out his scheme with complete success is in keeping with Chaucer's method throughout.[13]

[12] The Host's knowledge of technical terms is a bit shaky. "Cardynacle" is his corruption of "cardiacle." See Robinson, *Works*, 834.

[13] For example, the method is almost exactly the same at the end of the performance by the Pardoner (Robinson, *Works, CT*, VI, 946–55).

19. THE PARDONER

We have now reached the actor-Pilgrim whose presentation, in my opinion, involves the greatest degree of dramatic complexity.[1] The passages pertinent to any analysis of the Pardoner's character fall into eight definite divisions: first, the portrait of the Pardoner in the General Prologue (I, 669–714); second, the interruption by the Pardoner in the Wife of Bath's Prologue (III, 163–87); third, the Introduction to the Pardoner's Tale (VI, 318–28); fourth, the Pardoner's Prologue (VI, 329–462); fifth, the sermon (VI, 463–915); sixth, the benediction (VI, 915–918); seventh, the attempted sale (VI, 919–45); eighth, the quarrel with the Host (VI, 946–68).[2]

Through a consideration of these passages in sequence, my interpretation of the Pardoner will be presented: namely, that the physically handicapped Pardoner, having joined the pilgrimage with the definite purpose of extracting money from his traveling companions, most of whom he despises, by a refinement of his usual methods of salesmanship among peasants directs his actions and words throughout toward that end and fails, after almost succeeding, because he foolishly reverts to those usual methods at the crucial moment. Thus, the dramatic structure of the Pardoner's performance, which includes a tale that suits both his regular occupation and his present purpose, involves his bitter antagonism towards his physically well-adjusted companions and represents an unintentional self-revelation of his own in-

[1] The numerous studies of the Pardoner and his recital were surveyed by G. G. Sedgewick, *MLQ*, I (1940), 431–58. Subsequent references to Sedgewick throughout this section are to this article. See also C. R. Sleeth, *MLN*, LVI (1941), 138; M. P. Hamilton, *JEGP*, XL (1941), 48–72; A. L. Kellogg, *Speculum*, XXVI (1951), 465–81; A. L. Kellogg and L. A. Haselmayer, *PMLA*, LXVI (1951), 251–77; Johannes Swart, *Neophilologus*, XXXVI (1952), 45–50.

[2] See Sedgewick (p. 443), from whom I have borrowed several terms: e.g., "interruption" and "benediction." Among other of his terms, the rejection of "afterthought" for lines VI, 919–68 of the Pardoner's Tale is especially important for my analysis.

I trowe he were a geldyng or a mare

adequacies in the very field of endeavor—salesmanship—at which he feels most competent. Here the tale proper is more completely subordinated to the whole performance than in any other instance.

There is no need here to dwell on all the familiar details of the Pardoner's portrait in the General Prologue (I, 669–714). It will suffice to note the following facts: the Pardoner has just come from Rome; he is a friend of the Summoner; he is obviously indifferent to any adverse opinions the other Pilgrims may form concerning the moral lapses evident in his behavior; he has been a eunuch from birth; he has his relics and pardons with him; and he has been extremely successful in the past, because of his shrewdness, at extracting money from peasants.

A close similarity exists, I think, between Chaucer's Pardoner and Shakespeare's Edmund in *King Lear*. Like Edmund, the Pardoner is subject to the scorn of society at large through no fault of his own—in fact, the Pardoner, a eunuch, has even more cause for bitterness on this score than Edmund, a bastard. Like Edmund, the Pardoner is extremely intelligent and self-reliant. We may infer that the Pardoner, like Edmund, decides that circumstances force him to find an outlet for his considerable abilities outside the sphere of normal human behavior and usual moral laws. Edmund, not feeling bound to honest dealing, outwits his family and his associates and blazes a brilliant path upward to a generalship and near kingship, until his fatal mistake of not choosing between the two evil sisters proves his undoing. The Pardoner, barred from normal satisfactions by a misfortune of birth, finds his compensation in matching wits with normal folk and coming off best in the encounter. The money he thus makes (I, 703–704) and the luxuries he can thus afford (VI, 439–53) are important to him as clear evidence to the world of his success. Perhaps he could have enjoyed even greater wealth and luxury, and some satisfaction, as a "supersalesman" in the seemingly more honest employ of some "big businessman," such as the Merchant; but the satisfaction of so obviously outwitting people born without his handicap would have been lacking.

If we assume that the Pardoner feels a bitterness against the world similar to that which characterizes Edmund, a pertinent question needs asking here: Why did the Pardoner go on the pilgrimage? It will perhaps be objected that such a question is trivial; Chaucer is presenting a fictional cross section of the society he knew, and a pardoner must needs be present. But if the enveloping plan of the *Canterbury Tales* is to deserve, as it has often received, the highest praise for literary artistry as the framework within which we meet the actors in a Human Comedy, such a question is relevant. It does not, then, seem to me too conjectural to suggest that the Pardoner, upon his return from Rome, encountered his friend the Summoner and learned of the plans for the pilgrimage, and that he therefore decided to join the company, determined to match wits with his traveling companions and, if possible, to extract money from them. Certainly his past successes among peasants filled him with confidence in his own abilities; his "walet .../Bretful of pardoun, comen from Rome al hoot" (I, 686–87) makes him particularly well prepared for an extraordinary effort at this time; and the hope of success among a group more sophisticated and less friendly than his usual victims, a success which would give him the greatest possible pleasure and satisfaction, would have been highly intriguing for him. It is difficult to believe that the Pardoner, just arrived in England after a long journey from Rome, would at once make the leisurely trip to Canterbury for the pleasure of a vacation. Neither are sincere devotion and desire for social approval plausible reasons for his going on the pilgrimage. Perhaps an immediate return to labors among his usual peasant victims would have brought the Pardoner more money, but his vanity and his urge "to get even with the world" would thus have been satisfied to a lesser degree than by success among the Pilgrims. In his mind, the time had come for him to advance another rung on the ladder of success.

In that light, the actions of the Pardoner mentioned in his portrait need not be dismissed simply as "broadly comic" or coolly impudent.[3] Chaucer clearly intends these actions "to be arresting," and to the Pilgrims the Pardoner's behavior must have ap-

[3] Sedgewick, 443–44.

peared shockingly different from that expected of an individual having the power of confession, no matter how widespread such abuses were.[4] But this irregular behavior by the Pardoner may have a purpose behind it, for he is not the man for aimless joking. It seems to me that the Pardoner's joining with the Summoner in a lewd secular song and his aping of the newest fashions represent his effort to test the reactions of his newly met companions from whom he had earlier decided to attempt to extract money. The big problem for him is what approach he shall employ to accomplish his end. There is, however, no necessity for his choosing his tactics at once. He will be associated with this group of people, his possible victims, for several days. Also, the Host, a man in whom the Pardoner is later to be vitally interested, has not yet become the center of attention with his proposal for the storytelling game. When this proposal is made, the Pardoner is certainly not the one to offer objections, for the storytelling presents him with the opportunity he seeks of employing his oratorical wiles before the Pilgrims.

After the General Prologue, the reader catches no further glimpse of the Pardoner until his interruption of the Wife of Bath. One imagines, however, that the Pardoner is relieved at not being called on to perform early in the game, for he now has plenty of time during the earlier tales to look about him, observing his companions closely and deciding tentatively just what methods he will use in his effort to extract money from them when his turn comes to speak. When the Wife takes the center of the stage and begins her autobiographical performance, the Pardoner, still undecided about his tactics, is probably all attention, for he recognizes a kindred spirit in the Wife and catches from her what he considers a hint as to how he can most easily accomplish his purpose when his time comes.

The Wife first regales her audience for 162 lines with arguments concerning chastity and marriage. From her speech the Pardoner realizes that here is a person who considers herself outside the governance of the usual moral laws controlling marriage

[4] Bowden, *Commentary*, 277–83.

and the sexual relationship, and who is by no means afraid of defending her position. At once the Pardoner grasps the similarity between the Wife's position with regard to marriage and his own position with regard to religion. Both are unashamedly beyond the rules by which the mass of people are governed; and each is a rebel within his sphere of human behavior.

As a result of this realization, the Pardoner is intensely interested in the reaction of the other Pilgrims to what the Wife is saying. Long before she had taken the center of the stage, while the earlier stories were in progress, the shrewd Pardoner had ample opportunity to note that many of his companions were filled with pretensions of a sort not unusual among middle-class people. Exempting for the sake of argument the truly devout members of the company, the Pardoner still saw a considerable number of individuals whose human failings were fairly marked. And, as the Wife vehemently advances her unorthodox views on the question of marriage, a question not totally unrelated to the Pardoner's closer connection with religious doctrine, it becomes apparent to him, whose previous success has resulted from his exploitation of human failings, that the most noticeable of the not unusual human failings evident in the Wife's listeners is an assuming of the "man-of-the-world" attitude toward her arguments. It is noteworthy, it seems to me, that not even the genuinely devout among the Pilgrims enter any objection to the rebellion against established morality which the Wife is preaching. Thus, as the Wife talked, the Pardoner might well have said to himself: "See how she is getting away with it; not a one of them who isn't swallowing it all." For one may easily assume that the reaction of each of the Wife's listeners—again perhaps exempting the really pious—is, in effect: "Of course, what she is saying would not do for the masses; but I am a sophisticated person, a traveler. I have seen something of the world, and I know that not everything is as one reads in the Bible or hears in church. Anyway, she is a remarkably interesting person." And who is it among the Pilgrims that is characterized to the highest degree by this affected sophistication? The Host, Harry Bailly, guide and governor for the group, who in his dealings with various Pilgrims has shown himself at times annoyingly pompous, in love with authority, convinced of his ability to handle people, and smug about his judgment as a literary critic.

It may well be, then, that the Pardoner here tentatively decides, first, that when his turn comes he can best accomplish his desired end of extracting money from his companions by an appeal to their affectation of worldliness in regard to accepted moral laws, and, second, that the Host, already bested by various Pilgrims, is probably his most likely victim. Since the Pardoner is to operate in a group more complex than his usual peasant groups, he determines to test his tentative decision by an interruption of the Wife's speech (III, 163–68), in which he protests indirectly against the doctrine she has advanced. She has just said that no matter what the clerics preach she will not be chaste; her husband shall be both her debtor and her thrall and shall have his tribulation "upon his flessh." It has been noted elsewhere that the Pardoner, an expert professional speaker, interrupts the Wife fittingly "at the conclusion of one of her numerous little homilies."[5] He directs attention to her as a "noble prechour in this cas"; the "cas" is her divergence from established behavior in marriage, and he himself is a noble preacher in a similarly divergent "cas," the matter of confession and pardon. Having emphasized for the attentive Pilgrims the Wife's pronounced divergence from established behavior, he proceeds to protest against this divergence by concrete personal application. He says: "I was about to take a wife, but your alarming description of married life has dissuaded me." This statement is directly pointed towards testing the depth of the worldliness affected by the listening Pilgrims. Had the others rallied to the support of his objection, the Pardoner would no doubt have decided that the tactics he had tentatively selected for use when his turn arrived would have to be abandoned for some likelier plan.

One critic has explained the seeming inconsistency between the Pardoner's physical handicap and his talk of his imminent marriage as an attempt to conceal his physical condition from the other Pilgrims.[6] But the Pardoner was not so foolish as to think that anyone present had doubts about his physical state, which the Narrator correctly guessed at first glance (I, 691). Nor

[5] Sedgewick, 445. [6] Curry, *Sciences*, 68–70.

do I think that his putting himself forward as a bridegroom-to-be is mere"jocosity" and shameless impudence. As is clearly evident in his quarrel with the Host at the end of his tale, he resents having attention called to his physical lack, and would resort to such a device only for a purpose very important to him. Whatever "japes" he indulged in were for the purpose of deception which would bring him profits (I, 701–706), and his assuming the role of prospective bridegroom when he interrupts the Wife is his amazingly shrewd method of pointing to her as a breaker of established rules for behavior in marriage. Thereby he is able to determine the reaction of her listeners.

As already pointed out, not a single one of the Pilgrims joins in the Pardoner's protest against the Wife. She realizes the implications of his words and slyly attacks him on the score of his fondness for drink. Then she promises that her future remarks will reveal even more clearly the tribulations of a husband (III, 169–83). So far, the Pardoner has the answer he seeks: the worldliness which the Pilgrims affect is deep enough to allow them to accept without remonstrance the unorthodoxy which the Wife preaches. Thus, he is about ready to conclude that these same Pilgrims will not remonstrate vigorously against his own scurrilous activities if he skillfully appeals to their feigned sophistication. Remembering, however, that he is among a new element, he wants to assure himself fully before deciding finally on the tactics he will employ when his turn comes. Therefore, he tests the Pilgrims' reaction for the second time by a pretense of meekness which points even more forcibly than his earlier comment to the Wife as a rebel against accepted standards of behavior:

> Dame, I wolde praye yow, if youre wyl it were,
> ... as ye bigan,
> Telle forth youre tale, spareth for no man,
> And teche us yonge men of youre praktike.   III, 184–87

Here the Pardoner, as one of "us yonge men," presents the Wife to the Pilgrims as an older and experienced person who is misleading inexperienced youths with a dangerously unorthodox view of marriage. He as much as invites the Pilgrims to object by his "spareth for no man," and specifically calls attention to the nature of the Wife's arguments and actions by terming them "youre praktike." "Praktike" here means "immoral or dishonest dealing" rather than "customary methods." Furthermore, there is an inviting tone of ironical satire against the Wife and himself in the request that the Wife teach "us young men." But still not one of the Pilgrims suggests that the Wife should cease her shocking revelations. Therefore, the Pardoner concludes that the worldliness which the Pilgrims affect is thick enough to bear the revelation of his own gross tricks in an autobiographical confession similar to that of the Wife, another moral transgressor. He has now reached a final decision concerning the approach he will use, and it is perhaps not too farfetched to imagine him, after his interruption of the Wife, as impatient for his turn and saying under his breath: "Well, Madam, you can pat yourself on the back for your success in taking in these would-be worldly ones, but I will show you how it really should be done." Meanwhile, he casts his eye hungrily on the Host's purse.

The Pardoner's impatience is not soon satisfied, for he has to wait a considerable time before the Host calls upon him to perform. In the interval he has seen no reason to change the decision reached during the Wife of Bath's Prologue; in fact, he has had reason to become more confirmed in his early opinion that the Host is his most likely victim, for Harry's assumed sophistication has become even more evident. Now, in calling upon the Pardoner for a tale to drive away the pity he feels for Virginia, Harry uses a phrase carrying a leer and a pretense to a knowledge of French (VI, 318–19).

The Pardoner, who has waited long for this moment, replies with an immediacy so emphatic as to require more explanation than that it arises from "eager zest." He has carefully developed and tested his plan of attack, and is now fully prepared to go to work (VI, 320–22). As has been pointed out, there is in the first line of this speech "a hint of return thrust . . . in the Pardoner's echoing" of the "dubious saint" to whom Harry referred in praising the Physician.[7] The echoing is more than a hint of a thrust, I think; it is the first individual probing by the Pardoner of the Pilgrim he has picked as his most likely victim. Then, in the two

[7] Sedgewick, 447.

succeeding lines, the Pardoner demands that a halt be called in the pilgrimage so that he can have a drink and eat a cake. But the "gentils" have noted carefully the far-from-admirable traits which the Pardoner has been at no pains to hide since his first appearance, and, assuming that if such a person starts drinking he will surely tell some "ribaudye," they object to the halt for refreshments and demand "som moral thyng." The Pardoner quickly agrees to their demand, even implying in his "I graunte, ywis" (VI, 327) that they are foolish to expect other than doctrinal material from him; but he insists upon the halt. Shrewdly he inserts the idea of a bargain with the Pilgrims—"I will give you moral material if you agree to halt here"—and supports the bargain idea with a justification of the drink—it will give him time to recollect "som honest thyng"—in order to win his point.

A great deal of ink has been mixed into this draft of ale which the Pardoner demands. A usual explanation is that it is simply another touch in Chaucer's portrait of a thoroughly abandoned character who must have a drink at this point and who becomes so drunk from this one drink of ale that his later boasting confessions are to be explained thereby.[8] But the request for a drink was not then a certain indication that one was a drunkard, especially if the drink was needed to wash down a cake. Nor could the one drink result in extended intoxication. A more plausible suggestion is that the Pardoner needs a few moments to think before he can tell some moral piece creditably.[9] However, as has been indicated, it seems to me that the Pardoner long ago decided on his general plan and needs no moment's grace before beginning his speech. Thus a better explanation here is that the Pardoner first suggests the halt for refreshments and then, after the objection by the "gentils," shrewdly bargains to win agreement to that halt in order to get the Pilgrims into a group so that he can fix them with his eye and generally put on his performance with the greatest possible effect. He knew, as any experienced public speaker would have known, that most of his coming words would be lost if delivered under the casual and disrupting circumstances of traveling. To avoid that unhappy situation, he

[8] See, for example, the article by Swart cited in n. 1 of this section.
[9] Sedgewick, 447–48.

suggests, and then insists successfully upon, a halt. The Pardoner delivers his prologue and tale to a group which has halted and assembled.

This view, which approaches that advanced by a number of preceding writers, is almost what Professor Sedgewick calls "The Tavern Heresy." Although he is particularly opposed only to the view that the Pardoner's Prologue and Tale were delivered inside a tavern, he holds it "at least possible that, after a pause to suit the Pardoner's convenience, the Pilgrims rode on, their entertainer talking to the usual accompaniment of hooves and harness." To me, a pause to suit the convenience of so experienced a public speaker as the Pardoner would end only when he had finished his speech and the noise of the hooves and harness could no longer distract his audience or him. I consider the Pardoner not an "entertainer" but rather a man with definite business to accomplish, for whom an assembled audience was a necessity worth insisting upon and bargaining for. Four passages are relevant to the question, two of them in the Introduction to the Pardoner's Tale:

> . . . heere at this ale-stake
> I wol bothe drynke, and eten of a cake.   VI, 321–22

> . . . but I moot thynke
> Upon som honest thyng while that I drynke.
> VI, 327–28

One occurs in the Pardoner's Prologue:

> Now have I dronke a draughte of corny ale.   VI, 456

and one at the end of the Pardoner's Tale:

> Anon they kiste, and ryden forth hir weye.   VI, 968

The assumption that the Pardoner kept his audience halted and assembled before him throughout puts no strain upon the text.

It may well be that the "moral thyng," which the "gentils" so emphatically demanded, gives the Pardoner an important additional detail for the plan he proposes to follow in his speech, in that it suggests to him that his appeal will be much stronger if he can include a definite undertone of convincing morality within

[211

the self-revelatory harangue with which he plans to lead up to his attempted sale. How skillfully he accomplishes this combination will be indicated in the discussion which follows.

Having succeeded in halting the pilgrimage and in arranging his audience so that the fullest effect can result from his speech, the Pardoner delivers 133 lines in which he frankly and boastingly reveals his methods of extracting money from peasants (VI, 329–462). It is one of my chief contentions that these 133 lines, together with the tale that follows, are accompanied by an extremely important overtone of meaning and implication whereby the Pardoner says, in effect, to the Pilgrims: "You are sophisticated citizens of the world; you know that things cannot always be as they seem. Therefore, you will enjoy a detailed recital of the tricks I use when I am at work among ignorant peasants." The Pardoner fully intends as flattering his invitation to the Pilgrims to join with him in laughing at the gullibility of peasants. It will be recalled from the portrait in the General Prologue that "feyned flaterye" is one of the two specific methods at which the Pardoner is expert (I, 705). Also, he clearly refers in two instances (VI, 392, 437) to his usual victims as "lewd peple." The Pardoner's hope is that his acceptance of the Pilgrims into his confidence, added to the admiration for his shrewdness which the revealing of his tricks will arouse, will cause many of his listeners to desire the convenient absolution which he can sell them.

Another idea which the Pardoner may well have in mind is that frequent reference to his interest in money and to his past successes in making it will be a sure way of arousing admiration for him among such people as many of the Pilgrims are. Certainly he lays great stress on this matter (VI, 389–90, 400–406, 434–35, 439–53, 461), and such an intention would fall in neatly with his larger purpose of appealing to the pretended sophistication of his listeners. Even the Narrator sounds somewhat impressed by the Pardoner's financial success (I, 701–704).

Alongside this flattering appeal to the worldliness which the Pilgrims affect, the Pardoner carefully includes one other line of thought in his prologue. This secondary approach, artfully built into his prologue by means of several brief "defenses," can be stated as follows: "I am telling you frankly that I am a vicious man who practices the very sin he preaches against. You, as citizens of the world, understand the necessity for such methods. Notice, however, that, despite my methods, the absolution which I am fully qualified to sell and which I induce many of my usual peasant listeners to buy is as efficacious as can be found anywhere." The rather illogical insertion of a statement of his theme, "*Radix malorum est Cupiditas*," into his opening description of his platform tricks (VI, 333–34) seems to be an introductory effort toward establishing this idea. Somewhat later, having given an example of his preaching and having stated that he is completely motivated by avarice, the Pardoner uses the age-old defense, "Others do the same or worse." He says:

> For certes, many a predicacioun
> Comth ofte tyme of yvel entencioun;
> Som for pleasance of folk and flaterye,
> To been avaunced by ypocrisye,
> And som for veyne glorie, and som for hate.
>
> VI, 407–11

Shortly thereafter, as a part of a passage in which he restates his theme and purpose, he boldly declares that though he is himself avaricious, he can make other folk repentant for having practiced that sin (VI, 429–30). To drive home his point, he inserts his fourth defense just before the last lines of his prologue: "For though myself be a ful vicious man,/A moral tale yet I yow telle can" (VI, 459–60).

It may be argued that the Pardoner accomplishes in his prologue the combination of flattery with "defense" which I have attributed to him. At least, no one stops or interrupts his performance. That the Pardoner himself, not too sure of the reaction of his audience, fears being silenced at this point is indicated by the line with which he concludes his prologue: "Now hoold youre pees! my tale I wol bigynne."

The Pardoner rushes immediately into his tale, which falls into four divisions: the sermon (VI, 463–915), the benediction (VI, 915–18), the attempted sale (VI, 919–45), and the quarrel with the Host (VI, 946–68). The next-to-last line of the Prologue, in which the Pardoner describes the "moral tale" he plans to tell as one which he uses frequently when preaching to "wynne"—that is, before his peasant audiences—has an important transitional purpose. Through this line he points out to the Pilgrims that the part of his speech still to come will be, like that part just completed, a report on his sly methods among his usual audiences. Thus, he offers to the Pilgrims a continued opportunity to laugh with him at the ignorant peasants, and he carries over to his sermon the same flattery which lay beneath his prologue.

There has been considerable discussion stressing the apparent clumsiness with which Chaucer has put together in the Pardoner's sermon incongruous materials from different sources and failed to cover up the joints. This view is based on two assumptions: first, that the "riotoures thre" (VI, 661) are awkwardly introduced because previous mention had been made only of "a compaignye/Of yonge folk that haunteden folye" (VI, 463–64); and second, that the material included concerning sins other than avarice represents Chaucer's carelessness, for the Pardoner definitely states that his preaching is always directed against avarice alone. The second of these assumptions can, I think, be easily refuted by repeating Sedgewick's wise observation that the Pardoner preaches to make money, not to appear logical, and therefore includes a wide sweep of usual sins—gluttony, drunkenness, swearing, and gambling—along with avarice, in order to thrust at as many potential victims as possible. The first assumption demands lengthier consideration.

The art of storytelling and the psychology of audiences are matters at which the Pardoner is an expert of long standing. He has been asked for, and has promised to deliver, a "moral tale." When he does fulfill his promise, his story will be one in which the sinners are the Younger Generation, a situation which has immediate appeal for his predominantly middle-aged listeners. That tale of the search for Death by the three rioters is not, however, the matter with which the Pardoner is most concerned at the moment. He wishes to give first a thorough preachment against the usual sins. But he knows from long experience that audiences love "tales olde" and are quickly bored by sermons against sin. Therefore, he decides to hook his imaginary peasant audience, as well as his present listeners, by extending the narrative bait included in the opening lines describing the wicked company of young folk in Flanders (VI, 463–79). In any age, these lines would sound like the typical opening for a good story about some interesting sinners. Then, having thus caught the close interest of his audience, he inserts his exhortation against the sins (VI, 480–660) before seriously beginning his purely narrative material. He has thereby avoided the risk of losing the interest of his audience by opening immediately with his survey of the sins. The brevity of this section (only 180 lines) bears witness to the Pardoner's realization of the danger of boredom for his audience inherent in such material, as do the brief narrative interpolations and illustrations within it. The skill of the transition from his narrative opening into his sermon is another matter not to be overlooked (VI, 477–84). There is not even the pause which would arise from the end of a sentence between the two sections.

Furthermore—looking now at the end of the Pardoner's harangue against the sins and at his introduction of the three rioters —it is perhaps beside the point to demand that the narrative-opening concerning the company in Flanders have close connection with the three rioters. From the Pardoner's point of view, that opening is connected with the sermon, and has served its purpose well by assuring him of his audience's close attention to that material. For his tale of the three rioters he provides a new introductory device, which also serves to call back the attention of any listeners who may have become bored with even so short an attack upon the sins: "But, sires, now wol I telle forth my tale." And in the following line, with which he begins the story, he does not say: "These three rioters of whom I told earlier"; he says: "These three rioters of whom I [shall] tell now." The Pardoner, at least, makes no effort at this point to recall the narrative-opening describing the company in Flanders, which, so far as he is concerned, has already served its purpose. He is far more interested in establishing continuity between his preachment and the conclusion to his sermon (VI, 895–915), in which he vigorously summarizes the sins against which he has spoken and

[215

then gives an example of his usual sales talk. The story of the three rioters is adroitly sandwiched between these two sections. It may well be that neither of the two assumptions which have been made in support of a claim that Chaucer has failed to cover up the joints is valid.

Earlier it was maintained that the Pardoner skillfully and purposely combines in his prologue an appeal to the affected worldliness of some of the Pilgrims with the idea that, in spite of his evil methods, absolution from him is thoroughly efficacious. In his prologue the latter idea stood in the background. Now, in his sermon, the Pardoner reverses their positions in the minds of his listeners; he uses the appeal to the Pilgrims' assumed worldliness as background, and moves to the fore the implication of the worth of what he has to offer as confessor.

The suggestion was also made earlier that the Pardoner, by means of line 461, carries over from his prologue to his sermon the invitation to the Pilgrims to continue laughing with him at the gullibility of his peasant audiences. This invitation establishes the background from which the Pilgrims view the whole sermon as his continued report of how he performs among peasants. Within this background the Pardoner is trying during his sermon to replace, in the minds of his listeners, the imaginary peasant audience with his present audience, the Pilgrims themselves. He is trying to do this for the same reason that he inserted the four "defenses" in his prologue: to establish in their minds the value and convenience of the absolution which he can sell them. He is slowly but surely bringing them to a receptive attitude for the sale which he has had in mind from the beginning. It is for this reason that the tone of the whole sermon (VI, 463–915) is so noticeably more solemn and serious than the excerpt (VI, 352–89) from one of the Pardoner's typical performances given in his prologue. The moving solemnity of the *exemplum* of the three rioters, noted by almost all who have had anything to say about the Pardoner, is itself an effort in that direction. He is now preaching with the same purpose he has always had—to make money, not alone for the sake of the money itself, but for the satisfaction of outwitting these normal people who have come into the world without his handicap. It also bears repeating here that he is now putting on a "superperformance" in an effort to advance from peasant audiences to middle-class groups, such as the Pilgrims.

Several other and less important details support the contention that the Pardoner is now preaching directly to the Pilgrims. Note the repetition of the form of address "lordynges," used first in the opening line of the Pardoner's Prologue, later in the midst of the harangue (VI, 329, 573). Such a form of address would not be usual in speaking to peasants. There is also an especial directness about the rhetorical question near the end of the story proper: "What nedeth it to sermone of it moore?" (VI, 879). Finally, the rapidity of the transition from the sermon to the story proper suggests that a desire for full effectiveness upon the present audience has become more important than an invitation to that audience to laugh at an imaginary gullible peasant group. When the story proper is completed and the Pardoner passes immediately to the conclusion of his sermon, he fully intends the powerful summary of the sins and the sales appeal to have almost as much effect on the Pilgrims as it would have had on his humbler audiences. No critic has denied that the Pardoner succeeds in creating that effect, not only on his listeners, but on his (or his creator's) readers also.

The next section of the Pardoner's performance is his benediction, which is quoted in full:

> And lo, sires, thus I preche.
> And Jhesu Crist, that is oure soules leche,
> So graunte yow his pardoun to receyve,
> For that is best; I wol yow nat deceyve.   VI, 915–18

A great part of the discussion by earlier writers concerning the character of the Pardoner has hinged around these four lines. Everyone agrees that the "And lo, sires, thus I preche" ends the pretense that the Pardoner is addressing any other audience than the Pilgrims. Now the imaginary audience is gone. Kittredge took this benediction as evidence of a moment of sincerity in the Pardoner;[10] Curry considered it a "preparation for his proposed masterstroke of deception";[11] Carleton Brown saw it as merely

---

[10] *Atlantic Monthly*, LXXII (1893), 831–32. See also Robinson, *Works*, 837.
[11] Curry, *Sciences*, 66–67.

the expected grave ending to the sermon;[12] and Sedgewick believed it to be a traditional and sincere farewell.[13]

Most of the critics take the lines of the benediction as meaning something about as follows: "The pardon which I hope Jesus Christ will grant you is better than mine; I will not deceive you who are my friends, as I have deceived former audiences." But perhaps the lines do not mean that at all. The assumption that the Pardoner suggests, by saying "Christ's pardon is better than mine," that he holds a position similar to Christ's but has inferior wares seems to me rather illogical. All absolution came ultimately from Christ, no matter if His agent was pardoner, friar, parish priest, or any other qualified individual. It is also difficult to believe that the Pardoner, having just worked so hard to replace, in the minds of his listening Pilgrims, the imaginary peasant audience with themselves, would intentionally toss away that advantage by recalling to them his humbler victims. Perhaps the benediction is really an even better preparation for the coming attempted sale than Curry claimed. The line "And lo, sires, thus I preche," which serves as transition between the sermon and the benediction, need not mean primarily: "There, ladies and gentlemen, I have shown you how I outwit gullible peasants." Rather, it may be aimed more at calling the Pilgrims' attention in retrospect to the good which the Pardoner accomplishes among his usual peasant audiences and can accomplish, despite his evil methods, among his present listeners. It is his preaching which he mentions specifically, not his "skinning" the gullible, and he has earlier made quite clear that much worthwhile preaching comes from "yvel entencioun," and that folk do give up their sins because of his preaching. Thus, with this one line, the Pardoner causes the picture of the peasant audience to fade entirely from the minds of his listeners, and brings fully to the foreground the value of what he has to offer. To emphasize this idea and to complete the foundation for his coming attempt to sell, he delivers the next three lines, the kind of traditional and fitting ending for his sermon that the Pilgrims would expect. The seemingly sincere devotion implied by these last three lines increases greatly their effectiveness on the Pilgrims. The Pardoner

[12] *The Pardoner's Tale,* xxiv–xxv.   [13] *Loc. cit.,* 450–51.

mentions that Christ is the true physician of "oure soules," and expresses the wish that He will grant His best-of-all pardons to the Pilgrims. The implication which stands out boldly in this traditional, expected, devout, and apparently sincere wish is that the Pilgrims should win Christ's best-of-all pardons through the medium of His agent the Pardoner, who is not only thoroughly qualified and readily available, but is also a "good fellow," the kind of spiritual guide who can "understand" such sophisticated citizens of the world as are many of the Pilgrims. Then, as a last clinching blow in his preparation for the attempted sale, he assures his listeners in the most straightforward way—not by indirection as in his earlier comments—that there will be no chicanery to have an ill effect on the value of the absolution he can sell them: "I wol yow nat deceyve." Certainly, the futurity included in this statement indicates that the Pardoner hopes to have further dealings with his listeners.

We should now recall that, as long ago as his interruption of the Wife, the Pardoner may have selected the Host, as the member of the company most filled with certain pretensions, for his most likely victim. Further, Harry's position as "gyde," "governour," "juge," and "reportour" would have suggested him to the Pardoner as the wisest choice for his first potential victim; if Harry sought absolution from the Pardoner, there would be a not inconsiderable number of the other Pilgrims who probably would follow suit.

We come now to the Pardoner's attempted sale.[14] Having skillfully maneuvered the Pilgrims into what he justly considered a receptive mood, the Pardoner offers his wares. Up to this point, if one accepts the interpretation presented above, the Pardoner has been completely successful. The attempt is, however, not a success. It is true, of course, that to a certain extent "poetic justice" dictates to Chaucer that such an individual as the Par-

---

[14] Sedgewick considers the attempted sale and the quarrel as a unit, which he calls the "afterthought." It may be observed that to use this term is to beg the question of what the Pardoner had in mind. Here, as in Sedgewick's earlier similar begging of the question by use of the term "Tavern Heresy," the matter is open to dispute.

doner must come to grief. But that is not an explanation of how the Pardoner fails; it is merely a demand that the Pardoner's failure be interpreted in the light of his previous words and actions. It is necessary, therefore, to examine carefully the nature of the attempted sale and to point out in detail just where the Pardoner erred.

Following the benediction, he says that he has forgotten to mention one thing: he has his relics and pardons from the Pope's hand with him (VI, 919–22). Then he issues a general invitation to the whole group to come up and buy his pardons now, or to "taketh pardoun" while traveling "at every miles ende" (VI, 922–30). Next, he stresses his qualifications and the convenience to the Pilgrims of his presence—a good appeal, he thinks, to a would-be worldly audience (VI, 931–40). Finally, he specifically invites the Host "to offre first anon" (VI, 941–45).

What methods has Chaucer used here to bring about the Pardoner's failure? An explanation lies, I think, in the fact that the Pardoner foolishly breaks the spell which his sermon and benediction have cast upon the Pilgrims; reverting in this crucial moment to his habitual methods among peasants, he establishes an atmosphere too undignified to be at all flattering in its appeal to his listeners. Note how the opening line, "But, sires, o word forgat I in my tale," with its reference to the mechanics of his speech, dispels the serious and solemn effect resulting from the sermon and the benediction. Omit that line and the spell is not broken. Second, the general invitation to take pardon at every mile's end is too jocular for acceptance by the Pilgrims. It is doubtful that the Pardoner meant for his listeners to take this invitation literally, as numerous critics have done; but he would have had more chance of success if he had changed "al newe and fressh at every miles ende" to "whenever you wish." Third, the illustration suggesting a possible fatal fall from a horse, by which the Pardoner is trying to emphasize the convenience for the Pilgrims of his presence on the pilgrimage, is too implausible and macabre to please his audience. He should have omitted that illustration altogether (VI, 935–40), for the Pilgrims surely understood by now that his services were readily available. Fourth, the whole of the specific invitation to the Host is badly done. The tone of that invitation should have been sincere and devout rather than bantering. There is no reason for him to state why the Host has been selected to offer first (VI, 941). The suggestion of kissing the relics (VI, 944), implying gullibility and superstition, should have been omitted. Also, there should have been no direct mention of money in the invitation to the Host; high regard for a "grote" is one of Harry's predominant traits.

It is here that we see the Pardoner's unintentional self-revelation of his inadequacy as a salesman. Among ignorant peasants he is a master of the psychology of supersalesmanship; but among his companions on the pilgrimage he fails. Despite a brilliant performance in laying the foundation for his attempted sale, the Pardoner fails because he reverts at the crucial moment, perhaps through force of habit or overconfidence, or perhaps through nervousness caused by the importance success in this venture had assumed in his mind, to the same crude level of appeal which he was accustomed to employ in his sales talks among peasants. Certainly the similarity in tone and structure between his benediction and attempted sale to the Pilgrims (VI, 916–45), on the one hand, and his typical sales talk to a peasant audience (VI, 904–15), on the other, is striking. The key to the dramatic structure of the Pardoner's performance lies, I think, in this explanation of his failure.

The last glimpse of the Pardoner comes in his quarrel with the Host, which follows the frustrated sale. Here Harry looses a vigorous stream of abuse upon the Pardoner. It is noteworthy that Harry's first statement in support of his refusal to "offre" is a negation (VI, 948–50) of the true worth of the Pardoner's absolution, the idea which the Pardoner had suggested indirectly in his prologue and had brought to the fore in his sermon. Then Harry makes the sharpest possible counterattack by direct reference to the Pardoner's physical misfortune. The Pardoner is speechless with anger, and the Host refuses to "pleye" any longer with him. The Knight settles the quarrel and forces the Host to kiss the Pardoner. With peace restored, the members of the company regain their usual merriment and "riden forth hir weye."

One critic saw in the Pardoner's being speechless with anger after the Host's abuse an evidence of disgust with his own evil

Y delnesse is roten slogardye

ways. Others have set forth the likelier explanation whereby the Pardoner is quite understandably speechless with anger because of the direct references to his being a eunuch. There is, in addition to this cause for his anger, the quick realization that his own bungling of the sale brought about the failure of his carefully laid and tested plan. By stupidly reverting to his habitual level of appeal, the Pardoner robbed himself of the satisfaction of outwitting the Pilgrims and thereby progressing to a class of victims higher than his usual peasant audiences.

20. THE SECOND NUN

The Second Nun receives only brief mention in the General Prologue. At the end of the Prioress' sketch come the lines: "Another Noone with hire hadde she,/That was hir chapeleyne, and preestes thre" (I, 163–64). A traveling prioress was required to have at least one nun in attendance, and the attendant nun usually served as chaplain or secretary.[1]

Whatever characteristics Chaucer might have decided to give the Second Nun had he completed the *Canterbury Tales*, it is doubtful that he could have assigned material more suitable for her to relate to the company of Pilgrims than the prologue and tale she delivers in Fragment VIII. Her prologue begins with four stanzas on idleness, which seem to be original with Chaucer; then come eight stanzas which form the Invocation to Mary "based primarily on St. Bernard's prayer at the beginning of Canto xxxiii of Dante's Paradiso." The last five stanzas of the prologue present etymological interpretations of Cecilia's name and come from the *Legenda Aurea*.[2] The Second Nun says that

[1] Eileen Power, *Medieval English Nunneries c. 1275 to 1535*, pp. 62–64; F. J. Furnivall, *Anglia*, IV (1881), 238–40.

[2] My summary of sources is based on the chapter by G. H. Gerould in *Sources and Analogues*, 664–84. See also Mary-Virginia Rosenfeld, *MLN*, LV (1940), 357–59; J. S. P. Tatlock, *MLN*, XLV (1930), 296–98.

she has both "the wordes and sentence/Of hym that at the sein-
tes reverence/The storie wroot" (VIII, 81–83), and a rubric
found in two manuscripts suggests that Jacobus de Voragine is
the writer of the Legend of Saint Cecilia to whom the Second
Nun refers. However, as Professor Gerould has pointed out, in
our present state of ignorance about the manuscript history of
the *Legenda Aurea* we cannot be sure just what Chaucer's copy
of the *Golden Legend* contained.[3]

This last point has important meaning for our present concern
with the workings of Chaucer's dramatic principle. Almost without exception scholars have considered the Second Nun's Tale a
translation which Chaucer did long before he had the idea for
the *Canterbury Tales*, and which he later thrust into his collection without any effort to adapt it to its teller.[4] One point regularly cited in support of this view is that Chaucer is here translat-
ing very closely from the original; therefore, since we think that
he did a number of other close translations early in his writing
career, it is argued that the Second Nun's Tale must also be an
early work. But if, as Gerould stated, we cannot be sure about the
exact make-up of Chaucer's source in this case, then we cannot
say definitely that the Second Nun's Tale is a close translation;
thus one part of the argument for Chaucer's not having adapted
the tale to its teller appears premature.

There is, however, one other claim that is always advanced to
show that Chaucer did not prepare the Legend of Saint Cecilia
especially for the Second Nun to relate to the Pilgrims. In line
62 of her prologue the Second Nun calls herself "unworthy sone
of Eve," and therefore it is regularly assumed that Chaucer assigned the story first to a man. Several scholars have even suggested that "sone" meant Chaucer himself when he translated
the legend as a part of his earlier work and that he failed to make
the necessary revision when he assigned the tale to the Second
Nun. Recently, however, W. B. Gardner has shown—convincingly, I think—that the words "sone of Eve" are not inappropriate in the mouth of the Second Nun.[5] He says:

[3] *Sources and Analogues*, 670.
[4] See, for example, Robinson, *Works*, 15, 862.
[5] University of Texas *Studies in English*, XXVI (1947), 77–83.

When Chaucer had the Second Nun refer to herself as a "sone of Eve," he was merely using a word-pattern from the *Salve Regina* which he knew every Religious actually used every day of her life in reciting the Divine Office whether in Latin or English: "Hail, quene, modir of merci, oure liyf, oure swetnesse & oure hope, hail! to thee we crien, exciled sones of eue." The most natural thing in the world was to have the Second Nun at the height of her panegyric to the Virgin use a phrase taken from a prayer with which she was most familiar. . . . To have the Second Nun at the height of her impassioned prayer revert to a familiar word-pattern, change it from the plural to the singular, and refer to herself as "unworthy sone of Eve" is another example of Chaucer's genius for molding old matter into imperishably new forms.

It seems, then, that the "sone of Eve" may as easily mean "child of Eve," and therefore the second part of the charge that Chaucer did not adapt the tale to the Second Nun is also doubtful.

Turning to the positive side of the situation, we find that Chaucer fittingly assigned to the Second Nun not just any saint's life but the life of a female saint. Legouis enumerated several other details peculiar to this particular saint's life which suit it to a nun:

The impassioned eulogy to virginity preserved even after marriage, the ironical and half hysterical outburst of the saint before a kindly judge, the intemperate virtue and holiness depicted to us—all this becomes, as it were, the expression of the fanatic Nun, and ceases to have an imperative significance outside her. It is less the truthful account of the life of a saint than the truthful revelation, by means of this account, of the feelings of a nun and of the atmosphere which reigns in a monastery.[6]

While Legouis' statement may be somewhat exaggerated, it is nevertheless true that this particular saint's life is far better suited for recital by a nun than many another saint's life would have been. And there is no reason for us, perhaps too hastily, to deprive Chaucer of credit for bringing about this dramatic suitability.[7]

[6] Émile Legouis, *Geoffrey Chaucer* (English trans.), 185.
[7] See Gardner's article cited in n. 5 of this section(pp. 82–83); Sister Mary Hostia, *College English*, XIV (1953), 351–52.

That slidynge science hath me maad so bare

21. THE CANON'S YEOMAN

When the Second Nun completes her life of St. Cecilia, there occurs one of the liveliest events of the whole pilgrimage. Two additional travelers join the company: a canon, who is an alchemist, and his yeoman, or servant. The resulting performance, which has been the subject of relatively little critical comment, is representative of Chaucer's art at its best, and no source has been discovered for either the Canon's Yeoman's autobiographical revelations or his tale proper.[1] Perhaps there is no reason to look farther than the contemporary scene as sufficient explanation for the presence of this material. Although the history of alchemy in the fourteenth century is far from clear, we do know that this "science" was widely practiced in England during Chaucer's time—in fact, strict laws prohibiting it were passed early in the fifteenth century—and there is even a record of a contemporary canon at Windsor, William Shuchirch, an alchemist, who has been named as a possible model for the canon in the Yeoman's story. These facts have led to various suggestions that Chaucer, as an afterthought, included the Canon's Yeoman's performance in the *Canterbury* collection as a satirical exposé of all alchemy, or as an attack on false alchemists and a defense of true practitioners of this science, because he was himself fleeced by Shuchirch when he invested money in a similar get-rich-quick scheme.[2]

Such speculations seem to me very tenuous, however, for there is no particular reason to believe that Chaucer did not plan the addition of the Canon and his Yeoman to the group from the time

[1] See the chapter by J. W. Spargo in *Sources and Analogues*, 685–94.
[2] Thomas Tyrwhitt, *Canterbury Tales*, IV, 181; H. G. Richardson, *Transactions of the Royal Historical Society*, Ser. 4, V (1922), 38–39; S. F. Damon, *PMLA*, XXXIX (1924), 782–88; Manly, *New Light*, 235–52.

he hit upon his general scheme for the *Tales*;[3] and the argument
that *Pars Secunda* must have been written for another purpose
before the Yeoman was created, and then poorly adapted to him,[4]
is completely unconvincing. This argument rests on two suppo-
sitions. First, it is maintained that lines VIII, 992–1011 could be
appropriately addressed only to a group of canons, of which there
are none among the Canterbury company. But, as one commentator has observed,[5] these lines do not seem incongruous when
viewed as a rhetorical device employed by the Yeoman to emphasize the treachery of the canon in his tale, and such a device
is paralleled by the Physician's apostrophe to governesses and
parents (VI, 72–104), and by the Nun's Priest's appeal to lords
(VII, 3325–30). The second supposition is that the conclusion
of this performance (VIII, 1388–1481) is, because of its learned
nature, not acceptable as coming from an ignorant, impetuous,
loquacious fool like the Yeoman. This contention is obviously
dependent upon the estimate one makes of the Yeoman, and, as
the most recent writer to treat the matter in detail has shown, the
Yeoman is not elsewhere unacquainted with learned material.[6]

In any event, the chief necessity here is not to decide upon possible connections between the Canon's Yeoman's performance
and Chaucer's biography, but to analyze the dramatic techniques
which Chaucer employed in making this performance come
alive. As usual, the central emphasis is steadily kept upon the
character of the teller. The Canon's Yeoman's story of a treacherous alchemist inevitably fits into, and grows out of, the context
provided by the dramatic antagonism that he feels against "this
cursed craft" and its practitioners, in general, and against his
master, in particular. Yet, by the difference between the major
theme of his performance and the theme which he thinks he is
emphasizing most strongly, the Yeoman unintentionally reveals
more of his own state of mind than he intends. Even though he admits his own folly in continuing to work at alchemy, he seems to
aim primarily at showing that alchemists are treacherous evil-

[3] G. L. Kittredge, *Transactions* of the Royal Society of Literature (London), XXX
(1940), 87; O. F. Emerson, *PQ*, II (1923), 94–96.

[4] P. F. Baum, *MLN*, XL (1925), 152–54.

[5] Robinson, *Works*, 868.

[6] E. H. Duncan, *MP*, XXXVII (1939–40), 241–62.

doers who make dupes of poor innocents like himself, and little is said of the innocents' greed; but his autobiographical prologue and his narrative proper make more clearly evident the fact that anyone whose greed leads him into being victimized by alchemists is behaving in an exceedingly stupid manner. We shall now see in some detail how this disclosure is worked out.

First of all, note the skill with which Chaucer in the first twenty-seven lines builds up our interest in, and curiosity about, the two newcomers by having us view the fast-approaching Canon and his servant through the curious eyes of the Narrator as he rapidly observes each detail of their horses, baggage, and dress in an effort to decide just who and what they are. We follow this observation point by point until the Narrator concludes that the former must be "som chanoun" (VIII, 569–73). Our chief impression from these introductory lines is that the Canon and his Yeoman have had to flee pursuers, for the Canon is traveling light, and the Narrator dwells with pleasure, in his realistic, earthy description, upon the way the horses and men are sweating from hard riding.[7] But, in greeting the company, the Canon gives no hint of such flight. He explains the hard riding as the result of his desire to join such a "myrie compaignye," and his Yeoman supports this statement by remarking that the Canon "loveth daliaunce." The Host, ever eager to take advantage of an opportunity to increase the jollity of the trip, asks the Yeoman whether or not his master can tell a good tale or two. The Yeoman's answer is emphatically affirmative, but he quickly passes into his routine speech aimed at stirring up some alchemical business for the Canon. With confidential vagueness the Yeoman tells Harry that the Canon is a man of great skill, who can carry out large and important enterprises, a man from whose acquaintance Harry can profit; and, the Yeoman points out, the humility with which the Canon rides in this group should not lead Harry to underrate him.

The Host, though the first man to be interested in a profit, is impatient with such vague claims and bluntly asks whether the Canon is a cleric or what. The Yeoman continues in his previous vein and states that his master is much greater than any cleric,

[7] G. R. Coffman, *MLN*, LIX (1944), 269–71.

and, moving on to specific illustration for this point, says that the Canon has secret skills that would enable him to turn the road from here to Canterbury upside down and "pave it al of silver and of gold." This extravagant assertion strains Harry's credulity, for, in his experience, men who can command wealth dress the part; therefore, he wants to know why the Canon's clothes are so cheap, tattered, and dirty if he can afford better.

This question causes the Yeoman to change his tune completely, and in his answer we first glimpse his disturbed mental state:

> Why? . . . wherto axe ye me?
> God help me so, for he shal nevere thee!
> (But I wol nat avowe that I seye,
> And therfore keepe it secree, I yow preye.)
> He is to wys, in feith, as I bileeve.
> That that is overdoon, it wol nat preeve
> Aright, as clerkes seyn; it is a vice.
> Wherfore in that I holde hym lewed and nyce.
> For whan a man hath over-greet a wit,
> Ful oft hym happeth to mysusen it.
> So dooth my lord, and that me greveth soore;
> God it amende! I kan sey yow namoore.
>
> VIII, 640–51

Obviously this yeoman is brimful of complaints against his master, complaints which only his fear compels him to withhold. But the Host is now sure that he has hit upon a source of good fun, and, after flattering the Yeoman a bit, asks for further information: "Where dwelle ye, if it to telle be?" Throwing aside all discretion, the Yeoman says that they have to hide in corners and alleys like thieves. At once Harry is in full chase and quickly attempts to draw more facts from the Yeoman by asking why his face is so discolored. The latter proceeds to give details of his work, and it becomes fully clear that the Canon is an alchemist. The Yeoman's job has been to blow the fire, but always the experiments fail.

The Canon understandably does not like such talk and commands his servant to be silent. But the Host, delighted at the progress of events, urges the Yeoman to take no notice of the

Canon's threats. Reassured by Harry's support, the Yeoman decides to rebel against the Canon's command. At this, the Canon "fledde awey for verray sorwe and shame." Now that he is firmly established in the center of the stage, the Yeoman promises to tell the company all that he knows about alchemy.

At the end of this introductory scene, we glimpse another important aspect of the Yeoman's state of mind (VIII, 708–19). Here we see that he is pulled by two opposing forces: he is disgusted with himself for being connected with such a bootless game as alchemy (VIII, 710); yet it holds such fascination for him that he cannot give it up (VIII, 712–14). But he does not want to accept full responsibility for his situation; in fact, he blames the alchemist who first brought him into this work (VIII, 708–709). The opposing forces have built up considerable tension within the Yeoman, tension which causes him to undertake this rebellion against his master; and the two parts of his performance can best be regarded as his method of resolving the inner conflict and releasing this tension.

In *Prima Pars* the Yeoman shows the complete hopelessness of achieving the alchemical goal and the consequent folly of staying in that game. In this autobiographical confession he combines personal details and reactions (VIII, 720–49, 830–51, 862–97, 962–71) with a chronological account of a notable failure to "multiplie" (VIII, 750–829, 852–61, 898–961). He makes easily apparent his own gullibility and seems to feel himself therefore less blameworthy than his audience may have earlier considered him. He also includes another reference to the bittersweet fascination which alchemy holds (VIII, 877–83). Consequently, by the time he reaches the end of *Prima Pars*, he is able to suggest that the blame in the chicanery he has just described should be attached not at all to him but to his lord, the Canon, who was, of course, the master of ceremonies for the experiment (VIII, 960–71). In fact, the Yeoman claims here that the Canon—who seemed wisest and truest—is in the last analysis a fool and a thief. But, most certainly, someone among the Canterbury Pilgrims must have thought to himself at this point that the Yeoman is the greater fool and an equal thief for continuing to take part in alchemical experiments.

Pars Secunda, the Yeoman's Tale proper, illustrates further the perfidy of alchemists. Here a canon who, the Yeoman says, knows a hundred times more "subtiltee" than the Canon whom we saw momentarily on the pilgrimage (VIII, 1088–92), dupes a priest. The Yeoman's sympathy is wholly with the priest; he heaps an inordinate amount of invective upon the alchemist, with but slight mention of the priest's stupidity and avariciousness. Actually, however, the priest well deserves the treachery he receives. This priest is an "annueleer" who has lived in London for many years, and who is "so plesaunt and so servysable" to the woman with whom he boards that she does not charge him for his meals and clothes, and presumably furnishes him with sufficient "spendyng silver" (VIII, 1012–18). But the Yeoman, who sounds a bit envious of the cleric's situation, does not want to direct attention to the priest's shallowness and greed; he therefore says quickly: "Therof no fors" (VIII, 1019). The point, of course, is that the Yeoman is trying to impress the company with the evil represented by the canon, hoping thereby to shift attention from his own greed, which certainly matches that of the duped priest. We find little difficulty, however, in seeing the Yeoman and the priest as rogues potentially equal to the two canons.

In the last section of his performance (VIII, 1388–1481), the Canon's Yeoman rises to a climax in denouncing alchemy. "Multiplying" is the cause of great scarcity of gold; philosophers are so vague that no alchemist will ever be successful in discovering their secret. "This lusty game" makes men unhappy and poor, and all who meddle with alchemy should at once leave it. To prove these points the Yeoman says: "I wol yow tellen heere/ What philosophres seyn in this mateere." He then quotes Arnoldus de Villa Nova and Hermes Trismegistus and tells a story involving Plato, to show that the secret of the philosophers' stone cannot be discovered.

The Yeoman's familiarity here with learned material does not fit the conception of him, held by a number of critics,[8] as an ignorant, garrulous fool who on the pilgrimage holds the center of the stage for the first time in his life, and enjoys pouring forth

[8] See, for example, Manly, *New Light*, 239.

helter-skelter, without understanding them, the tags of alchemical knowledge which he has managed to pick up. As a matter of
fact, the technical talk of alchemy in *Prima Pars* is well organ-
ized and shows considerable understanding of the accepted steps
in the process.[9] Also, the Yeoman's entire performance follows a
careful pattern aimed at shifting the responsibility for his own
connection with alchemy. He is not at all the unschooled dolt
some commentators have made him out.

His performance concludes with the following lines:

> Thanne conclude I thus, sith that God of hevene
> Ne wil nat that the philosophres nevene
> How that a man shal come unto this stoon,
> I rede, as for the beste, lete it goon.
> For whoso maketh God his adversarie,
> As for to werken any thyng in contrarie
> Of his wil, certes, never shal he thryve,
> Thogh that he multiplie terme of his lyve.
> And there a poynt; for ended is my tale.
> God sende every trewe man boote of his bale! Amen.
>
> VIII, 1472–81

When we think back over the Yeoman's whole recital, this passage has a definitely uncalled-for moral smugness about it. The
Yeoman, who is not a "trewe man," has devoted his meager funds
and his constant labor to alchemy for at least seven years, and we
have had a sample of his usual method of enticing others into his
master's trap. Further, he has stated that the game so fascinates
him—presumably by its appeal to his greedy desire to get rich
quick—that he can never give it up. In addition, he has throughout his performance attempted to suggest a picture of himself as
the poor innocent led astray by him "that me broghte first unto
that game," and by his master, the Canon. The Yeoman is certainly a wonderfully entertaining fellow, who gives an excellent
performance for the Pilgrims, but a full estimate of his character
produces an individual torn between his awareness of the inevitable failure of the alchemical experiments, and his ever-present
greedy hope for success. His autobiographical confession and

[9] See the article by Duncan cited in n. 6 of this section.

Ay biforn and in good staat

illustrative tale represent his effort to clear himself of guilt, but Chaucer has skillfully manipulated him into revealing to the Pilgrims and to us more of his real character than he intends.

22. THE MANCIPLE

Although some critics find no indication that the tale of the talkative crow was written for the Manciple,[1] there is what seems to me good evidence here of Chaucer's usual concern for dramatic suitability.[2] In brief, the situation is this: the Manciple is given to dishonest dealings, of which the Cook is aware; by foolishly talking in such a way as to arouse the Cook's anger, he risks having his dishonesty made public by the Cook; he then tells a tale the theme of which "exalts expediency rather than morality." Thus not only is the tale a suitable one for its teller in this situation, but it also functions dramatically as a part of the Manciple's effort to smooth over his quarrel with the Cook.

From the sketch in the General Prologue (I, 567–86) we learn that the Manciple works in one of the Inns of Court in London. His job is probably "to stock the buttery; to attend the cook; to examine and keep account of the meat bought, and to see that there was no waste of it; to collect money from the lawyers and students who ate in Commons."[3] Furthermore, we have the individualizing fact that this particular Manciple makes money dishonestly by "padding" his accounts; in fact, he "sets the caps" of all his more than thirty masters, even though a dozen of them are capable of managing the largest estate in England:

[1] For example, Robinson, *Works*, 16, 870.
[2] My treatment of the Manciple and his recital depends heavily upon the essay by J. B. Severs, *JEGP*, LI (1952), 1–16, which includes references to the earlier discussions. For a different view, see Wayne Shumaker, *UTQ*, XXII (1953), 147–56.
[3] Bowden, *Commentary*, 257.

> Now is nat that of God a ful fair grace
> That swich a lewed mannes wit shal pace
> The wisdom of an heep of lerned men?   I, 573–75

Since a manciple would have regular supervisory duties over a cook, and more particularly since a manciple in Chaucer's day would have had to buy his provisions from a cookshop, neither the Cook's knowledge of the Manciple's chicanery nor the antagonism between the Manciple and the Cook, which appears in the Manciple's Prologue (IX, 1–104), is difficult to accept.[4] In that prologue the Cook is so drunk that he cannot stay awake, keep up with the group, or sit his horse securely. The Host, who also has professional reasons for seeking any opportunity to ridicule the Cook, notices his condition, calls on him to tell a tale, and then jokes at his drunken sleepiness, even suggesting that he may have spent the night with "som quene." The Cook rallies enough to say that his only desire is to sleep. At this point, the Manciple steps in with mock courtesy and humility to inform the Cook that he will be glad to tell a tale in order to do him a service. But the Manciple goes on to berate the Cook roundly for having a breath which "stynketh," and for being ridiculously drunk. Such talk can easily give rise to anger.

The Cook is still sufficiently aware of what is going on to take offense at the Manciple's jibes. In anger he swings at the Manciple but topples ingloriously from his horse: "This was a fair chyvachee of a cook!" Now comes one of the funniest scenes in the *Canterbury Tales*, when the other Pilgrims labor mightily to get the drunken Cook out of the mire and back on his horse. After this has been accomplished, Harry Bailly apparently feels that it is time to restore order. He therefore states that the Cook is too drunk to tell a decent tale and instructs the Manciple to begin his story. But the Host cannot let pass this opportunity to reprove the Manciple for talking too much. He therefore says:

> But yet, Manciple, in feith thou art to nyce,
> Thus openly repreve hym of his vice.
> Another day he wole, peraventure,

[4] Frederick Tupper, *JEGP*, XIV (1915), 261–65.

> Reclayme thee and brynge thee to lure;
> I meene, he speke wole of smale thynges,
> As for to pynchen at thy rekenynges.
> That were nat honest, if it cam to preef.   IX, 69–75

Harry knows that the Manciple overcharges the lawyers whom he serves, and the Host also is aware that the Cook knows this. Here is indeed a tightly knit group of city businessmen. The Manciple, quick to realize the folly of his talking so belligerently, claims that he berated the Cook in jest only. He takes further steps to make sure that he has not permanently estranged the Cook, and, to insure peace, offers him a drink of wine, though he remarks to Harry, presumably not in the Cook's hearing, that it will be a good joke to give the drunken Cook another drink. He very willingly takes the drink and, in perfect keeping with his present state of intoxication, seems to have forgotten completely his anger at the Manciple. After the drink he thanks the Manciple as if the latter were his one true friend. At this, Harry roars with laughter, lauds the efficacy of "good drynke," and asks the Manciple to tell his tale. The Manciple, having furnished a drink for the Cook, might well have felt that the latter's ire was adequately soothed. He seems desirous, however, of making clear to the company by means of his tale that he has learned a lesson, and that he will not in the future again run the risk of exposure because of excessive talk. Thus it is that he tells the story of the crow whose talking brings on misfortunes, and that he concludes his story with an unusually long section on the advantages of keeping one's mouth shut.

For the Manciple's little tale of Phebus and the crow that talks too much, we have no certain source. Chaucer could have used almost any Ovidian text for the story proper, and the material included in the several moralizing digressions which the Manciple inserts into the tale was common property in the Middle Ages.[5] When Phebus' wife is unfaithful while he is away, the crow tells his master of her act. In anger Phebus kills his wife, and in grief

---

[5] See Gardiner Stillwell, *PQ*, XIX (1940), 133–38; the chapter by J. A. Work in *Sources and Analogues*, 699–722; and the article by Severs cited in n. 2 of this section.

and remorse then turns upon the crow as treacherous informer. He makes the white crow black, deprives it of speech, and slings it out of the house.

Now comes the Manciple's lengthy concluding statement stressing the moral "Kepe wel thy tonge, and thenk upon the crowe." Apparently, the Manciple has told a story the theme of which can be aptly applied to his own near disaster from talking too much in the preceding argument with the Cook. By means of the tale the Manciple as much as says: "I have learned my lesson; not holding my tongue almost led to the Cook's exposing my business activities." The story thus plays an important part in the drama of the Cook-Manciple controversy. Also such a statement in praise of expediency comes naturally from a man steadily engaged in a war of wits with his master-lawyers.

Several other aspects of this performance deserve notice here. One critic observed: "The general theme of the 'Manciple's Tale' is suitable to its narrator. But the Greek setting, the rather learned rhetorical development, and the moral disquisition are completely incongruous with the dishonest Manciple."[6] This view, it seems to me, is greatly overstated. The "Greek setting" of the tale is almost nonexistent. True, the story is about Phebus, and a number of his exploits are mentioned. But the name of his wife is not included, and the whole is cast into the form of a late medieval fabliau of cuckoldry, with the addition of an unusual amount of trite, sententious comment. Certainly the Manciple is a suitable teller for a story of cuckolding. Furthermore, the digressive comment on the folly of jealously guarding wives, on the perversity of both animal and human natural desires, on the necessity for plain speech, and on the danger of talking too much does more to mar the rhetorical development of the narrative than to give it a learned air. In fact, the Manciple's learning—represented only by his naming Plato, Solomon, David, and Seneca, by his monitory tone, by his knowledge of this story, and by his references to the "olde clerkes" and their writings—is easily explained by his steady association with lawyers, as is his glib familiarity with the phrase "noght textueel" (IX, 235, 316). A man shrewd enough to keep his financial dealings hidden from more

[6] J. R. Hulbert, *SP*, XLV (1948), 576.

than thirty lawyers could easily pick up such matters as these without any studying at all. Also, the moral disquisition, as was suggested above, results understandably from the Manciple's effort to show the company that he realizes the error of his quarreling with the Cook.

At other points in the tale we find touches perfectly suited to the "lewed" Manciple. After citing the "ensaumples" of the bird, the cat, and the she-wolf, he illogically states that he is talking only of unfaithful men, "and nothyng by wommen" (IX, 188); yet this story is of an unfaithful wife. A few lines later he indulges in a kind of exaggerated gentility when he apologizes for saying the word "lemman" (IX, 205); if this word was generally considered shocking, the Middle English audience must have been shocked with great regularity. The point is that the story does not at all have the ring of a learned teller.

23. THE PARSON

The Parson's Tale, the last[1] and longest performance in the *Canterbury* collection, is a prose sermon on penitence, into which is inserted a lengthy treatise on the seven deadly sins. For this piece, no direct source has been found.[2] That such a sermon is suited to the admirable Parish Priest permits no argument, and we are able here to see clearly just how Chaucer fitted the tale into the framework of a dramatic antagonism, which exists between the Parson and the Host. In this antagonism the tale proper functions as a whole; its very nature accomplishes its purpose in the controversy.

The Parish Priest is, of course, Chaucer's most sympathetic pic-

[1] On the presence and position of the Parson's Tale in the *Canterbury* collection, see W. W. Lawrence, *Chaucer and the Canterbury Tales*, chap. vi.
[2] See the chapter by Germaine Dempster in *Sources and Analogues*. 723–60.

ture of a contemporary churchman (I, 477–528). There has been extensive discussion, based in part on this sketch, as to whether or not Chaucer was a Wycliffite, and as to the extent to which he was familiar with, and sympathetic towards, the Lollard reforms widely urged during the late fourteenth century. Although this argument ranges from the claim that Chaucer's Parson is Wycliffe to the opinion that Chaucer was almost completely untouched by the religious ferment of his day, the point at issue is not of fundamental importance here. For us, the interesting aspect of the sketch is that in the character of the Parson strict observance of his duties as priest is blended with kindly tolerance and understanding. Though properly poor in material wealth, he is rich in holy thoughts and works. His wide learning he uses in devoutly teaching his parishioners, and no obstacle keeps him from visiting the most distant houses in his wide parish, "Upon his feet, and in his hand a staf," no matter whether the person visited is rich or poor. He believes firmly in setting a good example for his flock by his own actions and does not rent out his parish in order to live luxuriously in London, for "He was a shepherde and noght a mercenarie." Corruption seems to have been generally present throughout the fourteenth-century Church, but one may feel fairly confident that this parson's vigorous and exemplary devotion to duty prevented its flourishing in his parish.

Somewhat surprisingly, the Parson's absolute seriousness about his work is accompanied by unusual generosity, patience, tolerance, and humility. In an era when most parish priests seemed primarily interested in the financial benefits to be gained from their positions, the Parson is very hesitant to excommunicate his parishioners for nonpayment of tithes; instead, realizing the hard lot of the peasants who make up his flock, he often gives them a part of his own income, for "He koude in litel thyng have suffisaunce." And in times of trouble he is noted for his patient suffering. Despite his personal holiness and virtue, he does not treat sinners scornfully or speak to them in severe and haughty tones. Nor does he pretend to an overly refined conscience. On the contrary, in his handling of sinners he shows extreme consideration, in an effort to lead them by his own example to a better way

First he wroghte, and afterward he taughte

of life. Yet the Parson is no weakling when occasion demands forcefulness:

> But it were any persone obstinat,
> What so he were, of heigh or lough estat,
> Hym wolde he snybben sharply for the nonys.
>
> I, 521–23

He exhibits no trace of subservience when dealing with the rich and mighty; "But Cristes loore and his apostles twelve/He taughte, but first he folwed it hymselve." Truly the Parson's combination of active devotion with kindly tolerance merits Chaucer's emphatic statement: "A bettre preest I trowe that nowher noon ys."

Although he must not have been particularly pleased with the performances of the Miller, the Reeve, and the Cook, we hear nothing from the Parson until the Host addresses him after the Lawyer's Tale. With what seems a deliberate effort to provoke him to anger, Harry says:

> Sir Parisshe Prest, . . . for Goddes bones,
> Telle us a tale, as was thi forward yore.
> I se wel that ye lerned men in lore
> Can moche good, by Goddes dignitee!   II, 1166–69

But the Parson is too wise and experienced to furnish the Host the satisfaction of seeing him moved to anger by either his blasphemy or condescension. Instead of lecturing briskly, he briefly and skillfully throws the conversational ball back to Harry by wryly inquiring of the company at large: "*Benedicite!*/What eyleth the man, so synfully to swere?" The Host now feels that he must press on with his attack in order to stir the Parson to entertaining controversy. He therefore proclaims to the group that they shall now hear a sermon, for "This Lollere heer wil prechen us somwhat." Again the Parson refuses to rise to the bait, even though he has been called a Lollard. Instead—and probably to the Host's annoyance—the Shipman breaks in to say that he will tell a merry tale himself. The Parson-Host controversy has been set up by this scene, with the Parson winning the first round, and, although further exchange is postponed by the Shipman's intervention, neither is ready to let the matter drop. The company, however, must wait until the final performance on the pilgrimage to see the outcome of this antagonism.

When the Manciple completes his tale of the crow, the Narrator notices that the time is four in the afternoon. The Host, as manager of the group, points out that there is only one more tale to be told, and he prays that God will be good to the Pilgrim who tells the last tale. In the next line we learn, as Harry already knows, that this last teller is to be the Parson. Note that the Host, by asking God's blessing on the Parson, has completely changed his tune from the blasphemous approach he used in addressing him earlier. We assume that perhaps Harry has profited by his experience and is unwilling to risk being bested again. But immediately he reverts to the same kind of large condescension and blasphemy that characterized his earlier approach (X, 22–29). The only explanation I can see for his shift from a mild opening to his former discourtesy towards the Parson is that he suddenly decides that he has him just where he wants him: it is four o'clock in the afternoon and the journey is almost over; neither the late hour nor the probable impatience of the company to arrive at its destination favors the Parson's delivering a lengthy sermon. Harry takes further precaution against a sermon by his suggestion that the Parson tell an entertaining narrative. But "Juge" Bailly has badly misjudged the character of the Parson.

Although he could accept with tolerant good humor the Host's earlier condescension and blasphemy, the Parson feels that Harry has gone too far in suggesting that he tell a "fable." He therefore answers with noticeable immediacy—"al atones:"

> Thou getest fable noon ytoold for me;
> For Paul, that writeth unto Thymothee,
> Repreveth hem that weyven soothfastnesse,
> And tellen fables and swich wrecchednesse.
> Why sholde I sowen draf out of my fest,
> Whan I may sowen whete, if that me lest?   X, 31–36

The Parson's anger at the Host rapidly vanishes, once he has delivered this emphatic statement of his point of view, and he courteously tells the company that if they wish to hear "moralitee and vertuous mateere" and if they promise to listen to him, he will be pleased to perform as best he can. But he has one further warning: he is a Southern man and cannot recite "rum, ram, ruf" in the manner of the Northern and West Midland alliterative verse; consequently, he will speak in prose.

With considerable shrewdness the Parson seems to have guessed the reason, mentioned above, for the shift in the Host's manner toward him, and is working hard to arrange for Harry's getting his just deserts. He therefore does his best to cause the company to accept him as the last performer, and also to keep the Host, as well as the other Pilgrims, from thinking that he will deliver a lengthy technical sermon (X, 45–60). Part of the Parson's clever strategy is that he here promises a "merry tale" with which he will conclude the storytelling. Also, he remarks that he will not "glose"; "glose" is a verb with many meanings, two of which are "to comment upon a text, usually religious" and "to flatter." Although I may be giving the Parson credit for too much subtlety, it seems to me that he expects the company to understand his parenthetical remark—"I wol nat glose"—as meaning "I will not comment at length on religious texts," whereas he himself enjoys taking it as the equivalent of "I will not flatter the Host by giving the brief performance he is trying to jockey me into." Moreover, the Parson knows that the company as a whole can hardly refuse, as did the Shipman earlier, to allow him to show them the way for that "parfit glorious pilgrymage," a particularly suitable topic for this benedictory performance. Too, his assurance that he is "nat textueel" is aimed at keeping the group from thinking that he will belabor them with hair-splitting religious material, and his comment that he is interested only in the "sentence" seems to promise brevity. Finally, the humility with which he puts himself under the correction of scholars serves to suggest that he can be halted if necessary.

The company rapidly instruct the Host to ask the Parson to tell his tale, for, as he expected, they feel that a performance by him is a suitable way of bringing the storytelling and the pilgrimage to a proper conclusion. Harry therefore wishes the Parson well and commands him to begin his "meditacioun"; then, in a final effort to ensure brevity, the Host continues:

> But hasteth yow, the sonne wole adoun;
> Beth fructuous, and that in litel space,
> And to do wel God sende yow his grace!
> Sey what yow list, and we wol gladly heere.   X, 70–73

Apparently the whole company shares this hope for brevity, for the Narrator tells us that the Host in this speech "hadde the wordes for us alle." But the way is now cleared for the Parson's revenge for the treatment he has received from Harry Bailly, revenge which takes the form of the extremely long sermon called the Parson's Tale. And the Shipman must also suffer for his discourtesy. Although all readers may not be convinced that there is "solas" as well as "sentence" in the Parson's "merry tale in prose," we can hardly avoid granting him our admiration for the skill with which he repays the Host for ill-mannered behavior.

CONCLUSION

The Dramatic Principle

It was stated in Part I that the analyses of the twenty-three performances which make up the body of the *Canterbury Tales* lead to the conclusion that within the structure of the book as a whole Chaucer employed a principle which includes three stages of dramatic development, or three techniques of dramatic presentation. By way of summary and conclusion, I shall now restate these three steps or techniques in tabular form and arrange the various performances in their proper categories, according to the interpretations set forth in Part III.

A. Simple suiting of tale and teller.
   - The Second Nun
   - The Squire
   - The Prioress
   - The Knight
   - The Franklin
   - The Physician
   - The Sergeant of the Law
   - The Shipman
   - The Cook
B. Simple suiting of tale and teller, plus an externally motivated dramatic situation.
   - The Manciple
   - The Monk
   - The Parson
   - The Friar

      The Summoner
      The Miller
      The Reeve
      The Nun's Priest
      The Pilgrim Chaucer
      The Clerk

C. Simple suiting of tale and teller, plus an externally motivated dramatic situation, plus internally motivated and extended self-revelation of which the teller is not fully aware.

      The Merchant
      The Canon's Yeoman
      The Wife of Bath
      The Pardoner

Although there is some minor overlapping among and within these three categories, such an arrangement represents an ascending order of complexity in the employment of the dramatic principle involving the relationship between tales and tellers. Thus, in the first category, the Second Nun and the Squire have a single predominant trait, and the story each tells fits with that trait; the Prioress, the Knight, the Franklin, and the Physician are presented in the General Prologue as characters with double traits or interests, and their tales mirror both sides of their characters; then, in the cases of the Sergeant of the Law, the Shipman, and the Cook—the instances in which Chaucer's dramatic intentions are least clear and, in my opinion, least effective—we find some appropriateness of tales and tellers, and, in addition, a hint of the kind of controversy present in the performances which make up the other two categories.

In the second category the Monk and the Parson deliver material aimed at discomfiting the Host; the Manciple expediently tries to smooth over his error in dealing with the Cook; the Friar-Summoner and Miller-Reeve pairings represent open conflict; the Nun's Priest slyly defends the Host; the Pilgrim Chaucer exposes the Host on two counts; and the Clerk delivers a surprise burlesque of the Wife's views.

In the four performances making up the third category, the

Merchant's remarks about his unhappy married life are cautiously brief; the Canon's Yeoman is freer in his personal revelations; and the Wife of Bath and the Pardoner give unabashed, detailed pictures of their lives, both past and present.

This study of the principle which seems to control the dramatic interplay among the Canterbury Pilgrims leads to a further important conclusion concerning Chaucer's narrative artistry in the book. There can be no doubt, I think, that upon occasion Chaucer sacrifices absolute literary criteria in favor of dramatic decorum. In plainer words, Chaucer at times purposefully includes in the *Tales* a story not possessed of consistent literary merit because a tale lacking such merit is demanded by the dramatic context. The Parson's Tale is a good example of this. We are not to assume that Chaucer thought the Parson's sermon an excellent story, or that it is present only to represent a type of late medieval literature; rather, it has its part in the dramatic interplay. A similar example is the "Melibeus." Chaucer could hardly have considered this long didactic piece a literary gem simply because the fourteenth century seems to have been fonder of such material than we are. The point is that dramatic necessity called for a long didactic piece here, and Chaucer furnished the "Melibeus." The recitals by the Franklin, the Physician, and the Manciple are among other cases in point.

Thus, though certainly we must not read medieval literature wholly in modern terms, it does not follow necessarily that the *Canterbury Tales* can be most effectively read by limiting our perspective to the conventions which governed other storytellers than Chaucer in the fourteenth century, or that "modern" is the proper term for any alleged characteristic of the *Tales* not to be found in the writings of Chaucer's contemporaries. Neither extreme—disregard of those conventions, or disregard of all else—will serve satisfactorily; for the individual tellers and tales not only exemplify contemporary persons and storytelling, but are also fashioned for a larger purpose in accord with Chaucer's dramatic principle, a principle which contributes fundamentally to the lasting greatness of the *Canterbury Tales*.

Selected Bibliography

I. BIBLIOGRAPHIES

1908 Hammond, E. P. *Chaucer: A Bibliographical Manual.* New York, Macmillan.

1926 Griffith, D. D. *A Bibliography of Chaucer, 1908–24.* Seattle, University of Washington Press.

1935 Martin, W. E., Jr. *A Chaucer Bibliography, 1925–33.* Durham, Duke University Press.

1945 Wells, J. E. *A Manual of the Writings in Middle English, 1050–1400.* New Haven, Yale University Press, 1916. Nine supplements to this manual cover to December, 1945.

II. EDITIONS

1775–78 Tyrwhitt, Thomas. *Canterbury Tales.* 5 vols. London. Printed for T. Payne.

1894–97 Skeat, W. W. *The Complete Works of Geoffrey Chaucer.* Vols. IV, V. Oxford, Clarendon Press.

1928 Manly, J. M. *Canterbury Tales by Geoffrey Chaucer.* New York, Holt.

1933 Robinson, F. N. *Complete Works of Geoffrey Chaucer.* Boston, Houghton Mifflin.

1940 Manly, J. M. and Edith Rickert. *The Text of the Canterbury Tales.* 8 vols. Chicago, University of Chicago Press.

III. TRANSLATIONS

1912 Tatlock, J. S. P. and Percy MacKaye. *The Modern Reader's Chaucer.* New York, Macmillan.

1934 Nicolson, J. U. *Canterbury Tales.* New York, Garden City; a complete poetic version except for "Melibeus" and the Parson's Tale, which are translated in prose.

1935 Hill, F. E. *The Canterbury Tales*. London, Longmans, Green.
1948 Lumiansky, R. M. *The Canterbury Tales*. New York, Simon and Schuster. Rev. trans., New York, Rinehart, 1954. The revised translation is a complete version in prose.
1949 Morrison, Theodore. *The Portable Chaucer*. New York, Viking.
1952 Coghill, Nevill. *The Canterbury Tales*. Baltimore, Penguin.

IV. CONCORDANCE

1927 Tatlock, J. S. P. and Arthur G. Kennedy. *A Concordance to the Complete Works of Geoffrey Chaucer and to the Romaunt of the Rose*. Carnegie Institution of Washington, D.C.

V. HISTORICAL AND ANALYTICAL STUDIES

Baldwin, C. S. "Cicero on Parnassus," *PMLA*, XLII (1927), 106–12.
Baugh, A. C. "The Original Teller of the Merchant's Tale," *MP*, XXXV (1937–38), 15–26.
Baum, P. F. "The Canon's Yeoman's Tale," *MLN*, XL (1925), 152–54.
———. "Characterization in the *Knight's Tale*," *MLN*, XLVI (1931), 302–304.
Beichner, P. E. "Chaucer's Man of Law and *Disparitas Cultus*," *Speculum*, XXIII (1948), 70–75.
Block, E. A. "Originality, Controlling Purpose, and Craftsmanship in Chaucer's *Man of Law's Tale*," *PMLA*, LXVIII (1953), 572–616.
Bowden, Muriel. *A Commentary on the General Prologue to the Canterbury Tales*. New York, Macmillan, 1948.
Braddy, Haldeen. "The Cook's Mormal and Its Cure," *MLQ*, VII (1947), 265–67.
Brennan, M. J. "Speaking of the Prioress," *MLQ*, X (1949), 451–57.
Bressie, Ramona. " 'A Governour Wily and Wys,' " *MLN*, LIV (1939), 477–90.
———. "Chaucer's Monk Again," *MLN*, LVI (1941), 161–62.
Bronson, Bertrand. "Chaucer's Art in Relation to His Audience," *Five Studies in Literature*. Berkeley, University of California Press, 1940, 1–53.
Brown, Carleton (ed.). *The Pardoner's Tale*. New York, Oxford University Press, 1935.
Browne, W. H. "Notes on Chaucer's Astrology," *MLN*, XXIII (1908), 53–54.

Brusendorff, Aage. *The Chaucer Tradition.* London, Oxford University Press, 1925.

Bryan, W. F. and Germaine Dempster (eds.). *Sources and Analogues of Chaucer's Canterbury Tales.* Chicago, University of Chicago Press, 1941.

Caldwell, R. A. "Chaucer's *Taillynge Ynough, Canterbury Tales,* B² 1624," *MLN,* LV (1940), 262–65.

Camden, Carroll, Jr. "Query on Chaucer's Burgesses," *PQ,* VII (1928), 314–17.

Chute, Marchette. *Geoffrey Chaucer of England.* New York, Dutton, 1946.

Coffman, G. R. "Old Age from Horace to Chaucer. Some Literary Affinities and Adventures of an Idea," *Speculum,* IX (1934), 249–77.

———. "Canon's Yeoman's Prologue, G, ll. 563–566: Horse or Man," *MLN,* LIX (1944), 269–71.

Coghill, Nevill. *The Poet Chaucer.* London, Oxford University Press, 1949.

Coulton, G. G. *Five Centuries of Religion.* 3 vols. Cambridge, Cambridge University Press, 1923–36.

———. *Medieval Panorama.* New York, Macmillan, 1938.

———. *Chaucer and His England.* 7th ed. London, Methuen, 1946.

Cowling, G. H. *Chaucer.* London, Methuen, 1927.

Cummings, H. M. *The Indebtedness of Chaucer's Works to the Italian Works of Boccaccio.* University of Cincinnati *Studies,* No. 10, Part 2 (1916).

Cunningham, J. V. "The Literary Form of the Prologue to the Canterbury Tales," *MP,* XLIX (1951–52), 172–81.

Curry, W. C. *The Middle English Ideal of Beauty.* Baltimore, Furst, 1916.

———. *Chaucer and the Mediaeval Sciences.* New York, Oxford University Press, 1926.

Damon, S. F. "Chaucer and Alchemy," *PMLA,* XXXIX (1924), 782–88.

Dempster, Germaine. *Dramatic Irony in Chaucer.* Stanford, Stanford University Press, 1932.

———. "The Original Teller of the Merchant's Tale," *MP,* XXXVI (1938–39), 1–8.

Donaldson, E. T. "Chaucer the Pilgrim," *PMLA,* LXIX (1954), 928–36.

Donovan, M. J. "The *Moralite* of the Nun's Priest's Sermon," *JEGP,* LII (1953), 498–508.

Duffey, B. I. "The Intention and Art of *The Man of Law's Tale,*" *ELH,* XIV (1947), 181–93.

Duncan, E. H. "The Yeoman's Canon's 'Silver Citrinacioun,'" *MP,* XXXVII (1939–40), 241–62.

Emerson, O. F. "Some of Chaucer's Lines on the Monk," *MP*, I (1903–1904), 105–15.

——. "Some Notes on Chaucer and Some Conjectures," *PQ*, II (1923), 81–96.

Fairchild, H. N. "Active Arcite, Contemplative Palamon," *JEGP*, XXVI (1927), 285–93.

Forehand, Brooks. "Old Age and Chaucer's Reeve," *PMLA*, LXIX (1954), 984–89.

Francis, W. N. "Chaucer Shortens a Tale," *PMLA*, LXVIII (1953), 1126–41.

French, W. H. "The Lovers in the Knight's Tale," *JEGP*, XLVIII (1949), 320–28.

Frost, G. L. "Chaucer's Man of Law at the Parvis," *MLN*, XLIV (1929), 496–501.

Frost, William. "An Interpretation of Chaucer's Knight's Tale," *RES* XXV (1949), 289–304.

Furnivall, F. J. "Chaucer's Prioress's Nun-Chaplain," *Anglia*, IV (1881), 238–40.

Galway, Margaret. "Chaucer's Shipman in Real Life," *MLR*, XXXIV (1939), 497–514.

Gardner, W. B. "Chaucer's 'Unworthy Sone of Eve,' " University of Texas *Studies in English*, XXVI (1947), 77–83.

Gerould, G. H. "The Social Status of Chaucer's Franklin," *PMLA*, XLI (1926), 262–79.

——. *Chaucerian Essays*. Princeton, Princeton University Press, 1952.

Gibbons, R. F. "Does the Nun's Priest's Epilogue Contain a Link?" *SP*, LI (1954), 21–33.

Green, A. W. "Chaucer's Clerks and the Mediaeval Scholarly Tradition as Represented by Richard de Bury's 'Philobiblon,' " *ELH*, XVIII (1951), 1–6.

Hadow, Grace. *Chaucer and His Times*. New York, Holt, 1914.

Ham, E. B. "Knight's Tale 38," *ELH*, XVII (1950), 252–61.

Hamilton, M. P. "The Credentials of Chaucer's Pardoner," *JEGP*, XL (1941), 48–72.

——. "The Convent of Chaucer's Prioress and Her Priests," *Philologica: The Malone Anniversary Studies*. Baltimore, Johns Hopkins Press, 1949, 179–90.

Hammond, E. P. *English Verse Between Chaucer and Surrey*. Durham, Duke University Press, 1927.

Harper, G. H. "Chaucer's Big Prioress," *PQ*, XII (1933), 308–10.

Harrison, B. S. "The Rhetorical Inconsistency of Chaucer's Franklin," *SP*, XXXII (1935), 55–61.

Hart, W. M. "A Note on the Interpretation of the *Canterbury Tales*,"

Transactions of the American Philological Association, XXXIX (1908), *liii–liv*.

―――. "The Reeve's Tale: A Comparative Study of Chaucer's Narrative Art," *PMLA*, XXIII (1908), 1–44.

Haselmayer, L. A. "The Apparitor and Chaucer's Summoner," *Speculum*, XII (1937), 43–57.

Hemingway, S. B. "Chaucer's Monk and Nun's Priest," *MLN*, XXXI (1916), 479–83.

Hinckley, H. B. *Notes on Chaucer.* Northampton, Massachusetts, Nonotuck Press, 1908.

Hostia, Sister Mary. "The Prioress and Her Companion," *College English*, XIV (1953), 351–52.

Hotson, Leslie. "The *Tale of Melibeus* and John of Gaunt," *SP*, XVIII (1921), 429–52.

Hulbert, J. R. "What Was Chaucer's Aim in the *Knight's Tale?*" *SP*, XXVI (1929), 375–85.

―――. "The *Canterbury Tales* and Their Narrators," *SP*, XLV (1948), 565–77.

Ives, D. V. "A Man of Religion," *MLR*, XXVII (1932), 144–48.

Jefferson, B. L. *Chaucer and the Consolation of Philosophy of Boethius.* Princeton, Princeton University Press, 1917.

Jones, Claude. "Chaucer's Taillynge Ynough," *MLN*, LII (1937), 570.

―――. "The Monk's Tale, A Mediaeval Sermon," *MLN*, LII (1937), 570–72.

Jones, H. S. V. "The Clerk of Oxenford," *PMLA*, XXVII (1912), 106–15.

Jones, R. F. "A Conjecture on the Wife of Bath's Prologue," *JEGP*, XXIV (1925), 512–47.

Jusserand, J. J. *English Wayfaring Life in the Middle Ages.* English trans., 4th ed. New York, Putnam, 1950.

Kellogg, A. L. "An Augustinian Interpretation of Chaucer's Pardoner," *Speculum*, XXVI (1951), 465–81.

Kellogg, A. L. and L. A. Haselmayer. "Chaucer's Satire of the Pardoner," *PMLA*, LXVI (1951), 251–77.

Ker, W. P. "Chaucer," *English Prose.* Ed. Henry Craik. London, Macmillan, 1893.

Kimpel, Ben. "The Narrator of the *Canterbury Tales*," *ELH*, XX (1953), 77–86.

Kittredge, G. L. "Chaucer's Pardoner," *Atlantic Monthly*, LXXII (1893), 829–33.

―――. "The Canon's Yeoman's Prologue and Tale," *Transactions* of the Royal Society of Literature (London), XXX (1910), 87.

―――. "Chaucer's Discussion of Marriage," *MP*, IX (1911–12), 435–67.

————. *Chaucer and His Poetry*. Cambridge, Harvard University Press, 1915.

Knott, T. A. "A Bit of Chaucer Mythology," *MP*, VIII (1910–11), 135–39.

————. "Chaucer's Anonymous Merchant," *PQ*, I (1922), 1–16.

Knowlton, E. C. "Chaucer's Man of Law," *JEGP*, XXIII (1924), 83–93.

Kökeritz, Helge. "The Wyf of Bathe and Al Hire Secte," *PQ*, XXVI (1947), 147–51.

Kuhl, E. P. "Chaucer's Burgesses," *Transactions* of the Wisconsin Academy of Sciences, Arts, and Letters, XVIII (1916), 652–75.

————. "Notes on Chaucer's Prioress," *PQ*, II (1923), 302–309.

————. "Chaucer's Monk," *MLN*, LV (1940), 480.

Kuhl, E. P. and H. J. Webb. "Chaucer's Squire," *ELH*, VI (1939), 282–84.

Lawrence, W. W. "Satire in Sir Thopas," *PMLA*, L (1935), 81–91.

————. "The Tale of Melibeus," *Essays and Studies in Honor of Carleton Brown*. New York, New York University Press, 1940, 100–10.

————. *Chaucer and the Canterbury Tales*. New York, Columbia University Press, 1950.

Legouis, Émile. *Geoffrey Chaucer*. English trans. London, Dent, 1913.

Loomis, R. S. "Was Chaucer a Laodicean?" *Essays and Studies in Honor of Carleton Brown*. New York, New York University Press, 1940, 129–48.

Lounsbury, T. R. *Studies in Chaucer*, 3 vols. New York, Harper, 1892.

Lowes, J. L. "Simple and Coy," *Anglia*, XXXIII (1910), 440–51.

————. *Convention and Revolt in Poetry*. Boston, Houghton Mifflin, 1919.

————. *Geoffrey Chaucer and the Development of His Genius*. Boston, Houghton Mifflin, 1934.

Ludeke, Henry. *Die Funktionen der Erzählers in Chaucers epischer Dichtung*. Halle, Niemeyer, 1927.

Lyon, E. D. "Roger de Ware, Cook," *MLN*, LII (1937), 491–94.

Macauley, G. C. "Notes on Chaucer," *MLR*, IV (1910), 14–19.

McGalliard, J. C. "Chaucer's *Merchant's Tale* and Deschamps' *Miroir de Mariage*," *PQ*, XXV (1946), 193–220.

Madeleva, Sister Mary. *Chaucer's Nuns and Other Essays*. New York, Appleton, 1925.

Malone, Kemp. "Style and Structure in the Prologue to the *Canterbury Tales*," *ELH*, XIII (1946), 38–45.

————. *Chapters on Chaucer*. Baltimore, Johns Hopkins Press, 1951.

Manly, J. M. "The Stanza-Forms of Sir Thopas," *MP*, VIII (1910–11), 141–44.

————. *Some New Light on Chaucer*. New York, Holt, 1926.

Marckwardt, A. H. "Characterization in Chaucer's Knight's Tale,"

University of Michigan *Contributions in Modern Philology*, No. 5 (1947).

Mead, W. E. "The *Prologue of the Wife of Bath's Tale*," *PMLA*, XVI (1901), 388–404.

Meyer, Emil. *Die charakterzeichnung bei Chaucer*. Halle, Niemeyer, 1913.

Moffett, H. Y. "Oswald the Reeve," *PQ*, IV (1925), 208–23.

Neville, Marie. "The Function of the *Squire's Tale* in the Canterbury Scheme," *JEGP*, L (1951), 167–79.

Owen, C. A., Jr. "One Robyn or Two," *MLN*, LXVII (1952), 336–38.

———. "The Crucial Passages in Five of the *Canterbury Tales:* A Study in Irony and Symbol," *JEGP*, LII (1953), 294–311.

Owst, G. R. *Literature and Pulpit in Medieval England*. Cambridge, Cambridge University Press, 1933.

Patch, H. R. "Chaucer and Lady Fortune," *MLR*, XXII (1927), 377–88.

———. *On Rereading Chaucer*. Cambridge, Harvard University Press, 1939.

Power, Eileen. *Medieval English Nunneries c. 1275 to 1535*. Cambridge, Cambridge University Press, 1922.

Pratt, R. A. "Chaucer's Shipman's Tale and Sercambi," *MLN*, LV (1940), 142–45.

———. "Was Robyn the Miller's Youth Misspent?" *MLN*, LIX (1944), 47–49.

———. "The Order of the *Canterbury Tales*," *PMLA*, LXVI (1951), 1141–67.

Preston, Raymond. *Chaucer*. London and New York, Sheed and Ward, 1952.

Richardson, H. G. "Year Books and Plea Rolls as Sources of Historical Information," *Transactions* of the Royal Historical Society, Ser. 4, V (1922), 28–51.

Rickert, Edith. "Chaucer's 'Hodge of Ware,' " *TLS* (Oct. 20, 1932), 761.

———. *Chaucer's World*. Ed. C. C. Olson and M. M. Crow. New York, Columbia University Press, 1948.

Robertson, D. W., Jr. "Chaucerian Tragedy," *ELH*, XIX (1952), 1–37.

Robertson, Stuart. "Elements of Realism in the *Knight's Tale*," *JEGP*, XIV (1915), 226–55.

Root, R. K. *The Poetry of Chaucer*. Rev. ed. Boston, Houghton Mifflin, 1922.

Roppolo, J. P. "The Meaning of 'at erst': Prologue to *Sir Thopas*, B², 1884," *MLN*, LXIII (1948), 365–71.

———. "The Converted Knight in Chaucer's *Wife of Bath's Tale*," *College English*, XII (1950–51), 263–69.

Rosenfeld, Mary-Virginia. "Chaucer and the Liturgy," *MLN*, LV (1940), 357–60.

Schlauch, Margaret. *Constance and the Accused Queens*. New York, New York University Press, 1927.

———. "Chaucer's *Merchant's Tale* and Courtly Love," *ELH*, IV (1937), 201–12.

Sedgewick, G. G. "The Progress of Chaucer's Pardoner, 1880–1940," *MLQ*, I (1940), 431–58.

———. "The Structure of the *Merchant's Tale*," *UTQ*, XVII (1947–48), 337–45.

Severs, J. B. *The Literary Relationships of Chaucer's Clerkes Tale*. New Haven, Yale University Press, 1942.

———. "Chaucer's Originality in the Nun's Priest's Tale," *SP*, XLIII (1946), 22–41.

———. "Is the *Manciple's Tale* a Success?" *JEGP*, LI (1952), 1–16.

Shannon, E. F. *Chaucer and the Roman Poets*. Cambridge, Harvard University Press, 1929.

Shelly, P. V. D. *The Living Chaucer*. Philadelphia, University of Pennsylvania Press, 1940.

Sherbo, Arthur. "Chaucer's Nun's Priest Again," *PMLA*, LXIV (1949), 236–46.

Shumaker, Wayne. "Chaucer's *Manciple's Tale* as a Part of a Canterbury Group," *UTQ*, XXII (1953), 147–56.

Silverman, Albert H. "Sex and Money in Chaucer's *Shipman's Tale*," *PQ*, XXXII (1953), 329–36.

Slaughter, E. E. "Clerk Jankyn's Motive," *MLN*, LXV (1950), 530–34.

Sledd, James. "Dorigen's Complaint," *MP*, XLV (1947–48), 36–45.

———. "The *Clerk's Tale:* The Monsters and the Critics," *MP*, LI (1953–54), 73–82.

Sleeth, C. R. "The Friendship of Chaucer's Summoner and Pardoner," *MLN*, LVI (1941), 138.

Spurgeon, C. F. E. *Five Hundred Years of Chaucer Criticism and Allusion*. 3 vols. Cambridge, Cambridge University Press, 1925.

Stillwell, Gardiner. "Analogues to Chaucer's *Manciple's Tale* in the *Ovide Moralisé* and Machaut's *Voir-dit*," *PQ*, XIX (1940), 133–38.

———. "The Political Meaning of Chaucer's *Tale of Melibee*," *Speculum*, XIX (1944), 433–44.

———. "Chaucer's 'Sad' Merchant," *RES*, XX (1944), 1–18.

———. "Chaucer in Tartary," *RES*, XXIV (1948), 177–88.

Stobie, M. R. "Chaucer's Shipman and the Wine," *PMLA*, LXIV (1949), 565–69.

Stokoe, W. C., Jr. "Structure and Intention in the First Fragment of *The Canterbury Tales*," *UTQ*, XXI (1951–52), 120–27.

Swart, Johannes. "Chaucer's Pardoner," *Neophilologus*, XXXVI (1952), 45–50.

Tatlock, J. S. P. *The Development and Chronology of Chaucer's Works.* London, Chaucer Society, 1907.

———. "Chaucer and Wyclif," *MP*, XIV (1916–17), 257–68.

———. "Chaucer and the *Legenda Aurea,*" *MLN*, XLV (1930), 296–98.

———. "The *Canterbury Tales* in 1400," *PMLA*, L (1935), 100–39.

———. "Chaucer's *Merchant's Tale,*" *MP*, XXXIII (1935–36), 367–81.

———. "Chaucer's Monk," *MLN*, LV (1940), 350–54.

———. "Is Chaucer's Monk a Monk?" *MLN*, LVI (1941), 80.

ten Brink, Bernhard. *History of English Literature.* English trans. New York, Holt, 1889–96.

Trevelyan, G. M. *England in the Age of Wyckliffe.* 4th ed. London, Longmans, Green, 1909.

Tupper, Frederick. "The Quarrels of the Canterbury Pilgrims," *JEGP*, XIV (1915), 256–70.

———. "Chaucer's Sinners and Sins," *JEGP*, XV (1916), 56–106.

———. *Types of Society in Medieval Literature.* New York, Holt, 1926.

———. "The Bearings of the Shipman's Prologue," *JEGP*, XXXIII (1934), 352–71.

Utley, F. L. *The Crooked Rib.* Columbus, Ohio State University Press, 1944.

Watt, Francis. *Canterbury Pilgrims and Their Ways.* London, Methuen, 1917.

White, F. E. "Chaucer's Shipman," *MP*, XXVI (1928–29), 249–55, 379–84, and XXVII (1929–30), 123–28.

Willard, Rudolph. "Chaucer's 'Text That Seith That Hunters Ben Nat Hooly Men," University of Texas *Studies in English*, XXVI (1947), 209–51.

Williams, Arnold. "Chaucer and the Friars," *Speculum*, XXVIII (1953), 499–513.

Wilson, H. S. "The *Knight's Tale* and the *Teseida* Again," *UTQ*, XVIII, (1948–49), 131–46.

Wood-Legh, K. L. "The Franklin," *RES*, IV (1928), 145–51.

Woolf, H. B. "The Summoner and His Concubine," *MLN*, LXVIII (1953), 118–21.

Worcester, David. *The Art of Satire.* Cambridge, Harvard University Press, 1940.

Work, J. A. "Echoes of Anathema in Chaucer," *PMLA*, XLVII (1932), 419–30.

Young, Karl. "A Note on Chaucer's Friar," *MLN*, L (1935), 83–85.

Addendum, 1954-1980

The newer practice of citing volumes of journals in arabic rather than roman numerals is followed here. In addition to those listed on page 2, the following abbreviations are here used:

ChauR	*Chaucer Review*
CE	*College English*
ES	*English Studies*
MedSt	*Mediaeval Studies* (Toronto)
NM	*Neuphilologische Mitteilungen*

I. BIBLIOGRAPHIES

Baird, Lorrayne Y. *Bibliography of Chaucer*, 1964–73. Boston, G. K. Hall, 1977.

Bazire, Joyce, and David Mills. "Middle English: Chaucer," *Year's Work in English Studies*. London, John Murray for the English Association.

Crawford, W. R. *Bibliography of Chaucer*, 1954–63. Seattle, University of Washington Press, 1967.

Fisher, John H., et al. "An Annotated Chaucer Bibliography," *Studies in the Age of Chaucer*. The New Chaucer Society, Norman, University of Oklahoma. Appears annually; first volume (1979) covers publications in 1975–76.

Kirby, Thomas A. "Chaucer Research," *ChauR*. University Park, Pennsylvania State University Press. Appears annually.

"Chaucer," *MLA International Bibliography, Volume I*. New York, Modern Language Association of America. Appears annually.

II. EDITIONS

Baugh, Albert C. *Chaucer's Major Poetry.* New York, Appleton-Century-Crofts, 1963.

Donaldson, E. T. *Chaucer's Poetry.* New York, Ronald Press, second and expanded edition, 1975.

Fisher, John H. *The Complete Poetry and Prose of Geoffrey Chaucer.* New York, Holt, Rinehart, Winston, 1977.

Pratt, Robert A. *The Tales of Canterbury.* Boston, Houghton Mifflin, 1974.

Robinson, F. N. *The Works of Geoffrey Chaucer.* Boston, Houghton Mifflin, second edition, 1957.

The Variorum Edition of Chaucer's Works. In preparation at the University of Oklahoma. Paul G. Ruggiers, General Editor.

III. HISTORICAL AND ANALYTICAL STUDIES

Allen, Judson B. "The Old Way and the Parson's Way: An Ironic Reading of the *Parson's Tale,*" *Journal of Medieval and Renaissance Studies,* 3 (1973), 255–71.

Baker, Donald C. "A Crux in Chaucer's *Franklin's Tale*: Dorigen's Complaint," *JEGP,* 60 (1961), 56–64.

Baldwin, R. G. "The Yeoman's Canons: A Conjecture," *JEGP,* 61 (1962), 232–33.

Baldwin, Ralph. *The Unity of the Canterbury Tales* (Anglistica 5). Copenhagen, Rosenkilde og Bagger, 1955.

Beichner, Paul E. "Daun Piers, Monk and Business Administrator," *Speculum,* 34 (1959), 611–19.

———. "Chaucer's Pardoner as Entertainer," *MedSt,* 25 (1963), 160–72.

Beidler, Peter G. "The Pairing of the *Franklin's Tale* and the *Physician's Tale,*" *ChauR,* 3 (1969), 275–79.

Benjamin, Edwin B. "The Concept of Order in the *Franklin's Tale,*" *PQ,* 38 (1959), 119–24.

Benson, Larry D., and Theodore M. Andersson (eds.). *The Literary Context of Chaucer's Fabliaux.* Indianapolis, Bobbs-Merrill, 1971.

Berndt, David E. "Monastic *Acedia* and Chaucer's Characterization of Daun Piers," *SP,* 68 (1971), 435–50.

Birney, Earle. "After His Ymage—The Central Ironies of the *Friar's Tale,*" *MedSt,* 21 (1959), 17–35.

———. "Structural Irony Within the *Summoner's Tale,*" *Anglia,* 78 (1960), 204–18.

———. "Chaucer's Gentil Manciple and His Gentil Tale," *NM,* 61 (1960), 257–67.

Bloomfield, Morton W. "The *Miller's Tale*—An Un-Boethian Interpretation," *Medieval Literature and Folklore Studies . . . in Honor of Francis Lee Utley*. New Brunswick, New Jersey, Rutgers University Press, 1971, 205–11.

Bolton, W. F. "The *Miller's Tale*: An Interpretation," *MedSt*, 24 (1962), 83–94.

Brewer, Darek. *Chaucer and His World*. New York, Dodd Mead, 1978.

Broes, Arthur T. "Chaucer's Disgruntled Cleric: The *Nun's Priest's Tale, PMLA*, 78 (1963), 156–62.

Bronson, Bertrand H. *In Search of Chaucer*. Toronto, University of Toronto Press, 1960.

———. "Afterthoughts on the *Merchant's Tale*," *SP*, 58 (1961), 583–96.

Brosnahan, Leger. "Does the Nun's Priest's Epilogue Contain a Link?" *SP*, 58 (1961), 468–82.

Brown, Emerson. "The Poet's Last Words: Text and Meaning at the End of the Parson's Prologue," *ChauR*, 10 (1976), 236–42.

———. "Chaucer, The Merchant, and Their Tale: Getting Beyond Old Controversies: Part I," *ChauR*, 13 (1978), 141–56.

———. "Chaucer, The Merchant, and Their Tale: Getting Beyond Old Controversies: Part II," *ChauR*, 13 (1979), 247–62.

Burlin, Robert B. "The Art of Chaucer's Franklin," *Neophilologus*, 51 (1967), 55–73.

———. *Chaucerian Fiction*. Princeton, Princeton University Press, 1977.

Burrow, J. A. "Irony in the *Merchant's Tale, Anglia*, 75 (1957), 199–208.

Cadbury, William. "Manipulation of Sources and the Meaning of the *Manciple's Tale*," *PQ*, 43 (1965), 538–48.

Cespedes, Frank V. "Chaucer's Pardoner and Preaching, *ELH*, 44 (1977), 1–18.

Clark, John W. "Does the Franklin Interrupt the Squire?" *ChauR*, 7 (1972), 160–61.

Cohen, Edward S. "The Sequence of the *Canterbury Tales*, *ChauR*, 9 (1974), 190–95.

Corsa, Helen S. *Chaucer, Poet of Mirth and Morality*. Notre Dame, Indiana, Notre Dame University Press, 1965.

Cox, Lee S. "A Question of Order in the *Canterbury Tales*," *ChauR*, 1 (1967), 228–52.

David, Alfred. "Sentimental Comedy in the *Franklin's Tale*," *Annuale Mediaevale*, 6 (1965), 19–27.

———. "Criticism and the Old Man in Chaucer's *Pardoner's Tale*, *CE*, 27 (1966), 39–44.

———. *The Strumpet Muse: Art and Morals in Chaucer's Poetry*. Bloomington, Indiana University Press, 1976.

Donaldson, E. T. *Speaking of Chaucer*. London, Athlone Press, 1970.

———. "The Ordering of the *Canterbury Tales*," *Medieval Literature and Folklore Studies . . . in Honor of Francis Lee Utley*. New Brunswick, New Jersey, Rutgers University Press, 1971, 193–204.

Donner, Morton. "The Unity of Chaucer's Manciple Fragment," *MLN*, 70 (1955), 245–49.

Duncan, Edgar H. "The Literature of Alchemy and Chaucer's *Canon's Yeoman's Tale*: Framework, Theme, and Characters," *Speculum*, 43 (1968), 633–56.

Eisner, Sigmund. *A Tale of Wonder: A Source Study of the Wife of Bath's Tale*. Wexford, Ireland, John English and Co., 1957.

Fisher, John H. "Chaucer's Last Revision of the *Canterbury Tales*, *MLR*, 67 (1972), 241–51.

Fleming, John V. "The Antifraternalism of the *Summoner's Tale*," *JEGP*, 65 (1967), 688–700.

Friedman, Albert B. "The *Prioress's Tale* and Chaucer's Anti-Semitism, *ChauR*, 9 (1974), 118–29.

Friend, Albert C. "The Dangerous Theme of the Pardoner," *MLQ*, 18 (1957), 305–8.

Gardner, John. "The *Canon's Yeoman's Prologue and Tale*: An Interpretation," *PQ*, 46 (1967), 1–17.

Gaylord, Alan T. "*Sentence* and *Solaas* in Fragment VII of the *Canterbury Tales*: Harry Bailly as Horseback Editor," *PMLA*, 82 (1967), 226–35.

Gibbons, Robert F. "Does the Nun's Priest's Epilogue Contain a Link?" *SP*, 51 (1954), 21–33.

Ginsberg, Warren. " 'And Speketh so Pleyn': The *Clerk's Tale* and Its Teller," *Criticism*, 20 (1978), 307–23.

Gordon, James D. "Chaucer's Retraction: A Review of Opinion," *Studies in Medieval Literature*. Philadelphia, University of Pennsylvania Press, 1961, 81–96.

Grenberg, Bruce L. "The *Canon's Yeoman's Tale*: Boethian Wisdom and the Alchemists." *ChauR*, 1 (1967), 37–54.

Grennen, Joseph E. "Chaucer's 'Secree of Secrees': An Alchemical 'Topic,' " *PQ*, 42 (1963), 562–66.

———. "Saint Cecelia's 'Chemical Wedding': The Unity of the *Canterbury Tales*, Fragment VIII," *JEGP*, 65 (1967), 466–81.

Haller, Robert S. "Chaucer's *Squire's Tale* and the Uses of Rhetoric," *MP*, 62 (1965), 285–95.

Halverson, John. "Chaucer's Pardoner and the Progress of Criticism," *ChauR*, 4 (1970), 184–202.

Hamilton, Marie P. "The Dramatic Suitability of the *Man of Law's Tale*," *Studies in Language and Literature in Honour of Margaret Schlauch*. Warsaw, 1967, 153–63.

Hanson, Thomas B. "Chaucer's Physician as Storyteller and Moralizer," *ChauR*, 7 (1972), 132–39.

Harrington, David V. "The Narrator of the *Canon's Yeoman's Tale*," *Annuale Mediaevalia*, 9 (1968), 85–97.

Hartung, Albert. " 'Pars Secunda' and the Development of the *Canon's Yeoman's Tale*, *ChauR*, 12 (1977), 111–28.

Hatton, Thomas J. "Chaucer's Crusading Knight, A Slanted Ideal," *ChauR*, 3 (1968), 77–87.

Hazelton, Richard. "The *Manciple's Tale*: Parody and Critique," *JEGP*, 62 (1963), 1–31.

Heninger, S. K., Jr. "The Concept of Order in Chaucer's *Clerk's Tale*," *JEGP*, 56 (1957), 382–95.

Herz, Judith Scherer. "The *Canon's Yeoman's Prologue and Tale*," *MP*, 58 (1961), 231–37.

Hoffman, Arthur W. "Chaucer's Prologue to Pilgrimage: The Two Voices," *ELH*, 21 (1954), 1–16.

Howard, Donald R. "The Conclusion of the Marriage Group: Chaucer and the Human Condition," *MP*, 57 (1960), 223–32.

———. "Chaucer the Man," *PMLA*, 80 (1966), 337–43.

———. *The Idea of the "Canterbury Tales."* Berkeley, University of California Press, 1976.

Jones, George F. "Chaucer and the Medieval Miller," *MLQ*, 16 (1955), 3–15.

Jordan, Robert M. "Chaucer's Sense of Illusion: Roadside Drama Reconsidered," *ELH*, 29 (1962), 19–33.

———. "The Non-dramatic Disunity of the *Merchant's Tale*," *PMLA*, 78 (1963), 293–99.

———. *Chaucer and the Shape of Creation.* Cambridge, Harvard University Press, 1967.

Kaske, R. E. "The Knight's Interruption of the *Monk's Tale*, *ELH*, 24 (1957), 249–68.

———. "The 'Canticum Canticorum' in the *Miller's Tale*," *SP*, 59 (1962), 479–500.

———. "Chaucer's Marriage Group," *Chaucer the Love Poet*. Athens, University of Georgia Press, 1973, 45–65.

Keiser, George R. "Language and Meaning in Chaucer's Shipman's Tale," *ChauR*, 12 (1977), 147–61.

———. "In Defense of the Bradshaw Shift," *ChauR*, 12 (1978), 191–201.

Leicester, H. Marshall, Jr. "A General Prologue to the *Canterbury Tales*, *PMLA*, 95 (1980), 213–24.

Lenaghan, R. T. "The Nun's Priest's Fable," *PMLA*, 78 (1963), 300–7.

———. "The Irony of the *Friar's Tale*, *ChauR*, 7 (1973), 281–94.

Lepley, Douglas L. "The Monk's Boethian Tale," *ChauR*, 12 (1977), 162–70.

Luengo, A. "Audience and Exempla in the *Pardoner's Tale*," *ChauR*, 11 (1976), 1–10.

Lumiansky, R. M. "Chaucer's Cook-Host Relationship," *MedSt*, 17 (1955), 208–9.

———. "Chaucer's Retraction and the Degree of Completeness of the *Canterbury Tales*," *Tulane Studies in English*, 6 (1956), 5–13.

Madden, William A. "Some Philosophical Aspects of the *Knight's Tale*: A Reply," *CE*, 20 (1959), 193–94.

Major, John M. "The Personality of Chaucer the Pilgrim," *PMLA*, 75 (1960), 160–62.

Mandel, Jerome H. "Governance in the *Physician's Tale*," *ChauR*, 10 (1976), 316–25.

Mann, Jill. *Chaucer and Medieval Estates Satire: The Literature of Social Classes and the "General Prologue."* London, Cambridge University Press, 1973.

Manning, Stephen. "The Nun's Priest's Morality and the Medieval Attitude Toward Fables," *JEGP*, 59 (1960), 403–16.

Martin, Loy D. "History and Form in the General Prologue to the *Canterbury Tales*, *ELH*, 45 (1978), 1–17.

McCall, John P. "The *Clerk's Tale* and the Theme of Obedience," *MLQ*, 27 (1967), 260–69.

McGalliard, John C. "Characterization in Chaucer's *Shipman's Tale*," *PQ*, 54 (1975), 1–18.

Miller, Robert P. "Chaucer's Pardoner, the Scriptural Eunuch, and the *Pardoner's Tale*," *Speculum*, 30 (1955), 180–99.

———. "The *Wife of Bath's Tale* and Medieval Exempla," *ELH*, 32 (1965), 442–56.

——— (ed.). *Chaucer: Sources and Backgrounds.* New York, Oxford University Press, 1977.

Moore, Arthur K. "*Sir Thopas* as Criticism of Fourteenth-Century Minstrelsy," *JEGP*, 53 (1954), 532–45.

Moorman, Charles. "The Prioress as Pearly Queen," *ChauR*, 13 (1978), 25–33.

Morgan, Gerald. "The Design of the *General Prologue* to the *Canterbury Tales*," *ES*, 59 (1978), 481–98.

Muscatine, Charles. *Chaucer and the French Tradition.* Berkeley, University of California Press, 1957.

Neuse, Richard. "The Knight: The First Mover in Chaucer's Human Comedy," *UTQ*, 31 (1962), 299–315.

Olson, Glending. "A Reading of the *Thopas-Melibee* Link," *ChauR*, 10 (1975), 147–53.

Olson, Paul A. "Poetic Justice in the *Miller's Tale*," *MLQ*, 24 (1964), 227–36.

Olsson, Kurt. "Grammar, Manhood, and Tears: The Curiosity of Chaucer's Monk," *MP*, 76 (1978), 1–17.

Owen, Charles A., Jr. "Chaucer's *Canterbury Tales*: Aesthetic Design in Stories of the First Day," *ES*, 35 (1954), 49–56.

————. "Relationship Between the *Physician's Tale* and the *Parson's Tale*," *MLN*, 71 (1956), 84–7.

————. "The Development of the *Canterbury Tales*," *JEGP*, 57 (1958), 449–76.

————. "The Earliest Plan of the *Canterbury Tales*," *MedSt*, 21 (1959), 202–10.

————. "The *Tale of Melibee*," *ChauR*, 7 (1973), 267–80.

————. *Pilgrimage and Storytelling in the "Canterbury Tales": The Dialectic of "Ernest" and "Game."* Norman, University of Oklahoma Press, 1977.

Patterson, Lee W. "The 'Parson's Tale' and the Quitting of the *Canterbury Tales, Tradito*, 34 (1978), 331–80.

Paul, James. "A Defense of the Ellesmere Order," *Rackham Literary Studies* (Ann Arbor, Michigan), 5 (1974), 118–20.

Payne, Robert O. *The Key of Remembrance: A Study of Chaucer's Poetics*. New Haven, Yale University Press, 1963.

Peterson, Joyce E. "The Finished Fragment: A Reassessment of the *Squire's Tale*," *ChauR*, 5 (1970), 62–74.

Pittock, Malcolm. "The *Merchant's Tale*," *Essays in Criticism*, 17 (1967), 26–40.

Pratt, Robert A. "The Development of the Wife of Bath," *Studies in Medieval Literature*. Philadelphia, University of Pennsylvania Press, 1961, 45–79.

Reidy, John. "Chaucer's Canon and the Unity of the *Canon's Yeoman's Tale, PMLA*, 80 (1966), 31–7.

Reiss, Edmund. "The Pilgrimage Narrative and the *Canterbury Tales, SP*, 67 (1970), 295–305.

Ridley, Florence H. *The Prioress and the Critics*. Berkeley, University of California Press, 1965.

Robertson, D. W., Jr. *A Preface to Chaucer*. Princeton, Princeton University Press, 1962.

Rosenberg, Bruce A. "The Contrary Tales of the Second Nun and the Canon's Yeoman," *ChauR*, 2 (1968), 278–91.

Ruggiers, Paul G. "The Form of the *Canterbury Tales*: Respice Fines," *CE*, 17 (1956), 439–43.

————. "Some Philosophical Aspects of the *Knight's Tale*," *CE*, 19 (1958), 296–302.

————. *The Art of the Canterbury Tales*. Madison, University of Wisconsin Press, 1966.

Sands, Donald B. "The Non-Comic, Non-Tragic Wife: Chaucer's Dame Alys as Sociopath," *ChauR*, 12 (1977), 171–82.

Scheps, Walter. "Chaucer's Man of Law and the Tale of Constance," *PMLA*, 89 (1974), 285–95.

Severs, J. Burke. "Did Chaucer Rearrange the Clerk's Envoy?" *MLN*, 69 (1954), 472–78.

———. "Author's Revision in Block C of the *Canterbury Tales*," *Speculum*, 29 (1954), 512–30.

———. "Appropriateness of Character to Plot in the *Franklin's Tale*," *Studies in Language and Literature in Honour of Margaret Schlauch*. Warsaw, 1967, 385–96.

Shallers, A. Paul. "The *Nun's Priest's Tale*: An Ironic Exemplum," *ELH*, 42 (1975), 319–37.

Silverstein, Theodore. "Wife of Bath and the Rhetoric of Enchantment; or, How to Make a Hero See in the Dark," *MP*, 58 (1961), 153–73.

Stevens, Martin. " 'And Venus Laugheth': An Interpretation of the *Merchant's Tale*, *ChauR*, 7 (1972), 118–31.

Strange, William C. "The *Monk's Tale*: A Generous View," *ChauR*, 1 (1967), 167–80.

Strohm, Paul. "The Allegory of the *Tale of Melibee*," *ChauR*, 2 (1967), 32–42.

Sudo, Jun. "The Order of the *Canterbury Tales* Reconsidered," *Hiroshima Studies in English Language and Literature*, 10 (1963), 77–89.

Ussery, H. E. "The Appropriateness of the *Physician's Tale* to Its Teller," *Papers of the Michigan Academy of Science, Arts, and Letters*, 50 (1966), 545–56.

White, Gertrude M. "The *Franklin's Tale*: Chaucer or the Critics," *PMLA*, 89 (1974), 454–62.

Williams, Arnold. "The Limitour of Chaucer's Time and His Limitacioun," *SP*, 57 (1960), 463–78.

Wilson, James H. "The Pardoner and the Second Nun: A Defense of the Bradshaw Order," *NM*, 74 (1973), 292–96.

Wittock, Trevor. *A Reading of the "Canterbury Tales."* London, Cambridge University Press, 1968.

Wood, Chauncey. "Chaucer's Man of Law as Interpreter," *Tradito*, 23 (1967), 149–90.

Yunck, John A. "Religious Elements in Chaucer's *Man of Law's Tale*," *ELH*, 27 (1960), 249–61.

Index